Applying Coding Concepts:
Encoder Workbook

Applying
Coding Concepts:
Encoder Workbook

**Deborah Eid,
MHA, BS, CBCS
Program Director, Apollo College
Phoenix, Arizona**

THOMSON

™

DELMAR LEARNING

Australia   Canada   Mexico   Singapore   Spain   United Kingdom   United States

Applying Coding Concepts: Encoder Workbook
by Deborah Eid

Vice President, Health Care Business Unit:
William Brottmiller

Director of Learning Solutions:
Matthew Kane

Managing Editor:
Marah Bellegarde

Senior Acquisitions Editor:
Rhonda Dearborn

Product Manager:
Jadin Babin-Kavanaugh

Editorial Assistant:
Laura Pye

Marketing Director:
Jennifer McAvey

Senior Marketing Manager:
Lynn Henn

Marketing Manager:
Michele McTighe

Marketing Coordinator:
Andrea Eobstel

Production Director:
Carolyn Miller

Content Project Managers:
David Buddle, Brooke Baker

Senior Art Director:
Jack Pendleton

Library of Congress Cataloging-in-Publication Data
Eid, Deborah.

Applying coding concepts: encoder workbook / by Deborah Eid.
p.cm.
Includes index.
"This text includes a free trial CD of Encoder Pro by Ingenix"
ISBN-13: 978-1-4180-4845-7
ISBN-10: 1-4180-4845-3
1. Nosology—Code numbers.
2. Nosology—Code numbers—Problems, exercises, etc. I. Title.
RB115.E43 2008
651.5'04261—dc22
2007022659

NOTICE TO THE READER

Contents

Preface

Medical coding was once solely based on coding manuals, but it has now expanded to include coding using encoder software programs. This workbook integrates the traditional methodology of using coding manuals with the new practices of using encoder programs.

The author of this workbook saw a need for a student-centered, practice-based coding workbook that is easy to comprehend without a lot of the extraneous material found in most instructional coding textbooks. Throughout her years of teaching, she has found that students really respond to hands-on practice when learning coding concepts. She also saw the need to address encoder programs, since these are widely used in the medical office. The intent here is not to replace traditional coding methods with the use of encoders, but to familiarize students with this innovative tool that is available to complement traditional coding methods in the field.

This workbook opens with a chapter on basic encoder functionality to demystify encoder programs by providing step-by-step information on how to use an encoder, with screen shots to illustrate each feature. Because *Applying Coding Concepts: Encoder Workbook* is packaged with a free trial version of Ingenix Encoder Pro software, this chapter utilizes the Encoder Pro software product to illustrate the various concepts and functionalities of encoders.

The format of the workbook follows a step-by-step competency-based approach that covers all facets of medical coding. The chapters are written in a straightforward style with streamlined pedagogical features in order to get to the heart of the lesson, allowing generous opportunities for student practice, with room in the text to write answers. This workbook may be used to teach coding in various programs and courses, including Health Information Management, Administrative Medical Assisting, Medical Records Technician, Medical Office Assistant, and Medical Insurance. Students should have some basic knowledge of medical terminology and anatomy prior to using this workbook.

ORGANIZATION OF THE TEXTBOOK

This workbook consists of 14 chapters. Chapter 1 begins with an overview of encoder programs and provides step-by-step instructions on how to use an encoder to code. Chapter 2 discusses how to code for Evaluation and Management through step-by-step instructions and examples. Chapter 3 instructs the student in coding Anesthesia services. It includes anesthesia calculations. Chapter 4 discusses coding of the Surgery section, which includes the Integumentary System and Musculoskeletal System sections, surgical packages, and modifiers. Chapter 5 instructs the student in coding the Respiratory System, Cardiovascular System, and Lymphatic System sections. Chapter 6 directs the student in coding for the Digestive and the Urinary System sections. Chapter 7 discusses coding for the Reproductive, Endocrine, and Nervous System sections and includes the Eyes and Ears. Chapter 8 instructs the students on coding Radiology, which includes radiologic positioning, delivery, and treatment methods. Chapter 9 instructs the students on coding for Laboratory and Pathology procedures. Chapter 10 instructs the student on the correct coding of the Medicine section. It includes the sensory, motor, and mixed nerves of the body. Chapter 11 instructs the student on how to code for the different diagnoses. It includes the body system, ill-defined symptoms, and injury and poisoning. Chapter 12 discusses HCPCS Level II codes, which include durable medical equipment and national modifiers. Chapter 13 instructs the student in the methods of coding external causes for injury and poisoning. Chapter 14 discusses the reimbursement procedure, with instructions on completing the claim forms. Each chapter contains student practice exercises and an end of chapter review. Appendix A provides even more practice for students.

FEATURES AND BENEFITS

- Learning objectives listed at the beginning of each chapter help to focus the material
- Practice exercises throughout the chapters allow for immediate reinforcement of learned concepts
- Key terms are listed at the beginning of each chapter
- Illustrations and screen shots help the student to visualize concepts
- Chapter review exercises contain coding case studies to test application skills
- Appendix A contains additional exercises for coding practice
- Free trial CD-ROM of Encoder Pro, Ingenix's powerful coding software, is included

INSTRUCTOR'S MANUAL

The Instructor's Manual contains answer keys for all of the text exercises as well as the following:
- Additional texts and exams with answer keys

HOW TO USE THE ENCODER PRO 30-DAY FREE TRIAL CD-ROM

The Encoder Pro software included in the back cover of this textbook is a 30-day free trial of Ingenix's powerful medical coding solution that allows you to look up CPT, ICD-9 CM and HCPCS Level II codes quickly and accurately. This software can be used in conjunction with coding manuals to assign codes to any of the exercises in the textbook. Be sure to check with your instructor before installing and using the Encoder Pro software, because the CD-ROM bundled with your book will expire 30 days after installation.

Features and Benefits of Encoder Pro

Encoder Pro is the essential code look-up software for CPT, ICD-9 CM and HCPCS code sets. It gives users fast searching capabilities across all code sets. Encoder Pro can greatly reduce the time it takes to build or review a claim and helps improve overall coding accuracy. Should you decide to subscribe to the full version of Encoder Pro, the following tools will be available to you:

- **Powerful Ingenix CodeLogic search engine.** Improve productivity by eliminating time-consuming code lookups in outdated code books. Search all three code sets simultaneously using lay terms, acronyms, abbreviations, and even misspelled words.
- **Lay descriptions for thousands of CPT codes.** Enhance your understanding of procedures with easy-to-understand descriptions.
- **Color-coded edits.** Understand whether a code carries an age or sex edit, is covered by Medicare, or contains bundled procedures.
- **Quarterly update service.** Rest assured, you are always using accurate codes. You can code confidently throughout the year with free code updates.
- **Great value.** Get the content from over 20 code and reference books in one powerful solution.

For more information about Encoder Pro software, click on the Help menu from inside the free trial version and select Features by Product, or go to www.ingenixonline.com.

About the Author

Deborah Eid, MHA, BS, CBCS, earned her degrees at Rochville University. She is the Program Director at Apollo College and is a certified billing and coding specialist. She is a member of the Gerson-Lehrman Group, a worldwide consulting firm.

Acknowledgements

I would like to thank the staff of Delmar Publishing for their unending support in the publication of this workbook. Thanks to Adrian Williams and Dr. Karlen Bailie for their contributions of screen shots, and to John Lampignano for providing x-rays. I would like to specially thank my husband, Elie; without his support and inspiration, this workbook would have never been published.

Reviewers

For their valuable insights and advice, the author and publisher would like to thank the following:

Joan M. Cadenhead, MBA
Information Technology Management
Information Systems Business Analyst, Health Insurance Delivery
Valley Stream, New York

Adrienne L. Carter, M.Ed., BVE, RMA
Instructor in Medical Assisting
Moreno Valley Campus of the Riverside Community College
Moreno Valley, California

Candace M. Garland
Instructor, MCBS Certificate Program
Sanford Brown Institute
Springfield, Massachusetts

Leah Grebner, RHIA, CCS
Director of Health Information
Midstate College
Peoria, Illinois

Susanna M. Hancock, AAS, RMA, CMA, RPT, COLT
Medical Program Consultant
Former Medical Assistant Director-Instructor
American Institute of Health Technology
Boise, Idaho

Sharon E. Imperiale, CMA
Medical Assistant Instructor
College America
Phoenix, Arizona

Anne C. Karl, RHIA, CCS-P, CPC
Adjunct Professor
Rasmussen College
Eagan, Minnesota

Jane M. Kelly, PhD, CPC
Adjunct Professor
Davenport University
School of Health Professions
Merrillville, Indiana

Deborah L. Powers, CPC & AAPC Vendor
Medical Coding Basics
Rancho Cucamonga, California

Karen Reger, CRSO, RHIT
Part time Instructor
Mid-Michigan Community College
Harrison, Michigan

Technical Reviewer

Cynthia Harms, M.Ed., CMA, CPC, CPC-H
Instructor, Mildred Elley School
Latham, New York

AVENUE FOR FEEDBACK

The author and publisher would like to hear your comments about this text. Please go to www.delmarhealthcare.com to leave comments about this or any of our products.

Chapter 1
Introduction to Encoder Software

LEARNING OBJECTIVES

After completing this chapter, the learner should be able to:

- Describe the benefits and drawbacks of using encoders versus manual coding
- Understand the place of encoders in the medical office
- Describe basic encoder features and functionalities
- Use an encoder program to solve coding exercises

WHAT IS AN ENCODER?

Encoder programs are unique coding software programs that enable the new or experienced coder to locate the proper CPT, ICD-9 CM, and HCPCS codes quickly. Encoders contain all CPT and ICD-9 CM codes, and are available either on CD-ROM or as an Internet download. These programs not only give fast results, but some encoder programs also give code descriptions in lay terms. Most encoder programs will also allow you to place notes and bookmarks for quick reference. These applications are quickly and easily learned.

Although using encoder programs is the fastest way to look up codes, most encoder programs do not readily let the coder review the guidelines specific to that code. However, most do contain some type of guidelines that you can access through the click of a mouse. Most coders or billers must manually refer to the CPT or ICD-9 CM manual to view the guidelines of a specific code. An example of this is the code 64553. This code is used for the percutaneous implantation of a neurostimulator electrode for the cranial nerve. According to the guidelines, this procedure may be applied by both simple and complex stimulators. However, the encoder program does not show this information while the user is viewing the code or description of the procedure. All guidelines are located at the beginning of each section of the CPT and ICD-9 CM manual. You must know how to code before you can use an encoder as a quick reference. It is risky to try to use an encoder without the depth of knowledge and experience obtained by coding manually.

Types of Encoders

Encoder programs are readily available as Internet downloads or on CD-ROMs from various manufacturers. There are also Internet-based programs that provide some level of service for free: for example, you may be allowed to access the CPT portion of an Internet-based encoder but must pay to access the ICD portion or vice versa. Using an encoder allows for fast coding, but using an encoder to learn how to code is unthinkable. Even the most seasoned coder cannot report codes without first verifying the guidelines and rationales behind coding. Codes are updated every year, and coding guidelines are also updated. Therefore, codes that are acceptable one year may have been deleted or changed the following year.

Students who learn coding strictly from an encoder cannot pass a certification test, because they lack the ability to find the codes in the various coding manuals. (At this time, hospitals are experiencing the same problem.) Students who are experienced in both the use of the coding manuals and encoder software tend to prefer the manual. Learning to code from the CPT manual is a long process, but once you learn how to maneuver through the CPT manual and read the guidelines before coding, using an encoder will seem like child's play.

What users do like about encoder programs is the ease of use. Once you have gained knowledge of the toolbar, you are practically an expert at encoder use. Encoders also offer the ability to search for a specific code using the Search box. You may also use the Search box to locate a procedure or a diagnosis. This will usually show all the codes associated with that procedure or diagnosis. It is then up to you to investigate which code is appropriate for the procedure or diagnosis. Practically all encoder programs also provide the coder with the capability of placing notes for future use. More of these programs are becoming available, and there are many types of encoders on the market today. Most encoder programs provide all of these capabilities with the inclusion of relative value units (RVU). The RVU was developed to give CPT codes a basic unit value based on the physician's work, overhead and medical malpractice insurance.

The Unique Look of Encoders

Each encoder program has, like any other application, a special look of its own. These programs go from the very simple to the complex, but the one thing they all have in common is the set of codes used for reporting services. They all include CPT, ICD, and HCPCS codes. How they present them is completely different.

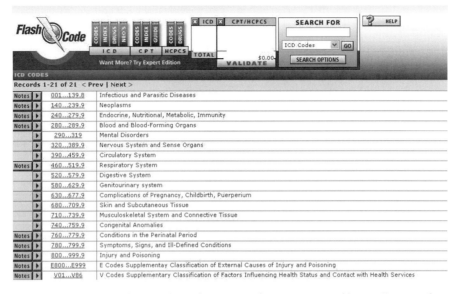

Figure 1-1 The Flash Code encoder software interface (Image used by permission of Flash Code)

Flash Code (Figure 1-1) is an Internet-based encoder program. As you can see, it readily lets the coder know where the CPT, ICD, and HCPCS codes are located within the toolbar. It further subdivides the CPT, ICD, and HCPCS codes and provides tools to readily access the index, drugs, neoplasms, and guidelines. This unique program also provides Medicare reimbursement rates and a primary and secondary diagnosis.

The 3M encoder is notable in the way the program is structured (see Figure 1–2). With most encoder programs, the coder must switch through various steps to find all the information that is readily available in just one screen with this encoder program.

The Ingenix Encoder Pro is a powerful search tool that allows you to search all three code sets from the toolbar. Encoder Pro provides lay descriptions for many CPT codes to aid understanding. In addition, it contains unique features that help to improve search time, such as bookmarks and sticky notes (see Figure 1–3).

BASIC ENCODER INTERFACE

Each encoder has its own functions and features, and once you have mastered these, using the encoder should be simple. All encoders will have certain features to facilitate code look-up and referencing. Because features are what set any product apart, these features will differ from encoder to encoder. For the purposes of this workbook, the Ingenix Encoder Pro interface will be used to illustrate various encoder features and functionalities because a free trial of this encoder program is packaged with this workbook. For information about how to install the 30-day free trial or about the full-version of Encoder Pro, please see the preface of this book.

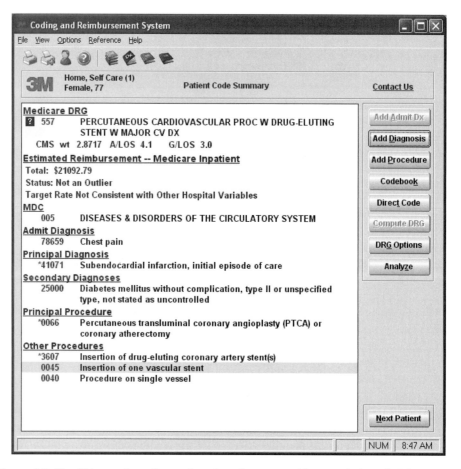

Figure 1-2 The 3M encoder software interface (Image used by permission of 3M)

Code Detail and Tabular Results Screen

When you enter a code, diagnosis, or procedure into the Search box, detailed information will appear in the Code Detail box. Viewing code information in the Code Detail screen is analogous to looking up codes in the coding manuals. Once the search results have been narrowed, select any code in the Tabular Results box to view it in the Code Detail box. The first panel of the Code Detail box (Figure 1–4A) lists the section of the specific coding manual that the code falls in, and the second panel (Figure 1–4B) lists the code description and the range of codes in which it falls. The third panel (Figure 1–4C) displays the color coded symbols applicable to the selected code, as well as any sticky notes attached to the code. You can proceed to the previous or next section of codes by using the hyperlinks at the top of the Code Detail panel.

The Tabular Results panel lets you specify the code types you are interested in accessing, which allows greater focus for your code search. Use the check boxes to limit the code sets you want to search in. The "Total matches:" area at the bottom will reflect the number of items in your search results.

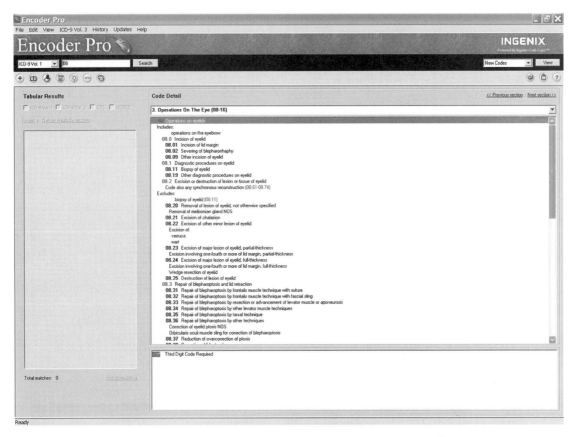

Figure 1-3 The Encoder Pro encoder software interface (Courtesy of Ingenix, Inc.)

Specifying only the code types you are interested in assists you in focusing your search. You can filter the displayed results by selecting or clearing one or more check boxes. For example, if you want to view code results only from ICD-9 CM Volume I, make sure that is the only box checked in the list. If a check box is grayed out, it means that no results were found for that code set and the check box cannot be selected for that particular search. Each time the results are filtered (by selecting or deselecting a check box), the "Total matches:" area reflects the number of results. You can also search in a particular code set by selecting the code set you want from the All Code Sets pull-down menu before hitting the Search button.

EXAMPLE

1. Using the free trial version of Encoder Pro in the back of this book, type the word *laminectomy* into the Search box and limit your search to ICD-9 CM Volume III by using the pull-down menu (see Figure 1–5).
2. The tabular results should display a range of codes associated with a laminectomy and show the total matches as 11 (see Figure 1–6). You then must narrow the search results accordingly.

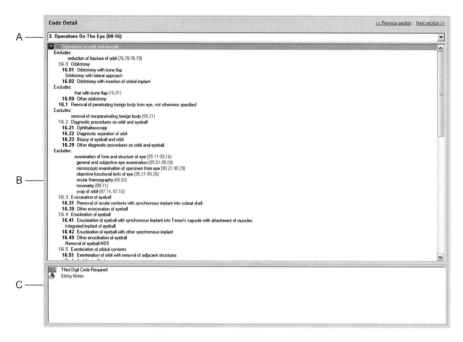

Figure 1-4 Code Detail panels of Encoder Pro: (A) Displays the coding manual section where the code falls, (B) Displays specific code description and range, (C) Displays symbols and notes applicable to selected code (Courtesy of Ingenix, Inc.)

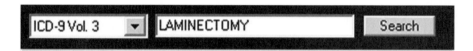

Figure 1-5 Searching for "laminectomy" using the ICD-9-Volume 3 code set (Courtesy of Ingenix, Inc.)

THE TOOLBAR

Once you are familiar with the **toolbar,** you should be able to use the encoder. The Ingenix Encoder Pro toolbar has three sections: an upper gray portion with various pull-down menus, a black search area with buttons and pull-down menus, and a second gray area with icons (see Figure 1–7). The first gray portion contains File, Edit, View, History, Updates, and Help menus. Please note that there is an additional menu that can appear between View and History, which will change depending on what code set you are currently working in: CPT, ICD-9 CM, or HCPCS. From this menu you can access information related specifically to whatever code set you are working with.

All of the functions within the upper gray toolbar area are also accessible by using the black toolbar area, with the exception of the History and Updates menu items. The History menu allows you to view the last 11 codes accessed using the software. The Updates menu allows you to log onto the Internet to receive the latest updates to Encoder Pro from Ingenix (requires a full subscription).

Figure 1-6 Tabular Results displayed for laminectomy search (Courtesy of Ingenix, Inc.)

Figure 1-7 Full toolbar of Encoder Pro: (A) Menus, (B) Search box area, (C) Icons (Courtesy of Ingenix, Inc.)

Figure 1-8 Encoder Pro icons from left to right: Add a Code, Bookmark, Sticky Notes, Notes, Annotations, Special Coverage, Color Coding Legend. Not shown: Printer, Notepad, Help icons. (Courtesy of Ingenix, Inc.)

The black portion of the toolbar contains the All Code Sets pull-down menu, Search box, New Codes pull-down menu, and View button (see Figure 1–7B). This is where code, diagnosis, or procedure searches are conducted. Once you have found the code you are looking for, you can perform various functions on that code using either the icons or the pull-down menus.

The lower gray portion of the toolbar contains buttons, or icons, that you use to add codes, bookmarks, sticky notes, or to access the notepad, annotations, special coverage instructions, color coding legend, printer function, and help features (see Figure 1–7C).

Toolbar Icons and Buttons

Now that we have explored the toolbar, let's identify the functions of each icon and button. Icons refer to the series of small circles, each of which contains a picture that relates to its particular function. (You can see all of the Encoder Pro icons in Figure 1–7, and a close-up of the left-side icons in Figure 1–8.) If you mouse over each icon, you will notice that a brief description will appear at the very bottom of the encoder screen to help you recall that icon's function. We will discuss each icon, from left to right across the toolbar, later in this section. There are only two buttons on the toolbar—the Search and View buttons.

When you click on an icon, a dialog box will open in the screen for more information. Buttons first require data to be entered, either by typing into the Search box or by using one of the pull-down menus located at either end of the toolbar.

All Code Sets Menu

The All Code Sets menu is located on the left side of the black portion of the toolbar (see Figure 1–9). This menu allows you to select a specific code from the ICD-9 CM, CPT, or

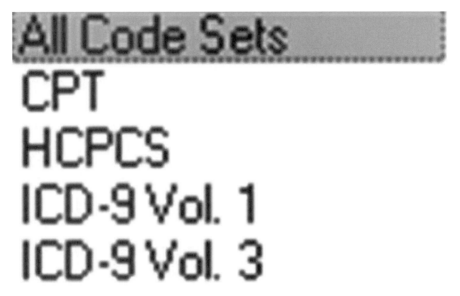

Figure 1-9 All Code Sets menu (Courtesy of Ingenix, Inc.)

HCPCS code sets, and is used in conjunction with the Search box. Using the All Code Sets menu and Search box, you can search for a specific code or code range.

Using the Search Box

The **Search box** enables you to search for a specific code or code range in a particular code set if that code or code range is known. Sometimes the code or code range will not be known, and you must enter medical terms into the Search box to find a particular procedure or diagnosis code.

EXAMPLE

1. Enter the word *fracture* into the Search box. All procedures that relate to fractures appear in the Tabular Results box.
2. At this point, you can narrow your search by clicking on the "Narrow results by section" option on the left side of the screen in the Tabular Results box. A dialog box will open, asking you to specify the codes you want to search by code set (see Figure 1–10).

View New, Revised, and Deleted Codes Menu

The pull-down menu located on the right side of the black portion of the toolbar works in conjunction with the View button that is located to the right of it (see Figure 1–11). This pull-down menu gives you the option to view new, revised, and deleted codes, as well as code book selections, for a given code.

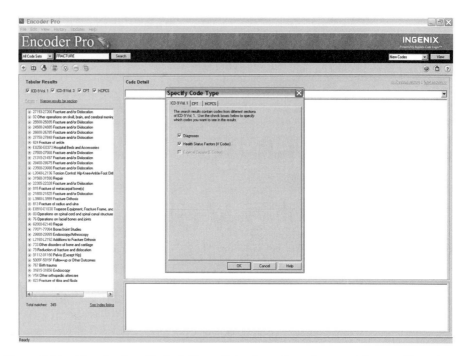

Figure 1-10 Using the Specify Code Type dialog box allows for search by specific code type (Courtesy of Ingenix, Inc.)

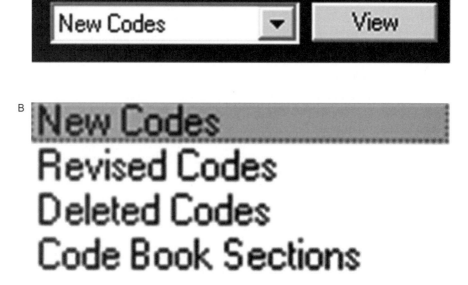

Figure 1-11 (A) View button and (B) Corresponding menu (Courtesy of Ingenix, Inc.)

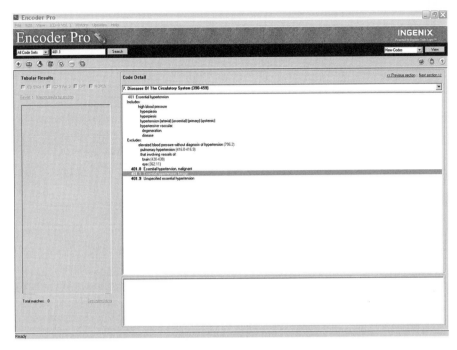

Figure 1-12 Code Detail screen for code 401 (Courtesy of Ingenix, Inc.)

Add Code Icon

The **Add Code icon** enables you to create sticky notes, add a code to the notepad, or bookmark a frequently used code. **Sticky notes** are personal notes you can create for specific codes; they function much like the yellow sticky notes often used in offices.

> **EXAMPLE**
>
> 1. Enter code *401.1* into the Search box and click the Search button. The code section appears in the Code Detail area, with code 401.1 highlighted (see Figure 1-12).
> 2. Now click the Add (+) icon or select Add from the Edit menu to open the Add Code dialog box. The code and its description appear along with the check boxes for bookmark, sticky notes, and notepad options (see Figure 1-13).

TIP: You can view all of your sticky notes, notepad, or bookmarks at any time by going up to the top of the screen and selecting the item you want to view from the View pull-down menu.

Bookmark Icon

Bookmarks are used as a reference for frequently used codes. Bookmarks make it easy for you to access multiple codes at one time and modify code descriptions. To add a bookmark, you must first conduct a search on the code you want to add to your bookmarks.

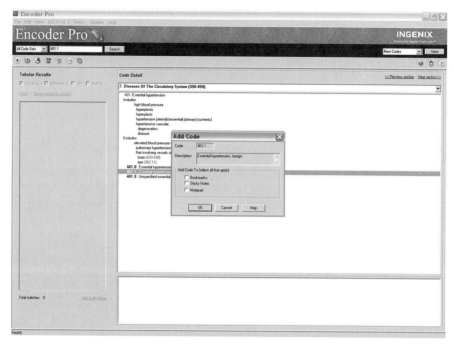

Figure 1-13 Add Code dialog box (Courtesy of Ingenix, Inc.)

EXAMPLE

1. Find the code for a radical resection of the sternum by entering the words *radical resection sternum* into the Search box. In the Tabular Results area, you will see a check mark next to CPT, signifying that this is a CPT code and not a diagnosis code. There is a range of codes given in the Tabular Results box. If you click on the plus signs to the left of the code ranges, you will be able to view the codes within each range. Highlight the code for a radical resection of the sternum. Now, the entire range of codes appears in the Code Detail box, with the selected code highlighted (see Figure 1–14).

2. Click the Add icon or right click to add this code to your bookmarks. Once the bookmark dialog box appears, you may place your bookmark in a category and modify the code's description. A category can be anything up to 35 characters that helps you identify your frequently used codes (see Figure 1–15).

3. Once you have completed this, click OK. You have now placed the code in your bookmarks for quick reference (see Figure 1–16). You may edit your bookmark by selecting Bookmarks from the View pull-down menu at the top of the screen. To delete a category, highlight it and use the Delete key.

Sticky Notes Icon

Sticky notes are reminder notes you create for selected codes. What makes Encoder Pro unique is that you can add sticky notes to one code or many codes.

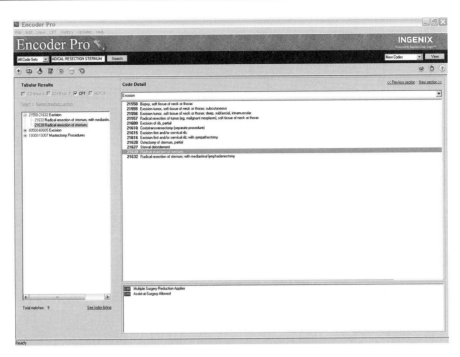

Figure 1-14 Selected code highlighted (Courtesy of Ingenix, Inc.)

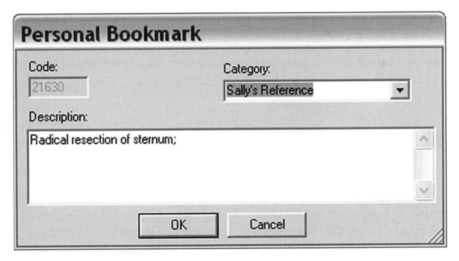

Figure 1-15 Changing category field on a personal bookmark (Courtesy of Ingenix, Inc.)

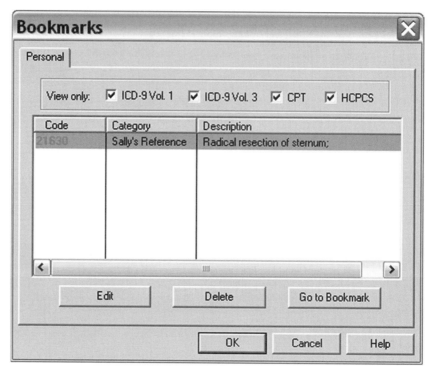

Figure 1-16 Bookmark category field changed (Courtesy of Ingenix, Inc.)

EXAMPLE

1. Enter code *99357* into the Search box. This is a prolonged service code.
2. Click the Add icon and select Sticky Notes, or click on the Sticky Notes icon to add the code into your sticky notes. The View Personal Sticky Note dialog box will appear onscreen (see Figure 1–17). You will see the code added to the dialog box named "Codes Assigned to Sticky Note." You may also assign a name to your sticky note.
3. Once you have added a code to your sticky notes, an icon will appear in the lower panel of the Code Detail screen as a reminder that there's a sticky note attached to this code.

TIP: You may also add a code to your sticky notes, bookmarks, and notepad by using a mouse shortcut. In order to do this, choose code 99357 so that it's highlighted and right click with the mouse. The Add Code shortcut menu appears. Now select the item you want to add the code to (bookmark, sticky note, notepad). This time, add the code to your bookmarks. Click OK, and the code has been added to your bookmarks.

Notes Icon

The Notes icon brings up instructional notes and references relevant to the selected code. This feature allows you to view procedures that may or may not be payable. For

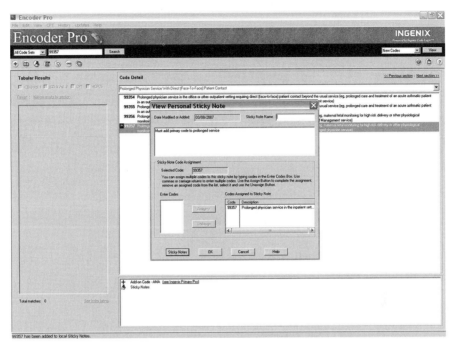

Figure 1-17 Personal Sticky Note dialog box (Courtesy of Ingenix, Inc.)

example, if you enter CPT code *99357* into the Search box, and then click on the Notes icon, a dialog box will open with tabs to notes on that particular code (see Figure 1–18).

Annotation Icon

The **Annotations** dialog box enables you to view more information regarding specific professional services. When using CPT codes, the annotations will provide lay (non-clinical) descriptions, which can be helpful for coding. To view an example, enter code *72880* into the Search box, then click on the Annotations icon. Not only does Encoder Pro fully explain the procedure, it also provides more information on the procedure itself. For another example, search on the HCPCS code *E0720* (see Figure 1–19). The Annotations dialog box explains what the TENS unit is used for, and that it may not be covered medical equipment.

Special CMS Coverage Icon

You can access special CMS coverage instructions by clicking on the CMS icon on the toolbar. Use this feature to view Medicare policy references regarding reimbursement for selected CPT or HCPCS codes.

EXAMPLE

1. Enter code *E0500* in the Search box and click on the CMS icon. Contained within the dialog box is a list of information regarding IPPB machines.

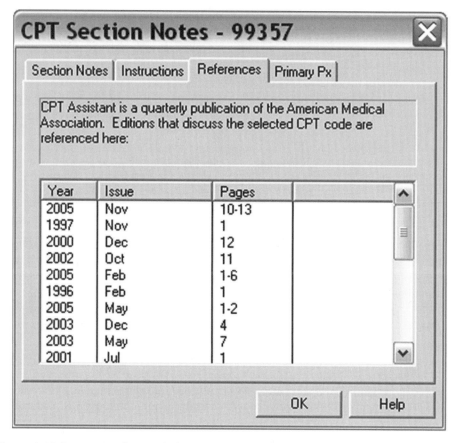

Figure 1-18 Instructional notes dialog box (Courtesy of Ingenix, Inc.)

2. Scroll down to view all of the information.
3. Now, enter code *E0720* in the Search box and click the CMS icon again. For this code, all of the information is listed under different publication numbers, which are listed on the tabs within the dialog box (see Figure 1-20).

Color Coding Legend Icon

The **color coding legend** enables the coder to quickly identify all codes associated with that specific color code. To view color codes, first determine if the color code is a CPT, ICD-9 CM, or HCPCS code. To view color codes for a CPT code, select CPT Color Code on the View pull-down menu. A dialog box with tabs will open. Each tab contains a Find field, which only accepts five digits. Enter code *99357* into the Find field. Encoder Pro automatically highlights the code, and in the box at the bottom of the Code Detail section of the screen, it will show various color codes listed for that particular code, as shown in Figures 1–14 and 1–17. The same procedure can be followed for both ICD-9 CM and HCPCS codes.

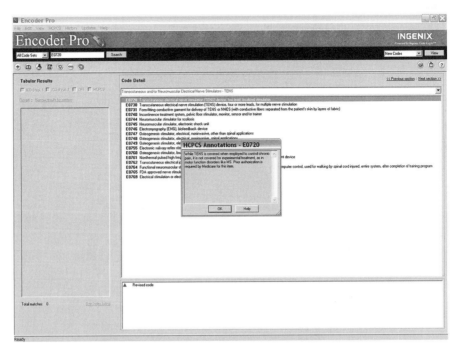

Figure 1-19 Annotations dialog box (Courtesy of Ingenix, Inc.)

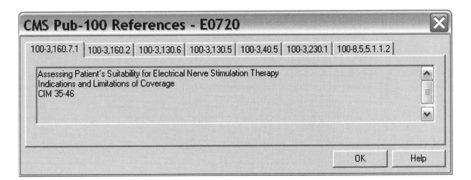

Figure 1-20 Special Coverage dialog box with tabs (Courtesy of Ingenix, Inc.)

To view the color code legend for a particular code set at any time, click on the Color Code icon, and the legend window for that code set will open (see Figure 1–21).

Printer Icon

This icon (on the right side of the toolbar) allows you to print any code-specific information in an open dialog box. You can also access the print function from the File menu at the top left of the toolbar.

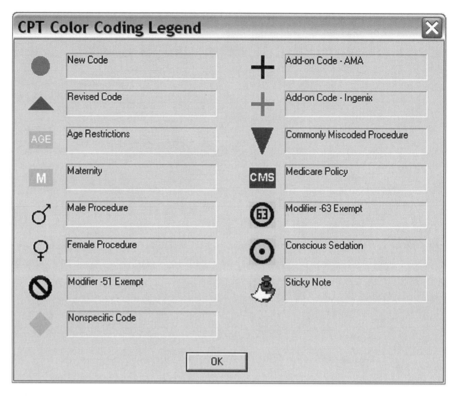

Figure 1-21 CPT Color Coding Legend (Courtesy of Ingenix, Inc.)

Notepad Icon

The **notepad** is used only to store temporary codes. These codes can be copied to the Windows clipboard, allowing you to perform several searches and send them all to the clipboard at once. To add a code to the notepad, click on the Notepad icon in the upper right corner of the screen. You can add a code from the dialog box by typing it in, or you can add a code to the notepad by first doing a search and then highlighting the code and using the shortcut right-click menu, just like the process used for sticky notes and bookmarks. You can view your notepad at any time by selecting Notepad from the View pull-down menu at the top of the screen.

You can select any code to make a new primary code; if a code has already been selected as primary, a dialog box will pop up and inform you of this. Once a code is marked as primary, a check mark will appear in the asterisk field (see Figure 1-22). To make a different code primary, click on Deselect Primary Code in the Notepad dialog box to remove it as primary code. To delete a code entirely from the notepad, select the code you wish to delete and click the Delete button from within the Notepad dialog box.

Help Icon

This pull-down selection gives you access to the indexed Help menu included with Encoder Pro.

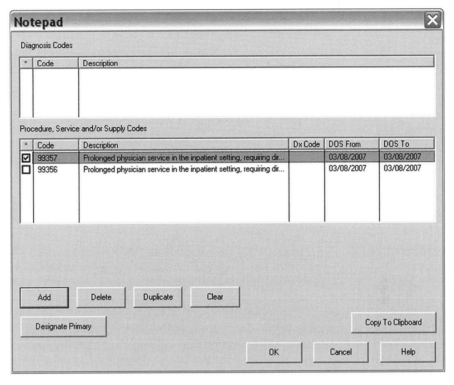

Figure 1-22 Notepad screen with primary code selected (Courtesy of Ingenix, Inc.)

CHAPTER REVIEW

Using Ingenix Encoder Pro, code the following exercises.

1. Insert the word *endoscopy* into the Search box. What is the code range for an endoscopy of the small intestines and stoma as located in the Tabular Results?

   Answer: _____

2. Insert the word *bronchitis* into the Search box and, using the pull-down menu, select ICD-9 Volume I, located next to the Search box. What are the total matches for bronchitis?

   Answer: _____

3. Using the ICD-9 Volume I, place the code *401.1* into the Search box. What is the description of this code as located within the Code Detail box?

   Answer: _____

4. Using code 401.1, click on the plus sign located in the gray toolbar. Which screen appears?

   Answer: _____

5. Type the word *repair* into the Search box and select CPT from the pull-down menu. Which screen appears?

   Answer: _____

6. Type the word *wound* into the Search box with All Code Sets in the pull-down menu. Click on "Narrow results by section." Which screen appears?

   Answer: _____

Chapter 2
Introduction to Evaluation and Management Coding

LEARNING OBJECTIVES

After completing this chapter, the learner should be able to:

- Identify all levels of evaluation and management
- Understand how to apply correct CPT codes
- Identify the difference between outpatient and inpatient

- Explain and understand modifiers
- Apply guidelines to coding procedures
- Understand the consequences of undercoding or overcoding

GETTING FAMILIAR WITH THE CPT MANUAL

Before we start, let's first understand what the CPT and ICD acronyms stand for. CPT is the acronym for Current Procedural Terminology and ICD is the acronym for International Classification of Diseases. The CPT manual is currently in its fourth edition (**CPT-4**). The CPT-4 is used to code physician procedures. The International Classification of Diseases (**ICD-9**) is in its ninth edition. It is used to code diagnoses. Both of these manuals are updated once a year to add, delete, or revise codes according to new procedures being performed and new technology. These manuals are used in conjunction with each other. Each procedure a physician performs (CPT-4) must have a diagnosis (ICD-9) to explain why the procedure was performed. Before you begin to use the CPT-4 manual, take a few minutes to leaf through the pages. You will find that this manual is divided into sections, seven to be exact. It is further divided into subsections, subheadings, categories, and subcategories that include anatomic locations and procedures performed. At first, this may seem overwhelming, but you will learn how to maneuver easily through the manual and locate codes and examples to properly report the procedures.

Let's get started by opening the front cover of the CPT-4 manual. Here you will find headings in bold print listing symbols, modifiers, patient status modifiers, and so forth. (As we learn to code, you will be using each one of these in the proper method.) The contents page lists the sections and code ranges of the CPT manual, which include Evaluation and Management (99201–99499), Anesthesia (00100–01999), Surgery (10021–69990), Radiology (70010–79999), Pathology and Laboratory (80048–89399), Medicine (90281–99199), and Category III codes. (The Introduction is not considered a section of the CPT manual.) As you can see, the guidelines are listed before each section in the manual. These guidelines are essential to read before choosing any code. Listed beneath each section are the subsections with their corresponding page numbers. You will also find at the end of the contents page a list of Category I Codes and Category II Codes, appendix A through appendix I, and the Index. Each of these appendices gives the coder a brief description of its contents. Note that appendix C contains clinical examples for correct code reporting. This will help the new coder when reporting Evaluation and Management codes. The index will only guide you to where specific procedure codes are located, and is not to be used in choosing a primary code. Although the procedure codes do give you a specific code, it may not be the correct code to report according to the guidelines.

Symbols

Mastering the proper use of symbols is a large part of learning how to code. The CPT manual contains symbols that are used throughout the manual and are printed at the bottom of each page. As technology advances, new codes, represented by a (•) bullet symbol placed in front of the code, will tell you the code is new. Codes that have been revised are identified by a (▲) triangle in front of the code. This informs the coder that the description has been revised in some manner. When the text within the description has been changed, (►◄) right and left triangles will appear in front and behind the text that was changed. The codes are updated each year in several different ways. They may be deleted altogether, the description may change, or additions may be added to the code. Complete listings of these updated codes are in Appendix B of the CPT manual. An add-on code is represented by a (+) plus sign. These codes must not be used alone; they must be used in conjunction with a primary procedure code. A complete listing of all add-on codes is located in Appendix D. Physicians who perform multiple procedures at one time will place modifier 51 at the end of the procedure code to indicate the services. But not all codes are allowed to be used with modifier 51: a (Ø) circle with a line through it will identify codes that cannot be so used. A code that represents multiple procedures will sometimes include the multiple procedures within the code itself. Complete listings of modifier 51 exempt codes are located in Appendix E. There are procedures that are performed under some type of sedation. One of these types is called conscious sedation. This is when the patient has not been placed under a general anesthesia and is awake and coherent throughout the procedure. Codes that reflect a conscious sedation are identified by a (☉) circle with a dot in the center. This symbol informs the coder that the procedure includes some type of conscious sedation.

LEARNING HOW TO CODE

The process of coding is not as complex as it may at first seem, once you understand how to select the correct codes. In order to completely understand how to select the codes, you must first understand how to identify the sections, subsections, subheadings, categories, and subcategories. So, let's start by taking a look at the Surgery section. (Skip the Surgery Guidelines for now.) On the first page of the Surgery section, you will find at the top of the page in bold print the word "Surgery." This is considered the **section** in which you will be identifying the code for surgical procedures (see Figure 2–1). Further down the page in bold print you will find the heading of "Integumentary System." The Integumentary System is the **subsection.** Just beneath the subsection in bold print is the heading "Skin, Subcutaneous & Accessory Structures." This heading is considered

Surgery	→ Section
Integumentary System	→ Subsection
Skin, Subcutaneous & Accessory Structures	→ Subheading
Incision and Drainage	→ Category

Figure 2-1 Divisions of a section

the **subheading.** The subheading tells you the location of the anatomic site on which the procedure is being performed. Listed under the subheading, you will find in bold print "Incision and Drainage." This is considered the **category.** The category tells the coder the procedure that is being performed on the identified anatomic site. **Subcategories** are used to identify the approach that the surgeon is going to use to perform the procedure. Since there are no different approaches used within this category, none is listed. Directly beneath is the code 10040. This begins the codes within the Surgery section of the Integumentary System of the Skin, Subcutaneous & Accessory Structures. So, let's practice what we have learned.

PRACTICE EXERCISE 2-1

Using your CPT manual, locate the code 21010. Identify the following.

1. Section: _____

2. Subsection: _____

3. Subheading: _____

4. Category: _____

How to Use the Index

Learning how to use the index is a fairly easy objective. The index is located at the back of the CPT manual and it basically resembles a dictionary. Each page lists the first procedure at the top of the page on the left side and the last procedure at the top of the page on the right side. The procedure codes are listed here in numeric order, starting with the lowest procedure number first. All of the terms associated with a procedure are listed here under the main term. For instance, under Anesthesia are procedures that are associated with the application of anesthesia, such as hernia repair (see Figure 2–2). The index then lists the range of codes in which anesthesia is given for a hernia repair (00830–00836). In this instance, the range of codes can easily be identified by a dash (–) between the two codes. As you can see, there are several codes associated with this procedure. But, not all procedures consist of a range of codes. The index may list only one code that is associated with a specific procedure: an example of this is code 28060

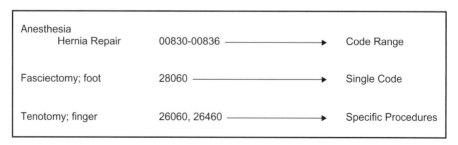

Figure 2-2 Types of index codes

(fasciectomy; foot). When there are two or three codes associated with a specific procedure, each code will be followed by a comma (tenotomy; finger, 26060, 26460).

The index is listed in alphabetical order for easy location of the main terms. These terms are listed under the type of procedure (cast, dialysis), the anatomic site (pelvis, chest) or the condition (abrasion, fracture). The index also includes synonyms, eponyms and abbreviations. A synonym is a word that has a similar meaning to another word, such as fingers (phalanges) or heart transplant (cardiac transplantation). Eponyms are procedures or things named after people, usually the person who developed the procedure or discovered a new technique. An example of this would be Mohs Micrographic Surgery (named after Frederic Mohs), in which tumors are removed one layer at a time. Abbreviations, such as MMR (measles, mumps, and rubella), are often used within the index. When abbreviations are used, the index informs you where to look ("see vaccines") to obtain the correct code. You may use any one of these methods to locate a specific procedure. Once again, coding from the index, even if only one code is listed, is not recommended. There are two reasons for this. The first is that the guidelines listed in front of the main section may rule against using that particular code for that specific procedure. The second reason is that there may be a more appropriate code listed under an HCPCS code that identifies the exact procedure performed. HCPCS codes are covered later in this book.

PRACTICE EXERCISE 2-2

Using the Index, locate the code or range of codes for the following.

1. Cauterization of a skin tag

   Code(s) _____

2. Gallbladder incision

   Code(s) _____

3. Repair of the pulmonary vein

   Code(s) _____

4. Fracture of the patella, open treatment

   Code(s) _____

5. Repair of a complex wound

   Code(s) _____

6. Paracentesis into the thorax

   Code(s) _____

7. Conscious sedation with an analgesic

   Code(s) _____

8. Biopsy of the liver

   Code(s) _____

9. Arthrodesis of the sacroiliac joint

   Code(s) _____

10. Creation of a temporary stoma

   Code(s) _____

Applying Codes from the Index

Now that you have learned to find codes in the index, let's apply them to the main sections of the CPT manual. Using your CPT manual, locate the code for an arthrodesis; pantalar (28705) within the index. Now locate the code within the main section (Surgery, Musculoskeletal System) of the CPT manual. You will find that the code 28705 is followed by a description of the code (see Figure 2–3). As you look at the codes, you will find that each code has a specific procedure relating to that code. Note that there is a semicolon after the word "arthrodesis." This code is called a stand-alone code because it contains the full description of the procedure. Codes that are indented only contain part of the procedure description, as you can see in codes 28715 and 28725. The difference between the two types of codes is that indented codes must include the description of the code preceding the semicolon of the stand-alone code. Therefore, an arthrodesis (stand-alone) can be performed on the indented codes 28715 (triple) or 28725 (subtalar).

PRACTICE EXERCISE 2-3

Using the CPT manual, identify the following codes as either stand-alone or indented.

1. Code 20205 is a/an _____.

2. Code 20525 is a/an _____.

3. Code 20552 is a/an _____.

4. Code 20662 is a/an _____.

5. Code 20694 is a/an _____.

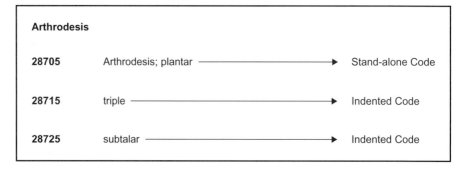

Figure 2-3 Stand-alone and indented codes

22521   percutaneous vertebroplasty, one vertebral body, unilateral or bilateral injection; lumbar

+22522   each additional thoracic or lumbar vertebral body

(use code 22522 in conjunction with 22521)

Figure 2-4 Add-on codes

Add-on Codes

Add-on codes are procedures performed in addition to the primary procedure. These codes are easily recognized by the plus (+) sign placed in front of the code. The code may also contain phrases such as "in addition to," "list separately in addition to the primary code," and "with." The CPT manual will also direct the coder by placing (in parentheses) a reminder beneath the add-on code using statements such as, "use code xxxxx in conjunction with xxxxx." When add-on codes are reported, they must be reported in addition to the primary procedure code and cannot be reported separately. Add-on codes are used for many different procedures. Physicians who perform surgical procedures on the vertebrae will use add-on codes for each vertebral segment that services are rendered on. An example of this would be code 22521 (percutaneous vertebroplasty, one vertebral body, unilateral or bilateral injection; lumbar) (see Figure 2–4). The add-on code +22522 is for each additional thoracic or lumbar vertebral body. Therefore, code 22522 cannot be reported without code 22521 being reported first.

GUIDELINES

Guidelines for coding a particular section are always located at the beginning of that section of the CPT manual. They give direct instructions on the proper use of all the codes within that section. The guidelines are used constantly by all coders to ensure proper reporting. When these guidelines are not reviewed before coding, several mishaps can occur. First and foremost, the wrong code leads to inaccurate reporting of the procedure performed. Second, the insurance company may reject or deny the code. This then results in the claim not being paid.

For the convenience of the new coder and for easy comprehension, the guidelines have been written into the text of this book. It is always better, however, to refer to the guidelines in the manual. Guidelines contain information on the terms and definitions within each section. They also contain special instructions on the use of specific code ranges. Guidelines are helpful in watching for the modifiers that may or may not be applicable to specific codes. Guidelines will also tell you when special reports are required before payment can be made. When guidelines are needed for a particular subheading, such as repair or excision, they will be listed at the beginning of that subheading. This gives you additional information you need to select the proper code available. When there is no code listed for the procedure performed, you must select an unlisted code. All coders must read both guidelines—section and subsection—before selecting a particular code. Not reading the guidelines is one of the largest mistakes a coder can make.

Unlisted Procedure Codes

You may be asking yourself, what is an unlisted procedure code, and how do I code a procedure if it is not listed? Each section of the CPT manual has codes that are considered unlisted. These codes are used when a physician performs some type of service or procedure for which no code has been established. This may be due to new procedures being implemented or new technology becoming available, or it may be that the service is not performed often enough to warrant a code. All unlisted procedure codes will end in 99, and they are listed at the beginning of each section in the guidelines. You will also find unlisted codes at the very end of a subsection or subheading in each section of the CPT manual: these represent the body site or the type of procedure performed. When using an unlisted procedure code, it is important to submit a special report. If no report is submitted with the claim, the claim may be denied or rejected.

PRACTICE EXERCISE 2-4

Give the unlisted code for the following procedures.

1. Unlisted procedure, arthroscopy

   Code(s) _____

2. Unlisted procedure, foot or toes

   Code(s) _____

3. Unlisted procedure, diaphragm

   Code(s) _____

4. Unlisted procedure, anesthesia

   Code(s) _____

5. Unlisted procedure, nervous system

   Code(s) _____

Special Reports

Special reports may be required to be filed with a claim for several reasons. First and foremost is when an unlisted procedure code has been reported. Other services that require a special report are new or unusual procedures. Special reports should be submitted for Category III codes or for codes that are seldom used. The report should include the type of service provided in detail, the extent of the procedure, and the need for the procedure. It should also include the equipment necessary to perform the procedure, the patient's symptoms, complexity of the patient's medical condition, any diagnostic or therapeutic procedures, time and effort, and the follow-up care for the patient. When special reports are not submitted with the claim, it may be denied or rejected due to the third-party payor not knowing the circumstances of the patient. Therefore, this information should be readily available from the patient's medical records. Documentation is a key element for proper coding.

MODIFIERS

Modifiers are listed on the inside front cover of the CPT manual. A more detailed explanation of modifiers is given in Appendix A of the manual. Modifiers are designed to give further explanation to the procedures performed by the physician. Modifiers consist of two numbers, a letter and a number, or two letters, but they all signify a specific explanation. They are placed after the CPT code by using a dash before appending the code. Let's look at an example. If a physician removes wax from a patient's ear, he or she would use code 69210 (cerumen removal, auditory canal, external). This code represents only one ear. If both ears had this procedure, a modifier –50 (bilateral procedure) should be appended to the original code of 69210. The correct placement of the modifier would be 69210–50. This informs the third-party payor that the procedure was performed on both ears. As you can see, the modifier does not change the code or the description of the code. It only provides additional information regarding the services that were rendered to the patient. It is important to understand that add-on codes are also modifier 51 exempt. The use or non-use of modifiers is also given in the guidelines before each section of the CPT manual. A good example of this is in the Anesthesia section. Now, let's review some modifiers from the inside cover of the CPT manual.

PRACTICE EXERCISE 2-5

Identify the correct modifier with the correct description below.

1. Multiple modifiers

   _____

2. Professional component

   _____

3. Decision for surgery

   _____

4. Prolonged Evaluation and Management Services

   _____

5. Two surgeons

   _____

CATEGORY II CODES

Category II codes consist of supplemental tracking codes. They are primarily used by administrations for the sole purpose of data collection. These codes have been developed to decrease chart reviews and measure the quality of patient care. They are also used by accrediting bodies and federal regulatory agencies. Category II codes are updated twice a year, in January and July. Coders working within the field may never have to use a Category II code.

CATEGORY III CODES

Codes listed within this section are considered temporary codes. As new technology emerges and new procedures are performed, there are no codes to report them. In the past, new procedures such as CT scans had to be reported using an unlisted procedure code. Therefore, these codes have been developed on a temporary basis to report these new procedures and new technology. Codes listed within this section may never become a Category I code within the CPT manual. A Category III code is archived after five years unless it can be proved the code is still needed. In order for a temporary code to be placed as a Category I code, it has to be used in multiple clinical locations and be approved by the FDA. All codes within the Category III section contain four digits followed by an alpha character, as in a cervicography, 0003T. These codes may be reported for services rendered if there are no appropriate codes listed elsewhere in the CPT manual. You will also find codes that have been deleted in Category III; this section will give you an appropriate code to report. Deleted codes are signified by the right and left triangle symbols.

HCPCS CODES

HCPCS codes are a set of national codes. These codes all begin with an alphabetical letter followed by four digits. They represent an array of services or equipment provided to the patient. The codes include but are not limited to durable medical equipment (crutches, wheelchairs), prostheses (artificial limbs), transport services (ambulance, flight helicopters), and even drugs that are administered to a patient. HCPCS also includes national modifiers, some of which are used to identify a specific anatomic site or a specific service. These codes are covered later within this workbook.

EVALUATION AND MANAGEMENT

The codes that are most often used are located in the **Evaluation and Management (E/M) section.** This section can also be the hardest for the new coder to learn, but with proper instruction and a little guidance, you can learn it quickly and easily. Let's review some of the basics of E/M assignment, which are based on several factors.

The first factor to consider is the **place of service.** This identifies the place or setting in which the service was provided. Some examples would be the physician's office, outpatient clinic, or inpatient hospital. The second factor in choosing the correct E/M codes is to identify the **type of service.** What was provided for the patient? Some examples of services provided would be an office visit, hospital admission, or flu vaccination. The third step in choosing the right code is to correctly identify the **patient status.** There are four types of patient status.

1. **New patient**—one who has not received professional services from the physician within the last three years or one who has never seen the physician.
2. **Established patient**—one who has received professional services within the last three years.
3. **Outpatient**—one who has not been formally admitted into a health care facility.
4. **Inpatient**—one who has formally been admitted into a health care facility.

KEY COMPONENTS OF THE MEDICAL RECORD

Once you have identified the place of service, type of service, and patient status, you are ready to locate the information in the medical record that identifies the key components of the service. The **key components** are the history, the examination, and the medical decision making (MDM). They consist of the chief complaint (CC); history of present illness (HPI); review of systems (ROS); past, family, and social history (PFSH); and time (represents the total amount or time and work associated with the service.)

Chief Complaint

The **chief complaint (CC)** is a concise statement made by the patient, describing the symptom, problem, or other reason for the visit or encounter. It must always be included in the history. The patient complaint is usually taken by a medical assistant when the patient is first placed in an examination room in an outpatient setting. It may include symptoms such as fever, stomach pain, headache, or any number of other reasons the patient is not feeling well. The CC is usually located within the first few lines of the patient's medical record, and may be recorded as either CC or S for subjective as in a SOAP note. (SOAP notes are used by physicians to document the encounter with the patient.)

History of Present Illness

The **history of present illness (HPI)** is a chronological description of the development of the patient's present illness from the first sign of the onset. The HPI may include the location (site on the body: leg), quality (characteristic: sharp, throbbing), severity (how intense the pain is on a scale of 1 to 10), duration (how long this episode or problem has lasted), timing (when does it occur), context (under what circumstance does it occur:

when I walk), modifying factors (what makes it better or worse: sitting down), associated signs and symptoms (what else is happening when it occurs: swelling).

Review of Systems

The **review of systems (ROS)** is an inventory of the body systems obtained through a series of questions that seeks to identify signs and symptoms that the patient may be experiencing. The physician will perform an ROS as part of the patient's physical examination. This may include a complete ROS (usually performed on new patients) or may only include one major body system (usually performed on established patients). The physician may also include body systems that are related to a patient's specific problem or complaint. The ROS may include **constitutional** (weight loss or gain, fever), **ophthalmologic** (eyes: cataract, glaucoma), **otolaryngology** (ears, nose, throat, mouth), **cardiovascular** (hypertension, chest pain), **respiratory** (asthma, cough, pneumonia), **gastrointestinal** (gallstones, ulcer, diverticulitis), **genitourinary** (menopause, UTI, kidney stones), **musculoskeletal** (arthritis, muscular dystrophy), **integumentary** (skin: rash, warts), **neurologic** (seizures, Alzheimer's, Parkinson's) **psychiatric** (anxiety, depression), **endocrine** (diabetes, estrogen imbalance), **hematologic/lymphatic** (leukemia, anemia, tonsillitis), and **allergic/immunologic (allergies, HIV, hepatitis).**

Past Family Social History

The **past family social history (PFSH)** is a review of the past family and social history of the patient. The physician decides on the extent of the PFHS according to the needs and diagnosis of the patient. Some examples of past medical history would include diagnoses such as hypertension or asthma. Previous surgeries would also be included. Medications that have or have not been prescribed to the patient such as Elavil or Humalog are always considered. Physicians also discuss and record the family history. Are the patient's parents still alive? Is there a family history of cancer or diabetes? The social history of the patient will also play an important role in the care of the patient. Does the patient state that he or she drinks or smokes? If so, how much and how often? What level of education does the patient have? Is the patient married? The physician also determines the level of history and the extent of the examination needed according to the present problem of the patient. These correspond to the four levels in the E/M services: problem focused, expanded problem focused, detailed, and comprehensive. For examinations, these levels consist of:

- **Problem focused examination**—a limited examination of the body area or organ system.
- **Expanded problem focused examination**—a limited exam of the affected body area or organ system with an additional examination to a related organ system.
- **Detailed examination**—an extended examination of both the affected area and related organ system.
- **Comprehensive examination**—a complete examination of a single organ system or a general multisystem examination.

For histories, these levels consist of:

- **Problem focused history**—chief complaint, brief history, or present illness.
- **Expanded problem focused history**—chief complaint, brief history.
- **Detailed history**—chief complaint, ROS, PFHS.
- **Comprehensive history**—chief complaint, extended history, ROS.

Elements of an Examination

During the examination, a physician must always take into consideration the appearance of the patient. This is called the **elements of an examination,** and includes various body areas (BA) and organ systems (OS), as well as an assessment of the patient's general appearance and condition (see Table 2–1). The three elements of an examination include general (constitutional), BA, and OS.

TABLE 2-1 THREE ELEMENTS OF A PATIENT EXAMINATION

General (constitutional)	• Blood Pressure (sitting, lying)
	• Pulse
	• Respiration
	• Temperature
	• Height
	• Weight
	• General appearance
Body areas	• Head (including face)
	• Neck
	• Chest (including breast and axillae)
	• Abdomen
	• Genitalia, groin, buttocks
	• Back
	• Each extremity
Organ system	• Ophthalmologic
	• Otolaryngologic
	• Cardiovascular
	• Respiratory
	• Gastrointestinal

TABLE 2-2 PROLONGED SERVICES

Total Duration of Time	Code
Less than 30 minutes	Not reported separately
30–74 minutes	99354 × 1
75–104 minutes	99354 × 1 and 99355 × 1
105–134 minutes	99354 × 1 and 99355 × 2
135–164 minutes	99354 × 1 and 99355 × 3
165–194 minutes	99354 × 1 and 99355 × 4

Time

When coding, **time** is a factor that should be included when choosing an E/M code. In some cases, the physician must spend more or less time with the patient than is allotted for that particular code. In these cases, *time* would represent the additional amount of time and work that is associated with that particular service for extenuating circumstances. (Time is never a factor when coding in the Emergency Department.) **Face-to-face time** is considered to be the amount of time the physician spends with the patient and/or family. **Non face-to-face time** is the amount of time the physician spends reviewing medical records and contacting other professionals. Time is considered a **prolonged service.** It is used in several different E/M services, including face-to-face and critical care. It may only be used once per day even if the service is not continuous. For example, if a patient was seen by a physician in the physician's office for a total amount of 1 hour and 15 minutes, you would code the primary office visit plus the prolonged service. Time may be the controlling factor when the physician spends more than 50 percent of his or her services face-to-face with the patient and/or family: this must always be documented in the patient's medical record. Prolonged services may also be billed without physician face-to-face contact in either an inpatient or outpatient setting. This code must be reported in addition to other services provided, including E/M, but it may only be used once a day even if the time is not continuous on that particular day. Prolonged service codes of less than 30 minutes total are not reported separately. (See Table 2–2.)

PRACTICE EXERCISE 2-6

Fill in the blank with the correct information or code.

1. Using code 99213, the typical time a physician spends with a patient face-to-face is _____ minutes.

2. Using code 99202, the typical time a physician spends with a patient is _____ minutes.

TABLE 2-3 LEVELS OF DECISION MAKING

Code	# of Diagnosis	Test/Data	Risk	Decision
99201	minimal	minimal	minimal	straightforward
99202	minimal	minimal	low	straightforward
99203	limited	low	moderate	moderate
99204	multiple	moderate	moderate	moderate
99205	extensive	extensive	high	high

3. Using code 99215, the physician spends a total of 1 1/2 hours with the patient. What prolonged service codes should be used in addition to the primary code?

    Code(s) _____

4. A new patient presents to the physician's office for management of hypertension. The physician spends a total of one hour with the new patient.

    Code(s) _____

Levels of Physician Decision Making

Upon examination, the physician must make a clinical judgment based on the patient's presenting problem. The complexity depends on four types of medical decision making (MDM), which are: straightforward, low complexity, moderate complexity, and high complexity (see Table 2–3). The possible number of diagnoses, risk of complications, diagnostic procedures, and tests determine the correct level. To select the correct E/M level, all of the key components must be met for two of three elements: history, examination, and decision making.

PRACTICE EXERCISE 2-7

Fill in the blanks with the correct information.

1. Using the encoder, the level of medical decision complexity for code 99204 is _____, the level of history is _____, and the examination level is _____.

2. The level of history using code 99214 is _____.

3. The level of examination using code 99211 is _____.

E/M HOSPITAL SERVICES

Within the E/M section, there are several types of hospital codes: initial hospital inpatient, observation, emergency department, consultations, critical care units, and hospital discharge (see Table 2–4). Key components for coding these services are equivalent to those used for coding the outpatient services. Most codes (excluding emergency and critical care services) must have two of the three key components. You may use the Easy Coder Quick Reference Guide to help in establishing the correct E/M codes. This feature may be accessed by clicking on the Notes icon and choosing "References."

Hospital Observation

Hospital observation codes (99218–99220) are used when a patient is not considered ill enough to actually be admitted into the hospital. For example, a patient presents to her family physician with a complaint of dizziness × 3 days. During a detailed examination, the physician discovers the patient was in an auto accident three days ago. The MDM is straightforward and the physician admits the patient into an observation status at a nearby hospital.

In this instance, the patient was not critically ill and the MDM was low complexity, qualifying the patient for initial observation care. To code this correctly, you must code only the observation room and not the office visit, since both services happened on the same day (the patient must spend eight hours in observation status).

When coding hospital observation, use the same codes for both new and established patients. These codes differ from postoperative observation or recovery room observation. (Hospitals are not required to have an observation room.) These codes also apply to patients who have been placed in observation status who reside in nursing homes or similar institutions. For patients admitted into the hospital on a date following an observation date, an initial hospital admission code should be used. For patients admitted into the hospital on the same day as an observation, the inpatient hospital admission code should be used. Do not code the observation discharge with an initial hospital admission. For patients admitted (as observation or inpatient hospital care) and discharged on the same day, use codes 99234 through 99236.

PRACTICE EXERCISE 2-8

Fill in the correct code(s) for the following.

1. A patient is placed in observation for chest pain. A detailed history was taken and the MDM was low complexity.

   Code(s) _____

2. Joe was placed in observation following a fall from a second-story window. A comprehensive examination and a decision of moderate complexity were taken before Joe was released ten hours later.

   Code(s) _____

3. Mary presented to the Emergency Room complaining of a severe headache. At that time she was placed in observation. When the headache did not subside, the attending physician performed an x-ray of Mary's head. After the x-ray

TABLE 2-4   EVALUATION AND MANAGEMENT

Brief	• Short in duration
	• Short in extent
	• Limited to the affected body area *or*
	• Limited to the organ system
	• Small or no risk factor
	• Self-limiting or minor problem
Expanded	• Limited to the affected body area
	• Limited to the organ system
	• Includes other symptoms or related organ systems
	• Low to moderate risk factor
Detailed	• Extended examination of the affected body area(s) *or*
	• Extended examination of affected organ system(s)
	• Longer length of time with patient
	• Moderate risk factor
Comprehensive	• General multisystem examination *or*
	• Complete exam of a single organ system
	• Larger number of possible diagnoses
	• Larger number of management options
	• Larger risk factor or complications
	• Large number of records to review, analyze, or obtain
Diagnosis	• 99201 or 99211 One diagnosis (usually not seen by physician)
	• 99202 or 99212 One diagnosis (seen by the physician)
	• 99203 or 99213 Two or three diagnoses
	• 99204 or 99214 Three or four diagnoses
	• 99205 or 99215 Three or more diagnoses

Diagnosis may be adjusted according to the severity of the illness, then use time.

revealed a small lesion, she was admitted into the hospital, but refused treatment. She was discharged on the same day.

Code(s) _____

Hospital Inpatient

Initial hospital codes (99221–99223) follow the rules for admission as stated in the E/M guidelines. They must contain two key components. These codes are used only to admit a new or established patient. Typically, the physician spends 30 to 70 minutes face-to-face with the patient and/or on the hospital unit upon admission, depending on the severity of the presenting problem. This includes the key components along with coordination of care and counseling the patient. Each additional day the patient is hospitalized is called **subsequent hospital care;** these codes range from 99231 to 99233. Note that this code range is typically used when the patient is not responding to treatment or has developed an additional problem. Now find code 99233. As you can see, the patient's complications are significant and the physician has spent approximately 35 minutes with this patient. At this time, the attending physician may consult with another physician for advice on a specific problem the patient is encountering. This is called a **consultation.** A consultation may be verbal or written and must be recorded in the patient's medical records along with the consulting physician's written report. When family members request a consultation for an inpatient, this must be coded as an office visit or confirmatory code. Consultation codes consist of: office consultation, initial inpatient consultation, follow-up consultation, and confirmatory consultation.

PRACTICE EXERCISE 2-9

Fill in the correct codes for the following.

1. The code range for a follow-up inpatient consultation is from code _____ to code _____.

2. The code range for a confirmatory consultation is from code _____ to code _____.

3. The code range for an initial inpatient consultation is from code _____ to code _____.

Emergency Room Services

Emergency room or emergency department services are used by patients who present with a need for immediate medical attention. Hospital-based emergency rooms are required by law to be open 24 hours a day. Patients requiring emergency treatment do not need to schedule appointments, but are seen on a triage system. This system is based on emergency services being given to the most critically ill patients first. In coding for emergency department services, there is no distinction between new and established

TABLE 2-5 PROLONGED CRITICAL CARE

Total Time Duration	Codes
Less than 30 minutes	Use E/M code
30–74 minutes	99291 × 1
75–104 minutes	99291 × 1 and 99292 × 1
105–134 minutes	99291 × 1 and 99292 × 2
135–164 minutes	99291 × 1 and 99292 × 3
165–194 minutes	99291 × 1 and 99292 × 4

patients. Codes are based on the medical decision making and time is not a key component. For example, with the code 99281, the MDM is straightforward. Patients presenting in the ER usually have a minor or self-limited problem, whereas patients requiring a code of 99285 usually have a life-threatening illness requiring an MDM of high complexity.

Critical Care

Patients requiring a higher level of treatment are considered **critical care** patients. Use these codes when an injury includes one or more vital organ systems. The same physician can provide critical care and other E/M services on the same day. Critical care codes (99291–99292) are based on the key component of time. Code 99291 is used to report the first 30 minutes of care, with code 99292 used to code each additional 30 minutes (see Table 2–5). Critical care services are the same for adults, children, and neonates. Inpatient Pediatric Care codes 99293 and 99294 are used for the E/M on a daily basis for infants aged 29 days through 24 months. Codes 99295 and 99296 are used on infants aged 28 days or less and are considered Inpatient Neonatal Critical Care. Sometimes an infant is not critically ill but still requires intensive care. This occurs when a neonate has a low birth weight (LBW) of less than 2500 grams, or very low birth weight (VLBW) of less than 1500 grams. In these cases, codes 99298 and 99299 are used.

Using the encoder, enter Critical Care *critical care code* in the Search box. Now double click on the Code Detail box, 99291—this code appears in the Code Detail box, along with code 99292. Highlight code 99292, and the add-on code message appears at the bottom of your screen. Click on the Instructions tab. As you can see, this code must be used in conjunction with code 99291. Now click on the Section Notes. The section note gives additional information on the context in which these codes may be used.

NURSING FACILITY SERVICES, ASSESSMENT AND DISCHARGE

Evaluation and management codes used for nursing facility services (NFS) include patients in longterm care facilities; skilled nursing facilities, intermediate care facilities, or a psychiatric residential treatment center. The codes are used for both new and established patients. Before a patient can be admitted into an NFS, an assessment must be conducted to establish functional capacity and any potential problems, using all three key components. Physicians typically spend 30 to 55 minutes with the patient or at the facility, developing a patient plan of care and documenting it in the patient's medical record. (Assessments can be performed at one or more sites.) Subsequent nursing facility care requires two of the three key components and is based on a 24-hour period. Patients who are discharged from a hospital and admitted into an NFS should be coded for a hospital discharge (99238–99239) and NFS admittance (99301–99303). A nursing facility must include 24-hour care and be a stand-alone facility. If psychotherapy treatments are provided in addition to E/M services, you should code them separately. When coding for a patient discharge, you should code the discharge based on time. The total amount of time should include the patient's final examination, preparation of discharge instructions, referral forms, and, if necessary, medications and continuation of care.

Domiciliary, Rest Home, or Custodial Care

Patients requiring these codes are unable to live independently. The services given in domiciliary, rest home, or custodial care include food, lodging, personal care, and leisure activities. Medical care such as physical therapy or occupational therapy must be coded in addition to codes in this section. These codes are based on a new or established patient and do not include a medical component. When you code for a new patient, the services must contain the three key components and be documented in the medical record. Services for established patients must contain two of the three components. Time is not a component within this section.

Home Services

Home service codes are used when physicians provide medical care to patients in a private residence. These codes are based on new or established patients. New patients require three key components while an established patient requires two key components. Let's compare code 99341 to code 99345. In code 99341, there is a straightforward MDM with a low severity problem, with the physician spending 20 minutes face-to-face, whereas in code 99345, the MDM is of high complexity. Here the patient has developed a significant new problem and the physician has spent approximately 75 minutes face-to-face.

PHYSICIAN STANDBY SERVICES

A standby service code (99260) is used when attending physicians request another physician to be available (on standby) in case his or her services are needed (see Table 2–6). The standby physician may not attend to any other patients and must have a total duration of standby of more than 30 minutes. Physicians using a standby code usually are

TABLE 2-6 PHYSICIAN STAND-BY SERVICES

Duration of Time	Code
Less than 30 minutes	Not reported
30–59 minutes	99360
60–89 minutes	99360 × 1
90–119 minutes	99360 × 2
120 minutes	99360 × 3

standing in attendance for surgical procedures or other procedures such as an EEG procedure or waiting for a frozen section for the laboratory. The code may not be used for hospital mandated services, nor if the standby physician's services were actually used. To code appropriately, you should code in increments of 30 minutes each.

Case Management

Case management codes include team conferences (99361, 99362) and telephone calls (99371, 99372). You will use these codes when the physician is in total and direct care of the patient. The codes are used to coordinate care with other health care professionals, without face-to-face services. They are usually not paid for by a third party.

Preventive Medicine Services

Codes used for preventive medicine are based on new (99381–99387) or established (99392–99393) patients and are based on the age of the patient (see Table 2-7). These codes are used for guidance and risk factor reduction interventions and are provided at the initial examination of a healthy individual. Other procedures such as x-rays, immunizations, or laboratory services are coded in addition to the preventive medicine codes. If any abnormality was found in the process of performing preventive medicine, then you should use the outpatient or new (99210–99215) or the established (99211–99215) codes in addition to the preventive medicine codes. This identifies a separate identifiable service.

COUNSELING AND RISK FACTOR REDUCTION INTERVENTION

Codes within this section refer to counseling individuals or groups of individuals. Counseling may include a single patient's laboratory results or a group encounter on substance abuse. You should not use them for patients with an established illness, but strictly for risk reduction intervention. Coding is based on the time component, lasting

TABLE 2-7 PREVENTATIVE MEDICINE

New Patient	Code	Established Patient	Code
Under 1 year	99381	Under 1 year	99391
Age 1–4 years	99382	Age 1–4 years	99392
Age 5–11 years	99383	Age 5–11 years	99393
Age 12–17 years	99384	Age 12–17 years	99394
Age 18–39 years	99385	Age 18–39 years	99395
Age 40–64 years	99386	Age 40–69 years	99396
65 years and older	99387	65 years and older	99397

from approximately 15 to 60 minutes. There are also two additional codes within this section, 99420 and 99429. The first code, 99420, is primarily used for a health hazard assessment. The last code, 99429, is an unlisted preventive service code, which you should submit with a special report explaining the services rendered.

Newborn Care

In coding newborn care, you should remember one important factor. These codes use several different settings and include codes for newborn stabilization and resuscitation. The codes include settings such as hospitals, birthing suites, and "other" newborn care settings. When coding an admission and discharge of a newborn on the same day, use the code 99435. Newborns discharged on a later date should be coded as a normal hospital discharge code of 99238.

Special E/M Services

Physicians other than the primary care physician use two of the three codes within this section. The codes are used to establish a baseline for medical disability, and are work-related. The primary physician to establish basic life and/or disability may use the other code. You will use code 99450 primarily when patients are required to obtain a certificate of health for purposes such as insurance. The services may be performed in any setting and are applied to both new and established patients.

Other E/M Services

The code 99499 is the only code listed in the "Other" section. It is an unlisted E/M service code that requires a special report to accompany the service. You should use this code only when no other code is available to describe the services rendered.

UNDERCODING AND OVERCODING

Typically, some new coders are afraid of overcoding and tend to undercode. **Undercoding** services results when the highest level of coding has not been achieved. It results in an underpayment of reimbursement from third-party payors. Other new coders become eager and want as much money for their physician as possible and tend to overcode. **Overcoding** services results when services performed are charged at a level that is higher than what was actually performed. Overcoding is considered fraud and may result in physician penalties and suspension of license. Therefore, it is important to read the guidelines and code each level of service appropriately.

CHAPTER REVIEW

I. Short Answer

1. The history level in code 99245 is _____.

2. The service performed in code 99361 is a/an _____.

3. The patient's age(s) in code 99396 is/are _____.

4. One who has not been formally admitted into a healthcare facility is called a/an
   _____.

5. Complexity depends on four types of medical decision making, which are:
   a. _____
   b. _____
   c. _____
   d. _____

6. Using an encoder, we find that the level of medical decision complexity for code 99204 is _____, the level of history is _____ and the examination level is _____.

7. The level of history using code 99214 is _____.

8. The level of examination using code 99211 is _____.

II. Coding Exercises

Using Encoder Pro, code the following.

9. Jamie presented to the emergency room complaining of severe stomach pain, which radiated into his back. Dr. Kelley performed an expanded history and MDM of moderate complexity and admitted Jamie with a diagnosis of appendicitis.

   Code(s) _____

10. John, who is an established patient of Dr. Stoddard, just purchased a life insurance policy. While performing the medical history and examination, Dr. Stoddard found John had an abnormally high blood pressure, completed the necessary

documentation for John's policy, and prescribed medication for the high blood pressure.

Code(s) _____

11. On March 3, 2007, Julie was admitted into the hospital for a coronary artery bypass by Dr. Sokol. For the next 21 days, Dr. Sokol spent approximately 25 minutes each day providing care for Julie. On March 25, Dr. Sokol discharged Julie, taking 30 minutes to prepare the documentation.

Code(s) _____

12. Naomi is a 25-year-old who presents to her regular physician for an annual check-up, with no presenting problems.

Code(s) _____

13. Joe, aged 67, has been a patient of Dr. Jeffery for many years. Today he has an appointment for a wellness visit. He presents with no complaints, but decides to receive a flu vaccine, which is billed to Medicare. (Code the visit only.)

Code(s) _____

14. Amy took her 3-month-old into Dr. Camry for his first visit. Dr. Camry examined the infant and diagnosed him as a normal, healthy three-month-old.

Code(s) _____

15. Dr. Newbury was called to the home of a longtime patient. The patient presented with a severe cough, wheezing, high fever, and overall malaise. Dr. Newbury performed an expanded problem focused history and examination, with an MDM of low complexity.

Code(s) _____

III. True/False

Indicate whether the sentence or statement is true or false.

___ 16. Marital status is indicated in a patient's social history.

___ 17. Consultation is a type of service.

___ 18. Moderate severity means there is a moderate risk of death without treatment.

___ 19. An outpatient setting is an example of a place of service.

___ 20. In the review of systems, an example of "constitutional" would include weight gain.

___ 21. A comprehensive exam only includes one organ system.

___ 22. Face-to-face time is the amount of time the physician spends with only the patient.

___ 23. Prolonged service codes of less than 30 minutes are always reported separately.

___ 24. Low complexity is a level of decision making.

___ 25. When coding hospital observation, different codes are used for new and established patients.

IV. Matching

Match the correct system to each examination element.

    a. Body system   b. Organ system

___ **26.** Allergic

___ **27.** Respiratory

___ **28.** Neck

___ **29.** Psychiatric

___ **30.** Arm

___ **31.** Cardiovascular

___ **32.** Back

___ **33.** Abdomen

___ **34.** Gastrointestinal

___ **35.** Head

Chapter 3
Anesthesia

LEARNING OBJECTIVES

After completing this chapter, the learner should be able to:

- Identify types of anesthesia
- Calculate anesthesia payments
- Understand anesthesia modifiers
- Understand relative values

ANESTHESIA

Anesthesia is defined as a partial or complete loss of sensation, with or without loss of consciousness. It is used to render patients insensible to pain and stress, to manage life functions under surgery, to relieve pain, and to help in the management of resuscitation. There are three stages in the progression of anesthesia. In the first and second stage, voluntary control is lost. In the last or third stage, total relaxation with no muscle rigidity and with deep regular breathing is present. The depths of anesthesia are based on the movement of the eyes, pupillary size, and respiration. There are approximately 40 different methods with which to administer anesthesia. Anesthesia can be partial or complete, with or without loss of consciousness, and with or without an analgesic. The most widely used administrations are local, general, regional, and spinal (which is also known as an epidural). Although these codes represent anatomical sites, there are also codes that must be used according to the specific procedure being performed. Pathology procedures (epidermal biopsy) and burns or debridement are examples.

Physicians are only one type of provider who can administer anesthesia. A certified registered nurse anesthetist (CRNA) can also administer anesthesia, but must use an additional modifier of QX, if under the direction of a physician, or QZ, without physician direction. Additional modifiers consist of AA (services performed by an anesthesiologist), AD (medical supervision by a physician with more than four anesthesia procedures), GC (resident physician under the direction of a teaching physician), QK (medical direction of two to four concurrent anesthesia procedures), and QY (anesthesiologist directing one CRNA). Materials and supplies (including sterile tray) may also be billed separately. These must be over and above those usually included in the office visit and should be identified by using code 99070.

Types of Anesthesia

Local

Local anesthesia is generally used to perform minor surgery or in the treatment of lacerations. It inhibits the nerve impulses by decreasing the flow of sodium ions into nerve cells. Generally, is it administered topically and absorbed through the skin. Local anesthesia can also be administered by the application of lidocaine (topically) or injected in the muscle (subcutaneously).

General

General anesthesia is a state of total unconsciousness, which is most widely used in surgical procedures. Methods of administration would include intravenously, rectally, by inhalation, and intramuscularly.

Regional

Regional anesthesia consists of blocking a nerve or a specific site, causing a loss of sensation over that particular area. Depending on the site to be blocked, it may take several injections to accomplish a regional block.

Spinal

A spinal block is also known as an **epidural.** It is accomplished by injecting an anesthetic into the spaces between the vertebrae.

Before you start coding for anesthesia, there are several factors you must consider:

- Calculating formula for payment
- What physical status modifiers apply
- With or without analgesia
- Whether the same physician is performing the services and administering anesthesia

- How many procedures are being performed
- Whether conscious sedation is being used

CALCULATING THE FORMULA FOR ANESTHESIA

The basic formula used in the calculation of anesthesia is measured in units—basic units, time units, and modifying units, or B + T + M—and then multiplied by the conversion factor. The **basic unit (B)** establishes national unit values based on the complexity of the service performed. The American Society of Anesthesiologists publishes the **Relative Value Guide,** which compares anesthesia services. The relative value guide is based on the type of procedure performed and establishes a **basic unit value** according to the complexity of the service. These guides are available from the Federal Register and The American Society of Anesthesiologists. Medicare also has a conversion factor for anesthesia services, based on the geological location in the United States. Each region has a carrier number and locality number (see Table 3–1). Be sure to check with your own state for the correct conversion factor.

Time Unit

Time unit (T) is calculated as each 15 minutes equalling 1 time unit. Multiple procedures are reported with the highest service units only (for two procedures during the same time period, one ranked at 10 units, the other 5 units, you should report only the 10 units). It is important to remember that modifier 51 (multiple procedure) is not usually used in anesthesia. Once the patient is anesthetized, it is the length of the service, not the number of procedures performed, that is reported. Therefore, "time" begins when the anesthesiologist first prepares the patient for services and ends only when the patient is no longer receiving care from the anesthesiologist.

Modifying Units

The **modifying unit (M)** characterizes the patient's physical condition, which is indicated by physical status modifiers P1 through P6. The anesthesiologist uses these modifiers to indicate the patient's physical condition and the complexity of the services to be provided (see Table 3–2). A P1 modifier is for a normal healthy patient, whereas a P4 modifier indicates a patient with a severe systemic disease. Therefore, a P4 modifier would indicate a more complex level of services. Modifier P6 is only used when a patient is declared brain dead and is donating his or her bodily organs. As you can see in Table 3–2, Physical status modifiers are also given a relative guide:

Physical Status

A **physical status unit** is a payment based on units assigned for the physical status rating and the qualifying circumstances. These codes range from 99100 to 99140. When reporting these codes, it is important to remember that they must not be reported alone.

TABLE 3-1 MEDICARE CONVERSION FACTOR

Carrier Number	Locality Number	Locality Name	Dollar Amount
00510	00	Alabama	17.04
00831	01	Alaska	29.66
00520	13	Arkansas	16.52
31146	26	Anaheim/Santa Ana, CA	18.68
31146	18	Los Angeles, CA	18.72
00824	01	Colorado	17.46
00591	00	Connecticut	18.60
00902	01	Delaware	17.88
00590	04	Miami, FL	19.93
00511	01	Atlanta, GA	17.99
00952	16	Chicago, IL	19.72
00953	01	Detroit, MI	21.10
00512	00	Mississippi	16.95
14330	04	Queens, NY	20.01
05535	00	North Carolina	17.03
00883	00	Ohio	17.58
00973	20	Puerto Rico	15.93
00870	01	Rhode Island	18.11
00880	01	South Carolina	16.59
05440	35	Tennessee	16.93
00900	31	Austin, TX	17.79
00900	20	Beaumont, TX	17.92
00900	09	Brazoria, TX	18.23
00910	09	Utah	17.10
00973	50	Virgin Islands	17.81

TABLE 3-2 PHYSICAL STATUS MODIFIERS

Physical Status Modifier	Description	Relative Value
P1	Normal healthy patient	0
P2	Mild systemic disease	0
P3	Severe systemic disease	1
P4	Severe systemic disease and threat to life	3
P5	Not expected to live without operation	4
P6	Brain dead	0

They must be reported as additional procedure numbers, qualifying the anesthesia procedure or service, and are only used as additional risk factors. These codes are also given a basic relative value according to the risk factor.

Qualifying Circumstances

Codes depicting **qualifying circumstances** begin with the prefix 99. These codes are used for patients whose condition makes it harder to administer anesthesia. They also have a relative value and so may not be used alone. For example, find code 99100; this code is used for patients of extreme age, under 1 year or over 70 years of age. This code has a relative value of 1. To code this correctly, you must add the patient status modifier and the qualifying circumstances together to get the sum of the modifying units.

EXAMPLE

To better see how to code anesthesia, let's look at this example. Enter code *11770* into the Search box (Excision of pilonidal cyst, simple), and use a basic value guide of 3. To use the formula B + M + T, let's review what we have learned in the following case scenario.

A 72-year-old male has been scheduled to remove a pilonidal cyst (the basic unit has a relative value of 3) at Dr. Hernandez's office in Utah. He has been previously diagnosed with a severe systemic disease, giving him a P4 physical status, with a relative value of 3. The procedure takes one hour to perform, a time unit of 4.

B	basic value	3	
M	modifier	4	(physical status 3, plus qualifying circumstance 1)
T	time	4	
Total units		11	

Because the locality of Dr. Hernandez's office is in Utah, which has a Medicare conversion factor of $17.10, the total amount of this anesthesia procedure would calculate to be $1882.10 (17.10 × 11).

ANALGESIA

Analgesia is the loss of or absence of the normal sensation of pain. There are several variations associated with anesthesia. **Preemptive analgesia** is administrated before surgery to reduce postoperative pain and disability. **Infiltration anesthesia** is injected into the nerve endings to reduce sensation in a localized area. **Continuous caudal analgesia** is an analgesia that is injected continuously into the sacral hiatus during childbirth. **Patient-controlled analgesia** permits the patient to administer analgesia at his or her own rate by using an infusion pump. All of these methods are used in conjunction with the various methods of administering anesthesia.

Conscious Sedation

Conscious sedation is a level of consciousness in which the patient is in a state of depressed consciousness but able to respond to physical and verbal commands and to breathe without assistance. A physician may administer both the analgesia and anesthesia in conjunction with performing a surgical procedure. Some examples of such procedures would be: endoscopic procedures, changing wound dressings, suturing lacerations, and so forth. Administration by the physician is often done when the surgical procedure is performed in an outpatient setting. These are considered minor procedures and the patients are able to resume their normal activity.

Additional Modifiers

Additional modifiers may also be used in coding anesthesia, as you learned in the previous chapters. These tell the third-party payor the circumstances under which payment may be effected.

CHAPTER REVIEW

I. Short Answer

Use the Medicare conversion table to answer the following questions.

1. What is the reimbursement for Austin, Texas? _____

2. What is the locality number of Puerto Rico? _____

3. How many locality numbers does Texas have? _____

4. What is the carrier number for Delaware? _____

5. Which state has the highest reimbursement? _____

6. Which state has the lowest reimbursement? _____

II. Coding Exercises

Use an encoder or coding manuals to code the following procedures.

7. Dr. Hines performed an appendectomy, which took four hours. How many units of anesthesia were used, based on the four hours?

   _____

8. Dr. Davies performed a parietal pleurectomy and lung biopsy, which took a total of 3 hours and 15 minutes. How many units of anesthesia were used?

   _____

9. Dr. Chow removed Tommy's tonsils, which took two hours. How many units of anesthesia were used? _____

10. Using the Anesthesia table, calculate the following payment. Dr. Reim performed a radical hysterectomy in Arizona. The procedure took a total of 2 hours and 45 minutes, on a patient with no presenting problems. The basic unit for the procedure is 3.

    Payment $ _____

11. Using the Anesthesia table, calculate the following payment and give the anesthesia procedure code. Sarah Hines, M.D. of Utah, rendered anesthesia for an intracranial subdural tap. The patient, aged 75, had a severe systemic disease but was expected to tolerate the procedure.

    Payment $ _____ Code _____

12. Using Encoder Pro, enter code *99100* in the Search box. The age of the patient is: _____. Notice that in the Code Detail box, all the codes for qualifying circumstances are given. Now, find the 99116. Anesthesia is complicated by _____

    _____

13. Enter code *99135* into the Search box. What is the diagnosis of the patient?

    _____

14. When would you use modifier P1?

    _____

    _____

III. Matching

Match the correct modifier with the correct description.

   a. modifier 21   b. modifier 99

   c. modifier 50   d. modifier 26

   ___ 15. Bilateral procedures

   ___ 16. Technical component

   ___ 17. Prolonged E/M service

   ___ 18. Multiple procedures

Chapter 4
CPT Surgery

KEY TERMS

allograft	external fixation	subcutaneous
autograft	internal fixation	surgical package
closed treatment	lesions	unbundling
debridement	manipulation	vertebral interspace
dermis	necrosis	xenograft
epidermis	open treatment	

LEARNING OBJECTIVES

After completing this chapter, the learner should be able to:

- Understand medical terms
- Identify open and closed treatments
- Apply correct CPT codes
- Apply correct modifiers
- Identify types of fractures
- Identify internal and external fixation devices

SURGERY

The surgery section is the largest section within the CPT-4 codes. When you are coding surgery, there are a few points to remember. Surgery is first coded by the body system (Integumentary System, Musculoskeletal System, etc.) then by the procedure (excision, incision, repair, etc.). It includes a surgical package, follow-up care, and materials supplied by the physician. It seems like a lot to try to remember what all of these services include and exclude. So, let's take it one step at a time.

Surgical Package, Follow-Up Care, and Materials

A **surgical package** refers to what is included when a physician performs surgery. Almost always, a surgical package will include:

- Topical anesthesia (if needed)
- One evaluation and management on the day of or just prior to the surgical procedure, which includes the history and physical
- Postoperative care, which includes writing prescriptions, dictating medical notes of the procedure performed, and speaking with family members regarding the procedure
- Additional written orders
- Evaluation of the patient immediately following the procedure (postoperative)
- Follow-up care during the postoperative period

Although the surgical package does include these, there are additional elements to a surgical procedure that may be billed separately. This would include complications from the surgery itself. Supplies and materials provided by the physician above the normal supplies used may be billed by using code 99070. Additional surgical trays or drugs may be coded by using the individual appropriate code.

To code appropriately, always click on the Annotations button to review the procedure and guidelines associated with that particular code. It's important to remember that the code you are using must match the surgical procedure documented in the patient's medical record. When the patient returns for a postoperative visit associated with the surgical procedure, always use code 99024 as an administrative purpose. This code may be used when extracting sutures used to close the procedure, and no charge is applied. If, however, a patient needs to see the physician during the postoperative period for a separate identifiable condition not associated with the surgical procedure, then it is billed separately, and a modifier is appended to the second code. When coding for diagnostic procedures, the postoperative care includes only the care needed to recover from that particular procedure only. If an additional procedure such as a biopsy is performed, it should be reported separately.

Multiple Procedures

During certain surgical procedures, a physician may perform a second surgical procedure that is associated with a particular disease or condition. An example of this would be a cardiac bypass. The physician must obtain an artery or vein from the patient in order to place it in the heart as a bypass. It requires more than one procedure to obtain the primary procedure being performed. Such an additional procedure is subject to the primary procedure. It is considered part of the surgical package and they are bundled into one code. When a surgical package is coded separately, it is considered **unbundling** and is an act of fraud. However, if a physician performs more than one procedure that is not a bundled service, each procedure may be reported. In these instances, modifiers are added to the additional procedure code.

> **TIP:** Add-on codes are used when a particular code does not provide enough information about the procedure. Codes requiring an additional add-on code are always designated with a + (plus) sign. You may also see terms such as "each additional," "use with," "in conjunction with," or "list separately." When add-on codes are used, they are never reported alone, so they do not need the use of a modifier.

INTEGUMENTARY SYSTEM

The Integumentary System section consists of the skin and its appendages (see Figure 4-1). Your hair, nails, and sweat glands are all part of the integumentary system. But coding involves much more than that. Over the next few pages, you will learn the different layers of skin, types of wounds, lesions, and various methods of repair and procedures.

Structure of the Skin

The skin consists of three distinct layers. The outermost layer is called the **epidermis.** This is the part of the skin you see every day, and it has five sublayers. The **dermis** is

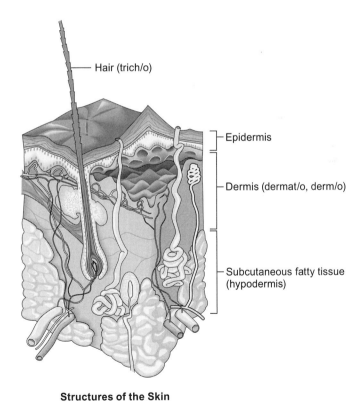

Structures of the Skin

Figure 4-1 The integumentary system

the middle layer of skin, which is the thickest layer. This layer contains muscle, nerve endings, hair follicles, blood vessels, and sweat glands. The **subcutaneous,** the deepest layer of skin, lies under the dermis. It is also called the superficial fascia. This is the part of the skin that contains most of the body's fat.

Types of Wounds and Lesions

To determine the best method to close a wound, physicians first must consider multiple factors, including the type of wound, size of the wound, and age of the patient (see Figure 4–2). They must also consider the possibility of infection. But that is not the extent of

A. Bruise, also known as a contusion, results from damage to the soft tissues and blood vessels, which causes bleeding beneath the skin surface. A bruise in a light-skinned individual will change from red to purple to greenish yellow before fading. In a dark-skinned person, the bruise will first look dark red, then darker red, brown, or purple, and slowly fade.

B. Abrasion, also known as a scrape or rug burn, results when the outer layer of skin is scraped or rubbed away. Exposure of nerve endings makes this type of wound painful, and the presence of debris from the scraped surface (rug fibers, gravel, sand) makes abrasions highly susceptible to infection.

C. Laceration, also known as a cut or incision, is caused by sharp objects such as knives or glass, or from trauma due to a strike from a blunt object that opens the skin, such as a baseball bat. If the wound is deep, the cut may bleed profusely; if nerve endings are exposed, it could also be painful.

D. Avulsion results when the skin or tissue is torn away from the body, either partially or completely. The bleeding and pain depends on the depth of tissue affected.

E. Puncture results when the skin is pierced by a sharp object such as a pencil, nail, or bullet. If a piece of the object remains in the skin, or if there is little bleeding due to the depth and location of the puncture, infection is likely.

Figure 4-2 Types of wounds

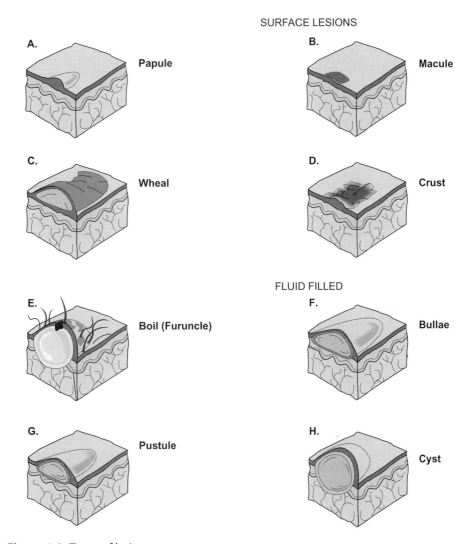

SURFACE LESIONS

A. Papule

B. Macule

C. Wheal

D. Crust

FLUID FILLED

E. Boil (Furuncle)

F. Bullae

G. Pustule

H. Cyst

Figure 4-3 Types of lesions

what they take into account when making their decisions. They must also consider the depth of the wound. Superficial wounds involve only the epidermis and dermis and require a simple closure. Full-thickness wounds involve the skin and subcutaneous layers; they require an intermediate closure. Deep wounds and complicated wounds involve a body cavity. (An example of a deep or complicated wound would be a gunshot wound.) Finally, physicians must also consider how the wound occurred. Of course, there are many types of wounds, so let's take some of the most obvious. These would include incised wounds from surgical cuts to open tissue to view; stab wounds; bullet wounds; and lacerated, contused, and crush wounds. These all require a different type of closure based on all of the factors that must be considered. You will code wounds based on type of repair, anatomical site, and then the size of the wound. Multiple wounds within the same anatomic group are added together, and the sum is then coded. When using more than one classification of wound repair, code the most complicated repair first (primary), leaving the less complicated to be coded last (secondary), with a modifier of 51 added to the secondary code.

Lesions are various types of skin disorder (see Figure 4–3). They also require different closures, based on the same principles as wounds. They do have a few exceptions, though. Benign and malignant lesions are coded independently, not added together. The lesion must include the margins of the lesion and thus should be coded by the greatest diameter (lesion plus margin). When lesions require more than a simple closure, report the intermediate or complex closure in addition to the simple closure.

PRACTICE EXERCISE 4-1

Find the code or range of codes for the following.

1. Wound of the forearm measuring 3.0 cm; simple

   Code(s) _____

2. Wound of the face measuring 3.0 cm; simple, with wound of the lip measuring 2.5 cm; simple

   Code(s) _____

3. Wound of the leg measuring 5.5 cm; simple, with secondary wound of the ear measuring 2.0 cm; simple

   Code(s) _____

4. Wound of the scalp measuring 8.0 cm; simple, with a secondary wound of the trunk measuring 4.5 cm; complicated

   Code(s) _____

5. Excision of a malignant lesion of the face measuring 1.0 cm; simple

   Code(s) _____

6. Excision of one benign lesion of the thigh measuring 2.0 cm; simple, with excision of a benign lesion of the thigh measuring 3.0 cm; complex

   Code(s) _____

7. Complex repair of the upper femur measuring 12.5 cm, with anesthesia

   Code(s) _____

8. Re-excision of a malignant lesion, including margins, on the trunk, measuring 4.0 cm, during the post-operative period

   Code(s) _____

Methods of Repair

In repairing a wound or incision, the physician must determine the most appropriate closure technique. This depends on the specific type, depth, and location of the wound.

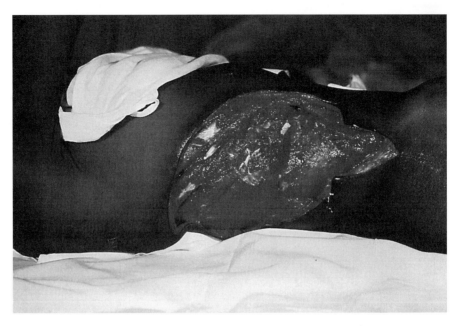

Figure 4-4 Severe tissue necrosis, post-debridement, prior to skin graft (Image courtesy of the Centers for Disease Control and Prevention)

While some wounds may require a suture, staple, or tissue adhesive technique, others (such as a skin tag) may require a simple removal or an incision and drainage. Certain types of wounds may need **debridement** (cleaning) of the wound to remove tissue **necrosis** (dead tissue) or foreign materials (see Figure 4–4). It is also important to remember that simple wound repair includes a local anesthesia, but intermediate and complex repair does not include anesthesia, which must be reported separately. A more extensive repair might include tissue transfer and skin grafts. Grafts may come from the individual patient (**autograft**), a donor (**allograft**), or an animal such as a pig (**xenograft**). If the physician performed a tissue transfer in the office, you should report the supply of this skin substitute separately. Materials used for a routine dressing are not reported separately. When coding for adjacent tissue transfer (the autograft that is necessary to close the wound), the secondary site is considered an additional procedure and is reported. You should also report surgical preparation of the site.

PRACTICE EXERCISE 4-2

Find the code or range of codes for the following.

1. Harvest of skin for tissue culture skin autograft, 90 cm

   Code(s) _____

2. Xenograft for temporary closure of the leg, 50 cm, infant

   Code(s) _____

3. Dermal autograft, trunk; 2% body area, infant

Code(s) _____

4. Surgical preparation of the recipient site by excision of an open wound, 100 cm

Code(s) _____

5. Full thickness graft, free, including direct closure of donor's site; arm, 40 cm

Code(s) _____

Burns, Destruction, and Reconstruction

When coding for a burn victim, code by the total body surface area. Report E/M codes separately, and include the applications of all dressings in the procedure. When coding for the destruction of a lesion, include any local anesthesia in the procedure. Destruction methods might include cryosurgery laser, electrosurgery, or chemical treatment. Reconstruction codes within the Integumentary System section are used to report the repair and reconstruction of the breast. The Integumentary System section includes the excision codes for breast biopsy and mastectomies. These codes do not include resections of chest wall tumors. Always remember, when reporting bilateral procedures, that you should use modifier 50. (See Figure 4–5.)

PRACTICE EXERCISE 4-3

Find the code or range of codes for the following.

1. Mastopexy

Code(s) _____

2. Excision of a chest wall tumor, including ribs

Code(s) _____

3. Complete mastectomy; simple

Code(s) _____

4. Unlisted breast procedure

Code(s) _____

5. Revision of reconstructed breast

Code(s) _____

6. Complete mastectomy, with immediate insertion of implant, including anesthesia

Code(s) _____

Incision and Excision

Incision codes within the Surgery section may be generalized. These include puncture aspirations, incision and removal of foreign bodies, and injection procedures. Some

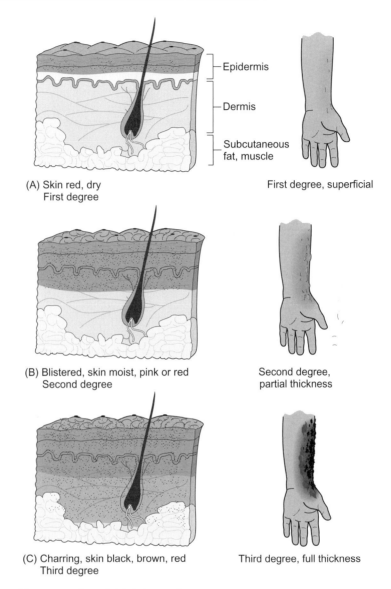

(A) Skin red, dry
First degree

First degree, superficial

(B) Blistered, skin moist, pink or red
Second degree

Second degree,
partial thickness

(C) Charring, skin black, brown, red
Third degree

Third degree, full thickness

Figure 4-5 First, second, and third degree burns

procedures may require the use of imaging guidance. Excision codes are based upon the body area. They include debridement of the skin, decubitus ulcers, and lesions.

PRACTICE EXERCISE 4-4

Find the code or range of codes for the following.

1. Incision and drainage of pilonidal cyst; simple

   Code(s) _____

2. Excision of a sacral pressure ulcer, with primary suture; with ostectomy

   Code(s) _____

3. Injection procedure only for mammary ductogram

   Code(s) _____

4. Puncture aspiration of an abscess

   Code(s) _____

5. Debridement; skin, full thickness

   Code(s) _____

6. Blepharoplasty of both upper eyelids, including anesthesia

   Code(s) _____

MUSCULOSKELETAL SYSTEM

In coding the Musculoskeletal System section (see Figures 4-6A and 4-6B), base the codes by the anatomical site, then by procedure. The first codes within the Musculoskeletal System section deal with general procedures. These codes include wound exploration, excision, introduction, removal, replantation, and grafts or implants. They include codes for both the muscles and bones. When coding wound exploration, you should be aware that these codes are only intended to describe surgical exploration. Codes from this section may also be used for enlargement of the wound, debridement, removal of foreign bodies, and ligation. Codes that do not require enlargement of the wound should be coded from the Integumentary System section. The excision codes within this section include biopsies of the bone and muscle. The introduction or removal codes include injections, aspirations, application of halos, and removal of foreign bodies. The replantation codes deal with specific procedures to replant an extremity or digits that have been amputated. You also should remember that these codes do not only refer to attaching the bone. During a complete amputation, nerves, muscles, and blood vessels also need to be attached. Report these codes separately with the addition of modifier 52. When an amputation is considered incomplete (partly attached), you still need to code each procedure independently from the repair section with the addition of modifier 52. The graft or implant codes deal with the bone, cartilage, and muscle. When coding from this section, you must remember not to append modifier 62. You may also report separately the incisions to obtain the graft, if these are not included in the code itself. These codes are identified by the keywords "includes obtaining graft."

PRACTICE EXERCISE 4-5

Find the code or range of codes for the following.

1. Removal of a foreign body in a tendon sheath; simple

   Code(s) _____

2. Replantation of the forearm due to amputation; with anesthesia

   Code(s) _____

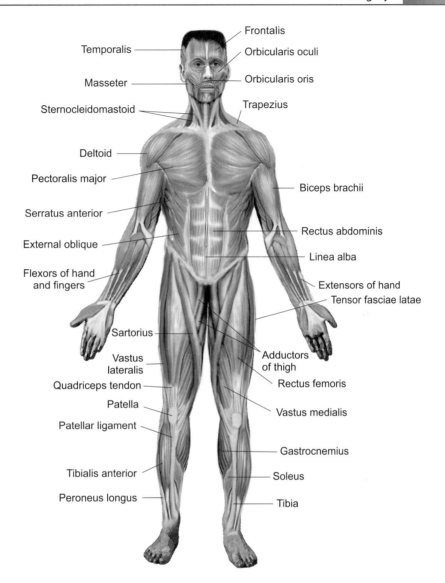

Figure 4-6A The muscular system, anterior view

3. Arthrocentesis, aspiration, and injection of a bursa of the finger

   Code(s) _____

4. Biopsy of the sternum using a trocar; superficial

   Code(s) _____

5. Removal of an external fixation system under anesthesia
   Code(s) _____

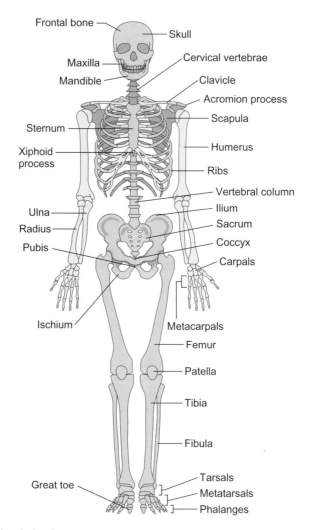

Figure 4-6B The skeletal system

Head

The anatomical sites of the head include the skull, facial bones, and temporomandibular joints (see Figure 4–7). The procedure codes include the incision, excision, introduction, repair, fractures, and other procedures. The incision codes contain only one code, which is an arthrotomy (incision) into the temporomandibular joint. Most of the codes in the excision section deal with benign or malignant tumors. When using these codes, you must make sure to add modifier 50 when doing a bilateral procedure. Also, you must always include the surgical sutures for wound closure (simple, intermediate, and complex). Remember to use the annotations on the toolbar to ensure proper coding. Codes in the Introduction section deal mostly with facial prostheses. You should use these codes only when the treating physician designs and prepares the prosthesis. They

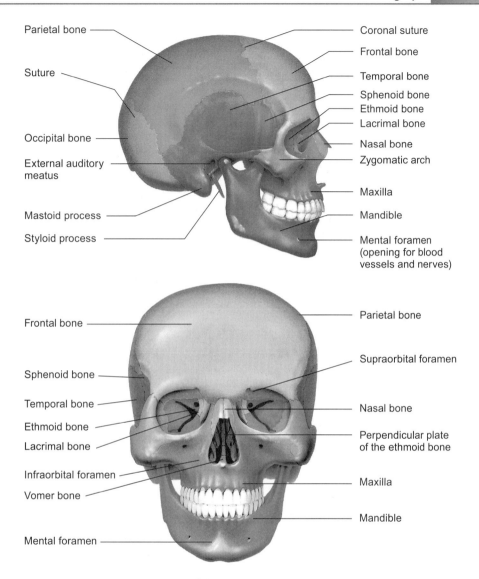

Figure 4-7 Bones and suture lines of the skull

include prosthetic codes for the eye, face, mouth, and nose. Within the Repair, Revision and Reconstruction section, the codes you'll mostly use deal with the reconstruction of the face. Some of these codes regard obtaining the autograft or prosthetic material. Codes that do not include bone grafts may need to be coded from another body system; an example of this would be codes used for certain types of cranioplasty. You should also keep in mind when coding from this section to always code the primary repair first. Use the secondary codes for additional repairs or revisions.

Fracture and dislocation codes are used for more extensive procedures throughout the musculoskeletal system. They incorporate several different types of treatment.

Before you begin to code from this section, there are several things to consider. First, determine the site of the fracture or dislocation. Second, identify if the treatment of the fracture is an open or closed treatment. An **open treatment** is considered as surgically opened to view. At this time, fixation devices may be used. A **closed treatment** is not surgically opened to view and may use manipulation or traction as the treatment procedure. **Manipulation** is a method used to restore the fracture to its original alignment by applying manual force to the skin with the use of straps. Another term you may see for this procedure is reduction. The third and final determination is to identify whether an internal or external or percutaneous fixation device is used in the treatment. **Internal fixation** means placing devices such as rods or pins into the bone to stabilize the treatment of an open fracture. The term **external fixation** is used when the stabilization devices extend out through the skin. Percutaneous fixation is not an open nor a closed treatment. Percutaneous fixation is using an x-ray to assist the placement of pins across the fracture site, thus stabilizing the fracture. When coding fractures or dislocations, you must remember that the type of fracture or dislocation doesn't drive any one specialized treatment. These codes may or may not include manipulation or fixation. They do include the first application and removal of casting material and traction devices. You should report any additional casting or traction using the code 99070, although most physicians use the code A4590 from the ICD-9 manual. When coding for fractures, report casts that are made of fiberglass (A4590) or plaster (A4580) separately by using the HCPCS supply code. Cast removals may be reported separately if another physician applied the cast. If crutches or any durable medical equipment were ordered, you must also report these separately. It is important to remember to code for the wound closure. You may also report the injection (J-codes) of any medication that was used.

PRACTICE EXERCISE 4-6

Find the code or range of codes for the following.

1. Excision of a facial bone for a bone abscess

   Code(s) _____

2. Open treatment of mandibular fracture, with external fixation

   Code(s) _____

3. Electrical stimulation to aid bone healing; noninvasive; with conscious sedation

   Code(s) _____

4. Application of a halo type appliance for maxillofacial fixation

   Code(s) _____

5. Open treatment of a nasal septal fracture, without stabilization

   Code(s) _____

Neck and Thorax

The Neck and Thorax codes refer to soft tissue. This is one of the smallest sections within the Musculoskeletal System section. Superficial wounds of the neck and thorax should be coded from the Integumentary System section repair codes. These codes are listed under the same procedures as before: incision, excision, fractures, and repair. So, let's code.

PRACTICE EXERCISE 4-7

Find the code or range of codes for the following.

1. Biopsy of the soft tissue of the neck

   Code(s) _____

2. Excision of a tumor from the soft tissue of the flank

   Code(s) _____

3. Division of sternocleidomastoid for torticollis, open; without casting

   Code(s) _____

4. Excision of first cervical rib with sympathectomy

   Code(s) _____

5. Unlisted procedure of the thorax

   Code(s) _____

Spine

The vertebral column includes the cervical, thoracic, and the lumbar spine, as shown in Figure 4-8. The spine is further divided into segments, each of which is considered a complete vertebral bone. A vertebral bone consists of two vertebral bodies containing the intervertebral disk, and the **vertebral interspace,** which is the non-bony compartment between the vertebral bodies. At first, you may find it very confusing to code for the spine. One point to remember: most procedures within this section are coded separately. It usually takes two surgeons to perform surgery on the vertebral spine. When coding, you must add modifier 62 to the primary procedure code for each surgeon as long as they work together as primary surgeons. Any secondary procedure performed should be reported with modifier 51 to indicate the multiple procedures, especially when arthrodesis is performed. Some procedure codes—such as 22585, 22614, and 22623—are considered add-on procedures, and modifier 51 should never be used with these codes. Do not report modifier 51 or 62 on bone grafts. Surgeons may also use spinal instrumentation and microscopy, which you should code in addition to a fracture, dislocation, or arthrodesis. When coding for spinal instrumentation, you may only use modifier 62 on codes for reinsertion of a spinal fixation device or removal of an anterior instrumentation.

PRACTICE EXERCISE 4-8

Find the code or range of codes for the following.

1. Closed treatment of a vertebral body fracture without manipulation, including casting

   Code(s) _____

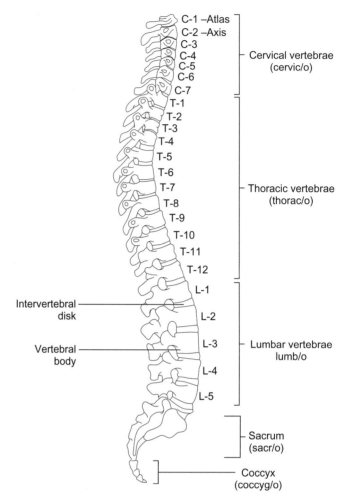

Figure 4-8 Spinal column

2. Incision and drainage of the sacral spine (open) for a deep abscess

   Code(s) _____

3. Osteotomy of the thoracic spine, posterior approach, one vertebral segment with arthrodesis

   Code(s) _____

4. Reinsertion of a spinal fixation device

   Code(s) _____

5. Manipulation of the cervical spine, requiring anesthesia

   Code(s) _____

Shoulder

Most people think the shoulder is a single bone connecting the arm. As coders, we know from appending codes that the shoulder contains the scapula, humerus head and neck, sternoclavicular joint, acromioclavicular joint, and shoulder joint. These codes are listed under the procedure that is being performed. They include, in specific order: incision, excision, introduction, and removal. Then, listed under category or subheading, are the Repair, Revision, and Reconstruction, followed by subheadings of Fracture and Dislocation. The last three subheadings are Manipulation, Arthrodesis, and Amputation. As always, be sure to read each code carefully. Codes throughout the Surgery section may or may not include anesthesia, biopsy, manipulation, or the removal of a foreign body.

PRACTICE EXERCISE 4-9

Find the code or range of codes for the following.

1. Reconstruction of a shoulder rotator cuff avulsion, chronic

   Code(s) _____

2. Manipulation under anesthesia of the shoulder joint, including application of a fixation device

   Code(s) _____

3. Claviculectomy; partial

   Code(s) _____

4. Excision of a benign tumor of the clavicle

   Code(s) _____

5. Closed treatment of a clavicular fracture with manipulation

   Code(s) _____

Humerus and Elbow

Codes within the Humerus and Elbow section include the head and neck of the radius and the olecranon process. Since the anatomic site is known, the procedure is now separated into basically the same subsections. Although the shoulder codes contain a subsection for manipulation under anesthesia, the codes for the humerus and elbow do not.

PRACTICE EXERCISE 4-10

Find the code or range of codes for the following.

1. Osteotomy, humerus, without internal fixation

   Code(s) _____

2. Tendon lengthening, upper arm, two tendons

   Code(s) _____

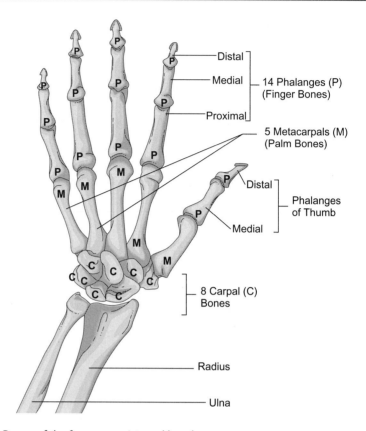

Figure 4-9 Bones of the forearm, wrist, and hand

3. Arthrotomy, elbow, including exploration and removal of a foreign body

   Code(s) _____

4. Sequestrectomy of the radial head

   Code(s) _____

5. Arthrectomy

   Code(s) _____

Forearm and Wrist

Codes within this section include procedure codes for the radius, ulna, and the carpal bones and joints. To better understand the anatomical location of these bones, refer to Figure 4–9. These codes also include the muscles and tendons associated with these bones. Treatment procedures may include manipulation and open or closed treatments, and may include more than one bone in the code. An example of this is code 25670. This code represents an open treatment of a radiocarpal dislocation, one or more bones. It is also important to remember that you must read the code carefully to ensure proper coding. Fractures that are closed may include manipulation.

PRACTICE EXERCISE 4-11

Find the code or range of codes for the following.

1. Transmetacarpal amputation; secondary closure

   Code(s) _____

2. Closed treatment of radial and ulnar shaft fractures with manipulation

   Code(s) _____

3. Arthrodesis; wrist; limited, without bone graft

   Code(s) _____

4. Centralization of wrist on ulna with pin insertion; unilateral

   Code(s) _____

5. Decompression fasciotomy, forearm and wrist, flexor and extensor compartment; without debridement of muscle and nerve

   Code(s) _____

Hand and Fingers

Procedures that deal with the fingers may be performed as a primary or secondary procedure (see Figure 4–9). Codes for procedures that lengthen, shorten, or release a tendon need to be reported separately if more than one tendon is repaired on the same finger or hand. If you are coding for the transfer of a tendon, and the procedure code is not available, use the code for "other method" used.

PRACTICE EXERCISE 4-12

Find the code or range of codes for the following.

1. Lengthening of two flexor tendons of the hand

   Code(s) _____

2. Arthrodesis of two interphalangeal joints with internal fixation

   Code(s) _____

3. Transfer finger to another position without microvascular anastomosis

   Code(s) _____

4. Percutaneous skeletal fixation of distal phalangeal fracture, thumb

   Code(s) _____

5. Tendon sheath incision

   Code(s) _____

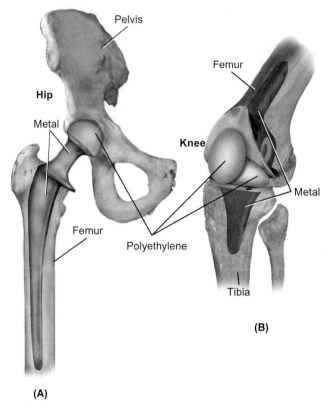

Figure 4-10 (A) Total hip replacement (B) Total knee replacement

PELVIS AND HIP JOINT

When it comes to coding for the pelvis, you might expect to need to determine first if you are coding for a male or female, since the pelvic region is associated with childbearing. Fortunately for coding purposes, there is no difference. In dealing with fractures of the hip socket (acetabulum), the fracture may be transverse, anterior, posterior, or a T-fracture. Dislocations of the hip may be traumatic or spontaneous. Spontaneous dislocations are mostly associated with elderly patients. Coding for this region also includes the neck of the femur (see Figure 4–10). The procedures are listed in the normal order, with incision first.

PRACTICE EXERCISE 4-13

Find the code or range of codes for the following.

1. Revision of a total hip arthroplasty; both components, without grafting, including anesthesia

Code(s) _____

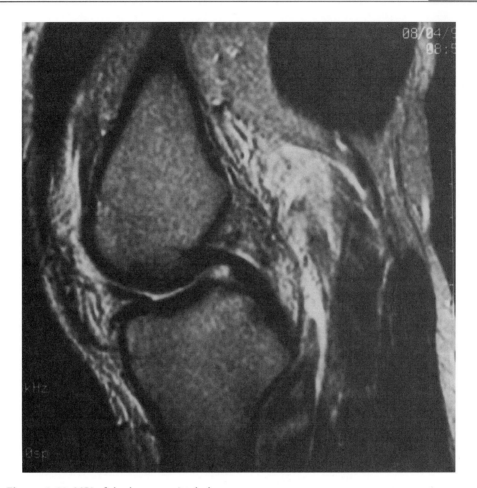

Figure 4-11 MRI of the knee, sagittal plane

2. Disarticulation of the hip

   Code(s) _____

3. Closed treatment of hip dislocation, traumatic; with anesthesia

   Code(s) _____

4. Injection procedure for hip arthrography; without anesthesia

   Code(s) _____

5. Osteotomy, iliac, with femoral osteotomy and with open reduction of hip

   Code(s) _____

Femur and Knee Joint

Coding for the femur (thigh region) and knee (patella) joint also includes the tibial plateaus (flat region) as seen in Figure 4–11. Some codes include sutures, fixation devices, and prostheses. When coding for a radical resection of a tumor; bone of the femur or knee (27365), do not miscode this procedure using the soft tissue code (27329). Make sure you read the procedures carefully to report the correct coding.

PRACTICE EXERCISE 4-14

Find the code or range of codes for the following.

1. Lengthening of hamstring tendon; multiple tendons, bilateral

   Code(s) _____

2. Manipulation of knee joint under general anesthesia, with the application of traction

   Code(s) _____

3. Decompression fasciotomy, thigh, with debridement of nonviable muscle and nerve

   Code(s) _____

4. Neurectomy, popliteal

   Code(s) _____

5. Arthrotomy with meniscus repair; knee

   Code(s) _____

Leg (Tibia and Fibula) and Ankle Joint

Codes used for the tibia and fibula are coded as "the leg" within this section unless otherwise specified. Some codes may or may not include anesthesia, may be with or without manipulation, may be primary or secondary procedures, and may be with or without skeletal fixation.

PRACTICE EXERCISE 4-15

Find the code or range of codes for the following.

1. Open treatment of a tibial shaft fracture, with fibular fracture, with screws, with cerclage and debridement, including removal of foreign material from the skin and subcutaneous tissue

   Code(s) _____

2. Repair, fascial defect of the leg

   Code(s) _____

3. Reduction of the ankle under general anesthesia with the application of traction

   Code(s) _____

4. Removal of an ankle implant

   Code(s) _____

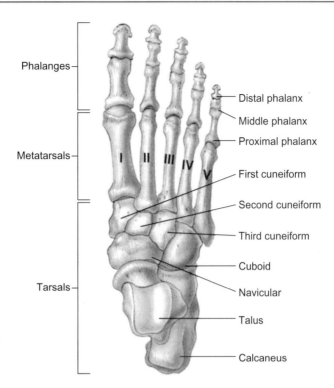

Figure 4-12 Right ankle and foot, superior view

5. Amputation, leg, through tibia and fibula, with immediate fitting technique and application of first cast

Code(s) _____

Foot and Toes

Codes that involve the toes may involve more than one fracture of each joint or bone (see Figure 4–12). If more than one toe is fractured, report the additional code. In such a case, remember to add an anatomical modifier (HCPCS) to specify each anatomic site. If you don't add a modifier in these instances, you risk the claim being denied as a duplicate. In cases of fractures, you also need to code for any x-ray obtained, which will be covered in Chapter 8.

PRACTICE EXERCISE 4-16

Find the code or range of codes for the following.

1. Excision, tumor, foot; subcutaneous tissue

Code(s) _____

2. Osteotomy, calcaneus, with internal fixation

Code(s) _____

3. Arthrodesis, great toe; interphalangeal joint

    Code(s) _____

4. Hallux rigidus correction with cheilectomy, debridement, and capsular release of the first metatarsophalangeal joint

    Code(s) _____

5. Flatfoot correction

    Code(s) _____

APPLICATION OF CASTS AND STRAPPING

When coding for the application of casting material, it is important to remember the first cast is included with the initial procedure. You may report any restorative treatment that is rendered by a physician who did not apply the first cast, strap, or splint. If the procedure is restorative, you may report the removal of the initial cast. If the physician prepares a temporary cast, splint, or strap, this is not considered part of the preoperative care, and you should not append modifier 56. When no other procedure is provided to the patient, you may report the supply code 99070 in addition to the E/M code. Always make sure you know what type of cast is being applied, since there are several types of applications and materials that are used. When the application of a halo type body cast is provided, you may report the insertion codes (20661–20663). The application of a cast, splint, or strap is not age related; codes may be reported for any patient at any age.

PRACTICE EXERCISE 4-17

Find the code or range of codes for the following.

1. Application of a figure-eight cast; short arm

    Code(s) _____

2. Bilateral wedging of clubfoot cast

    Code(s) _____

3. Strapping of a shoulder, patient aged 5

    Code(s) _____

4. Application of a leg splint; calf to foot

    Code(s) _____

5. Application of a Risser jacket, localizer, head and body

    Code(s) _____

ENDOSCOPY AND ARTHROSCOPY

When a physician performs an endoscopy or arthroscopy during surgery, the code always includes a diagnostic endoscopy or arthroscopy. But when an arthroscopy is performed during a procedure with an arthrotomy, you must append modifier 51. This procedure is mostly used during debridements, surgical repairs, resections, and removal of foreign bodies. Be sure to read the codes carefully. Some codes include the arthroscopy; in this case, you must not report it separately.

PRACTICE EXERCISE 4-18

Find the code or range of codes for the following.

1. Arthroscopy, hip, surgical; with removal of foreign body

   Code(s) _____

2. Diagnostic arthroscopy, metacarpophalangeal joint with synovial biopsy

   Code(s) _____

3. Endoscopic plantar fasciotomy

   Code(s) _____

4. Arthroscopically aided treatment of intercondylar spine and tuberosity fracture of the knee, with internal fixation and arthroscopy

   Code(s) _____

5. Unlisted arthroscopy

   Code(s) _____

CHAPTER REVIEW

I. True/False

Indicate whether the following sentence or statement is true or false.

___ 1. When coding for the pelvis, assume it is for a female.

___ 2. Surgical endoscopy never includes diagnostic endoscopy.

___ 3. A surgical package always includes written orders.

___ 4. All codes include anesthesia.

___ 5. When coding for fractures, you don't always code for x-rays.

___ 6. The shoulder is a single bone.

___ 7. Materials used in routine dressings are reported separately.

___ 8. Unbundling is an act of fraud.

___ 9. The subcutaneous layer of skin is called the superficial fascia.

___ 10. Add-on codes always use a modifier.

II. Multiple Choice

Identify the correct code.

___ **11.** Closed treatment of a calcaneal fracture without manipulation

    a. 28800   c. 28304

    b. 28400   d. 27760

___ **12.** Shortening of the humerus

    a. 24400   c. 24156

    b. 24500   d. 24420

___ **13.** Transfer of multiple muscles of the upper arm

    a. 23075   c. 24332

    b. 24301   d. 23395

___ **14.** Open treatment of distal radial extra-articular fracture with internal fixation

    a. 25607   c. 25622

    b. 25609   d. 25330

___ **15.** Closed treatment of a sesamoid fracture

    a. 28315   c. 28530

    b. 28496   d. 28531

___ **16.** Manipulation of the ankle under general anesthesia

    a. 27831   c. 27860

    b. 27871   d. 27860, 01462

III. Coding Exercises

Use an encoder or coding manuals to code the following procedures.

17. Injection procedure for a wrist arthrography

    Code(s) _____

18. Reinsertion of a spinal fixation device

    Cod.e(s) _____

19. Neurectomy of the gastrocnemius

    Code(s) _____

20. Excision of a single tendon of the palm

    Code(s) _____

21. Closed treatment of a sternum fracture

    Code(s) _____

22. Opponensplasty: superficialis tendon transfer type, one tendon

    Code(s) _____

23. Osteotomy of the pelvis, bilateral procedure

Code(s) _____

24. Lateral retinacular release, open procedure

Code(s) _____

IV. Coding Cases

Code the following cases using an encoder or coding manuals.

25. Patient presented into the outpatient surgery center for the removal of a benign lesion. Dr. Torrez cleaned the site with iodine and used one percent lidocaine for a local anesthetic, then excised the skin and subcutaneous tissue for hidradenitis, axillary with a complex repair.

Code(s) _____

26. Samantha presents to Dr. Stern's office with complaints of left shoulder pain. She has an increase of weakness and pain at night while trying to sleep. Upon examination, Dr. Stern discovers she has palpable tenderness at the greater tuberosity of the humerus and a limited range of motion. Dr. Stern diagnoses Samantha with ruptured musculotendinous cuff and schedules her for a rotator cuff repair. (Code the rotator cuff repair.)

Code(s) _____

27. Jack fell while learning how to ski at a local resort. With the help of the ski patrol, he was taken to the local emergency room. Upon examination, Dr. Radwin discovered Jack's leg was swollen, with a loss of sensation but good muscle strength. Jack also complained of pain upon toe movement. Dr. Radwin performed a closed treatment of a tibial shaft fracture with manipulation.

Code(s) _____

Chapter 5

The Respiratory and Circulatory Systems

aneurysm	myocardium	thrombus
cadaver	paranasal sinuses	tracheostomy
embolism	pericardium	trocar
fiber-optic endoscope	thromboendarterectomy	turbinates

LEARNING OBJECTIVES

After completing this chapter, the learner should be able to:

- Identify the structures of the respiratory system
- Apply correct codes to procedures performed
- Create correct codes by using modifiers
- Understand and apply guidelines to coding
- Recognize respiratory terminology

RESPIRATORY SYSTEM

In coding for the Respiratory System section, as shown in Figures 5-1A and 5-1B, codes will include the lungs, paranasal sinuses, larynx, trachea, bronchi, and lungs and pleural cavity. So, let's start coding with the nasal cavities. In order to report these codes correctly, you must remember the patient has two nasal passages. When reporting for procedures of the nose, be sure to use modifier 50 for all bilateral procedures. If a code includes a bilateral procedure, but only a unilateral procedure is performed, then use modifier 52 (reduced service). As always, the codes reflect the anatomic site first, then the procedure being performed, with the exception of the subheading of Fractures.

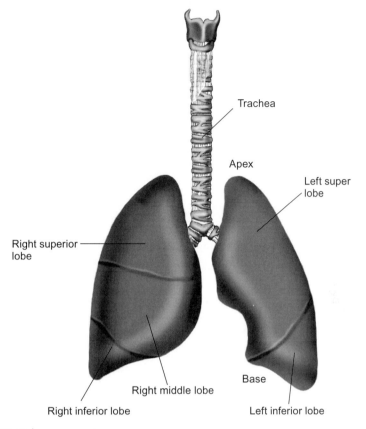

Figure 5-1A Pulmonary system

PRACTICE EXERCISE 5-1

Code the following procedures.

1. Rhinectomy; partial with closure 1.5 cm, with packing; simple

   Code(s) _____

2. Control of nasal hemorrhage, anterior, complex, bilateral

   Code(s) _____

3. Lysis intranasal synechia

   Code(s) _____

4. Therapeutic injection into turbinate

   Code(s) _____

5. Excision of a nasal polyp; simple

   Code(s) _____

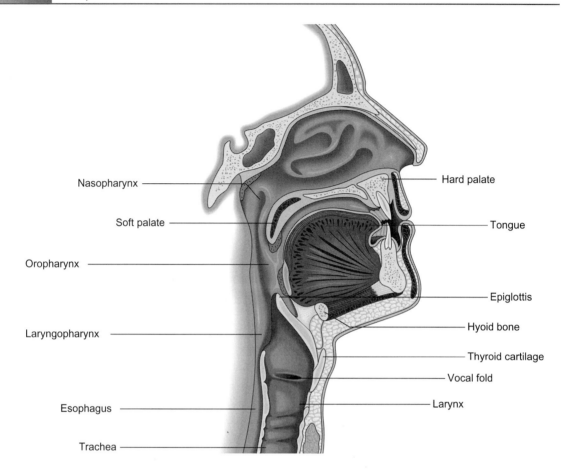

Figure 5-1B Respiratory system

Accessory Sinuses

Both the ethmoid and sphenoid bones are included in the accessory sinuses. They make up part of the **paranasal sinuses** that serve as the resonating chambers for the voice. When coding the accessory sinuses, you must remember that surgical endoscopy codes will always include a diagnostic endoscopy. These codes are usually unilateral; therefore, if a bilateral procedure is performed, append modifier 50. When reporting the procedure for diagnostic purposes, such as code 31231, then report only one code, even though in this case both the turbinates and the interior nasal cavity are evaluated. (**Turbinates** are a coil-shaped bone within the nasal cavity.) Also note that multiple procedures can be performed through a surgical endoscope. These codes may be reported separately and must be appended with modifier 51 for the multiple procedures.

PRACTICE EXERCISE 5-2

Code the following procedures.

1. Nasal/sinus endoscopy, surgical, with sphenoidotomy

   Code(s) _____

2. Nasal/sinus endoscopy, diagnostic, with maxillary sinusoscopy

   Code(s) _____

3. Lavage by cannulation; maxillary sinus

   Code(s) _____

4. Nasal/sinus endoscopy, surgical; with ethmoidectomy, partial, with maxillary antrostomy

   Code(s) _____

5. Ethmoidectomy; extranasal, total

   Code(s) _____

Larynx

Many codes within this section may include the use of an operating microscope or telescope. When these codes do not include a microscope or telescope, you may report the use of the device by appending code 69990 from the end of this chapter. These codes also reflect the approach, which may include direct, indirect, and the use of a flexible fiber-optic endoscope. A **fiber-optic endoscope** allows for the transmission of light through plastic fibers or glass. This permits the transmission of images around curves and corners. When the procedure calls for the use of a microscope and telescope, you should only code the procedure once. Diagnostic endoscopes should always be included in surgical procedures, and each anatomic site may be reported separately.

PRACTICE EXERCISE 5-3

Code the following procedures.

1. Diagnostic laryngoscopy direct, with tracheoscopy, for aspiration on a newborn

   Code(s) _____

2. Emergency intubation

   Code(s) _____

3. Laryngoscopy, flexible, with stroboscopy

   Code(s) _____

4. Laryngoplasty, cricoid split

   Code(s) _____

5. Laryngectomy; total, without radical neck dissection

Code(s) _____

Trachea and Bronchi

A **tracheostomy** is a procedure performed when there is an airway obstruction. The physician provides a temporary opening by making a surgical incision into the trachea and placing an endotracheal tube. When a tracheostomy is part of a larger procedure, it is not reported separately but is considered part of the procedure as long as it was performed within two years of the larger procedure; otherwise, it is considered a separate code. When reporting endoscopy procedures, each site that is examined is reported separately. When reporting a surgical bronchoscopy, you should always include the diagnostic bronchoscopy if the same physician performs the procedure. A bronchoscopy is used for a visual examination of the trachea and bronchi, which may be used in obtaining biopsies or removal of foreign bodies. You also must remember that for a biopsy of the upper airway and transbronchial, you only code the procedure once. These codes also include the use of fluoroscopic guidance.

PRACTICE EXERCISE 5-4

Code the following procedures.

1. Transtracheal injection for bronchography

   Code(s) _____

2. Bronchoscopy, rigid, without fluoroscopic guidance, with bronchial biopsy, single lobe; three biopsies

   Code(s) _____

3. Surgical closure tracheostomy; with plastic repair

   Code(s) _____

4. Transtracheal injection for bronchography

   Code(s) _____

5. Excision of tracheal tumor; thoracic

   Code(s) _____

Lungs and Pleura

When coding for the lungs, you must read the medical record very carefully. These codes may use the term lung or lungs, and they may also use the term segment or segments. Codes for the lungs or segments of the lung are bilateral procedures, so you should not use modifier 50. Procedures that require a fine needle aspiration must be coded from the Integumentary System section. Codes that require radiological supervision and interpretation include the biopsy codes and the introduction codes (coded from the Radiology section). The incision codes that require imaging guidance also are coded from the Radiology section. Endoscopy procedures are reported for each anatomic site and they always include the diagnostic procedure when the surgical procedure is performed.

PRACTICE EXERCISE 5-5

Code the following procedures.

1. Posttraumatic reconstruction of the chest wall, major

   Code(s) _____

2. Removal of lung, total pneumonectomy

   Code(s) _____

3. Thoracotomy, major; with open intrapleural pneumonolysis

   Code(s) _____

4. Pneumocentesis for aspiration

   Code(s) _____

5. Thoracoscopy, surgical; with lobectomy, segmental

   Code(s) _____

Lung Transplant

A lung transplant involves three distinct steps. First you must have a donor, usually a **cadaver** (a person who has expired); second, the cadaver must be prepared for the transplant. The last step in lung transplant is the transplant itself, which may be one or both lungs. If both lungs are transplanted, use the bilateral code 32856 and not the bilateral modifier.

PRACTICE EXERCISE 5-6

Code the following procedures.

1. Donor pneumonectomy from cadaver

   Code(s) _____

2. Lung transplant, single, without cardiopulmonary bypass

   Code(s) _____

3. Backbench standard preparation of cadaver donor lung allograft prior to transplant, including dissection of allograft from surrounding soft tissues to prepare pulmonary venous, pulmonary artery, and bronchus; bilateral

   Code(s) _____

4. Lung transplant, double, with cardiopulmonary bypass

   Code(s) _____

5. Donor pneumonectomy from cadaver donor with lung transplant, bilateral with cardiopulmonary bypass, with backbench standard preparation of cadaver donor lung allograft prior to transplantation, including dissection of allograft from surrounding soft tissues to prepare pulmonary venous, atrial cuff, pulmonary artery, and bronchus; bilateral

   Code(s) _____

CARDIOVASCULAR SYSTEM

Codes within the Cardiovascular System section are, as always, coded by anatomic site, then by procedure. They contain both diagnostic and therapeutic procedures. These codes can be very hard to the new coder, because of the medical terms used. For example, it is easy to confuse coronary artery and coronary vein. You must read the code description very carefully and use the annotations on the toolbar. In coding for the Cardiovascular System section (see Figure 5–2), you must also remember that other services and procedures may be performed at the same time. Laboratory services (Chapter 9) may be used and nonsurgical services such as the operation of pumps (Chapter 12) and monitors (Chapter 10). There are also specific orders (first, second, and third) when coding heart catheterizations. So, let's take this one step at a time, and learn how to code for the Cardiovascular System.

Heart and Pericardium

When we think of the heart and pericardium, we tend to think of the heart as a whole (see Figure 5–3A). But, let's divide it into the procedures for the **pericardium** (sac around the heart) and the **myocardium** (heart muscle). First, the Pericardium section deals with surgical punctures, excisions, and removal; the Myocardium section deals mostly with pacemakers and defibrillators. (See Figure 5–3B.) To code these correctly, you must understand the pacemaker. The pacemaker system creates mechanical contractions by emitting electrical discharges into the heart. The system may be a single chamber system that includes a pulse generator and electrode or it may be a dual chamber, which also includes a pulse generator and two electrodes. In a single chamber system, the electrode is inserted into the atrium or ventricle. In a dual pacemaker, one electrode is inserted into the right atrium and another into the right ventricle. Electrodes may be placed either through a vein or on the surface of the heart. When the electrode is placed on the surface of the heart (epicardial) the procedure requires a thoracotomy. Codes that include a wound of the heart do not include the removal of a blood clot (**thrombus**) unless a separate incision is required. If a thrombus is removed in conjunction with a cardiopulmonary bypass, then it requires a separate incision and you would report it by using the code 33315-59.

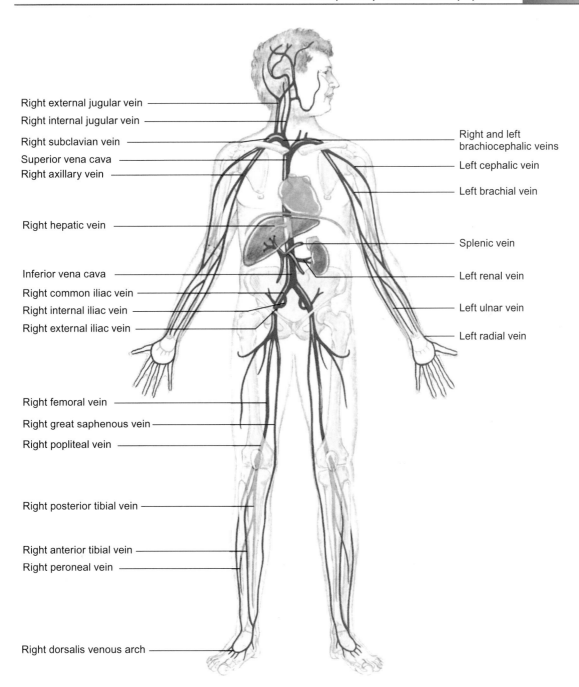

Right external jugular vein

Right internal jugular vein

Right subclavian vein

Superior vena cava

Right axillary vein

Right hepatic vein

Inferior vena cava

Right common iliac vein

Right internal iliac vein

Right external iliac vein

Right femoral vein

Right great saphenous vein

Right popliteal vein

Right posterior tibial vein

Right anterior tibial vein

Right peroneal vein

Right dorsalis venous arch

Right and left
brachiocephalic veins

Left cephalic vein

Left brachial vein

Splenic vein

Left renal vein

Left ulnar vein

Left radial vein

Figure 5-2 Circulatory system

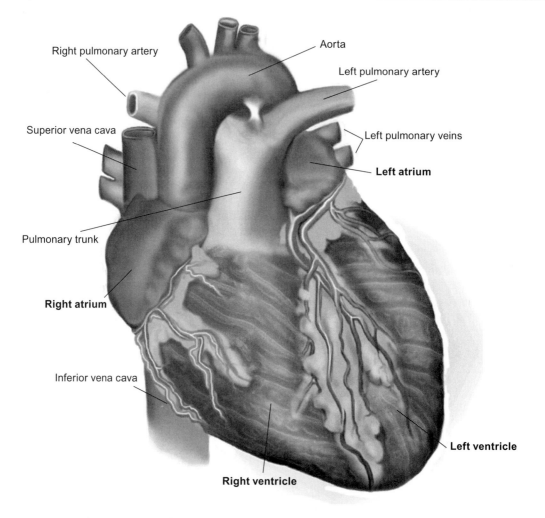

Figure 5-3A Cardiac system

PRACTICE EXERCISE 5-7

Code the following procedures.

1. Insertion of permanent pacemaker with transvenous electrodes; atrial and ventricular, and the insertion of pacing electrode, cardiac venous system for left ventricular pacing

   Code(s) _____

2. Implantation of patient-activated cardiac event recorder

   Code(s) _____

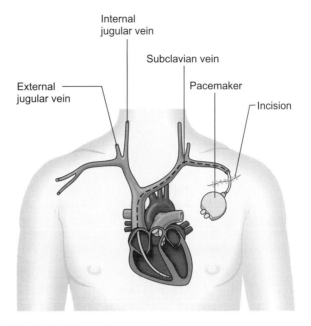

Figure 5-3B Cardiac defibrillator placement

3. Removal of permanent transvenous electrode by thoracotomy

   Code(s) _____

4. Repositioning of previously implanted transvenous pacemaker, right atrium

   Code(s) _____

5. Subcutaneous removal of single pacing cardioverter defibrillator pulse generator and electrode; by thoracotomy

   Code(s) _____

Cardiac Valves

Codes within this section deal with the removal and replacement of faulty valves of the heart. These valves include the aortic, mitral, tricuspid, and pulmonary valves (see Figure 5–4). In the event more than one valve is replaced, append modifier 51 to the second procedure.

PRACTICE EXERCISE 5-8

Code the following procedures.

1. Replacement of pulmonary valve

   Code(s) _____

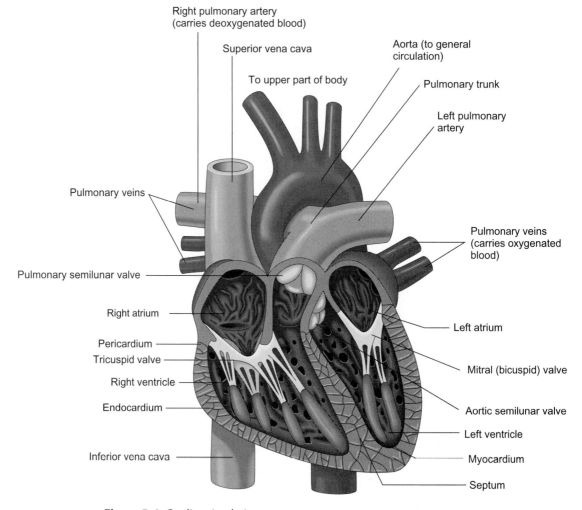

Figure 5-4 Cardiac circulation

2. Replacement of the aortic valve; with aortic annulus enlargement, noncoronary cusp with Konno procedure

   Code(s) _____

3. Valvotomy, mitral valve; closed heart procedure

   Code(s) _____

4. Construction of apical-aortic conduit

   Code(s) _____

5. Replacement of the mitral valve, pulmonary valve, and tricuspid valves with cardiopulmonary bypass

   Code(s) _____

Venous Grafting Only for Coronary Artery Bypass

Codes for grafting procedures within this section are used only for arterial coronary bypass. These codes also include the venous grafting when performed during the same procedure. They also include obtaining the saphenous vein graft. When reporting the harvesting of an upper extremity vein, you need to use code 35500 in addition to the bypass procedure. For harvesting of a lower extremity vein, you need to include 35572 in addition to the bypass procedure. Physicians who perform these procedures may also use a surgical assistant to perform the obtaining of the graft. If this is the case, then you will need to append modifier 80 to the grafting procedures.

PRACTICE EXERCISE 5-9

Code the following procedures.

1. Coronary artery bypass, two coronary venous grafts with procurement of a lower extremity vein

   Code(s) _____

2. Coronary artery bypass, vein only; single coronary venous graft, with a surgical assistant

   Code(s) _____

3. Coronary artery bypass, vein only; five coronary venous grafts, with a surgical assistant

   Code(s) _____

4. Coronary artery bypass, vein only; three coronary venous grafts using an upper extremity vein with a surgical assistant

   Code(s) _____

5. Coronary artery bypass, vein only; eight coronary venous grafts using upper and lower extremity vein segments with surgical assistant

   Code(s) _____

Combined Arterial-Venous Grafting for Coronary Bypass

When reporting codes within this section, it is very important not to report these codes alone. You must use two codes. The first codes are the combined arterial-venous grafting codes 33517 to 00523. The second codes to be reported from are the arterial graft codes 33533 to 33536. When reporting an upper extremity graft (saphenous vein) or lower extremity graft (femoropopliteal), report the appropriate codes in addition the primary bypass procedure. The only time you should report these codes separately is when an upper extremity artery such as the radial artery is involved. Do not append modifier 51 to these codes. Remember to use modifier 80 when a surgical assistant has performed the grafting procedure.

PRACTICE EXERCISE 5-10

Code the following procedures.

1. Coronary artery bypass, using venous graft and arterial graft; single vein graft

   Code(s) _____

2. Coronary artery bypass, using five venous grafts

   Code(s) _____

Single Ventricle and Other Complex Cardiac Anomalies

Cardiac and ventricle anomalies refer to something that has deviated from normal. It might be a valve, artery, or the ventricle itself that is abnormal. The types of procedures that are performed on infants should not be reported with modifier 63 (procedure performed on infants).

PRACTICE EXERCISE 5-11

Code the following procedures.

1. Repair of double outlet right ventricular with intraventricular tunnel repair

   Code(s) _____

2. Closure of semilunar valve by suture

   Code(s) _____

3. Repair of single ventricle with aortic outflow obstruction and aortic arch hypoplasia

   Code(s) _____

Septal Defect

A septal defect involves a defect of a dividing wall between two cavities. This could mean the wall between the left and right atria of the heart (atrioventricular) or a tetralogy, which means a combination of four (tetra means four) elements.

PRACTICE EXERCISE 5-12

Code the following procedures.

1. Banding of pulmonary artery

   Code(s) _____

2. Repair of a complete atrioventricular canal with a prosthetic valve

Code(s) _____

3. Repair of an atrial septal defect, secundum, with cardiopulmonary bypass with a patch

Code(s) _____

Shunting Procedures

Shunting procedures are performed to divert bloodflow from one artery to another artery. These procedures are performed when a cardiac bypass is performed; renal dialysis and bi-directional procedures may also be performed.

PRACTICE EXERCISE 5-13

Code the following procedures.

1. Shunt from the superior vena cava to pulmonary artery for flow to the right lung

Code(s) _____

2. Atrial septostomy; open heart with cardiopulmonary bypass

Code(s) _____

3. Shunt from the subclavian to pulmonary artery

Code(s) _____

Transposition of the Great Vessels

Transposition of the great vessels is a fetal deformity of the heart where the aorta arises from the right ventricle and the pulmonary artery arises from the left ventricle. The actual transposition happens when procedures are performed to relocate the vessels.

PRACTICE EXERCISE 5-14

Code the following procedures.

1. Repair of transposition of the great arteries with ventricular septal defect and subpulmonary stenosis with surgical enlargement of ventricular septal defect

Code(s) _____

2. Repair of transposition of the great arteries, aortic pulmonary artery reconstruction with closure of ventricular septal defect

Code(s) _____

Aortic Anomalies

These codes are used for the abnormalities of the aortic arch. They may include cardio-pulmonary bypass, grafting, and prosthetic material. Some codes are specified by the age of the patient.

PRACTICE EXERCISE 5-15

Code the following procedures.

1. Division of aberrant vessel with reanastomosis

   Code(s) _____

2. Repair of interrupted aortic arch using autogenous material with cardiopulmonary bypass

   Code(s) _____

3. Repair of patent ductus arteriosus by division in a patient less than 18 years old

   Code(s) _____

Endovascular Repair of Descending Thoracic Aorta

Codes within this section include all device introductions, deployment, manipulation, and positioning; they must not be reported separately. If it represents a family of procedures, report placement of an endovascular graft for the repair of the descending thoracic aorta. The only procedures you may report separately are fluoroscopic guidance, other interventional procedures performed at the time of endovascular repair of the descending thoracic aorta, open arterial exposure, and closure of arteriotomy sites. Medicare does not cover some codes within this section because the procedures are still in an experimental stage. Check the Special Coverage Procedures dialog box before reporting these codes to Medicare.

PRACTICE EXERCISE 5-16

Code the following procedures.

1. Open subclavian to carotid artery transposition performed in conjunction with endovascular repair of descending thoracic aorta by unilateral neck incision

   Code(s) _____

2. Placement of proximal extension prosthesis for endovascular repair of descending thoracic aorta leg

   Code(s) _____

3. Bypass graft with artery, transcervical retropharyngeal carotid–carotid, performed in conjunction with endovascular repair of descending thoracic aorta by neck incision

Code(s) _____

PULMONARY ARTERY

The pulmonary artery is located at the right ventricle of the heart and leads to the lungs. Therefore, codes within this section refer to procedures (repair, transection, and ligation) performed on the pulmonary artery.

PRACTICE EXERCISE 5-17

Code the following procedures.

1. Repair of the pulmonary artery arborization anomalies by unifocalization with cardiopulmonary bypass

Code(s) _____

2. Pulmonary artery embolectomy without cardiopulmonary bypass

Code(s) _____

3. Transection of pulmonary artery with cardiopulmonary bypass

Code(s) _____

Heart-Lung Transplantation

A heart and lung transplant involves three distinct components. The first involves the harvesting of the heart, the lung, or both, from a cadaver. (A cadaver is a dead body that is used for dissection.) The second component is the backbench work that is the preparation of a cadaver, which includes the removal of the organs and surrounding soft tissue. The final component consists of the actual transplant into the recipient.

PRACTICE EXERCISE 5-18

Code the following procedures.

1. Heart transplant with recipient cardiectomy

Code(s) _____

2. Donor cardiectomy-pneumonectomy

Code(s) _____

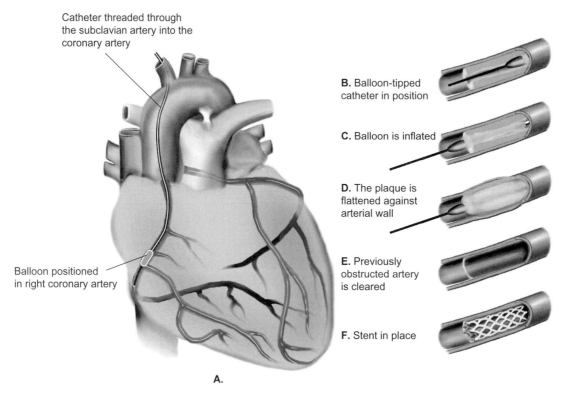

Catheter threaded through
the subclavian artery into the
coronary artery

B. Balloon-tipped
catheter in position

C. Balloon is inflated

D. The plaque is
flattened against
arterial wall

E. Previously
obstructed artery
is cleared

Balloon positioned
in right coronary artery

F. Stent in place

A.

Figure 5-5 Types of heart surgery

3. Backbench standard preparation of cadaver donor heart-lung allograft prior to
transplantation, including dissection of allograft from surrounding soft tissues to
prepare aorta, superior vena cava, inferior vena cava, and trachea for implant

Code(s) _____

Cardiac Assist

Codes within the cardiac assist section deal mainly with the insertion and removal of a
balloon. These balloons are attached to the end of a catheter and inserted into an artery,
a ventricle, or the aorta (see Figure 5–5).

PRACTICE EXERCISE 5-19

Code the following procedures.

1. Insertion of intra-aortic balloon assist device, percutaneous

Code(s) _____

2. Insertion and removal of a ventricular assist device, implantable intracorporeal, single ventricle

Code(s) _____

3. Insertion of intra-aortic balloon assist device through the ascending aorta

Code(s) _____

Embolectomy and Thrombectomy

An **embolism** is an obstruction of a blood vessel caused by a blood clot, bacteria, plaques, fat, or air. The obstruction may be removed by injecting enzymes (to dissolve a blood clot), or it may be surgically removed. Thrombectomy is the removal of a clot. Methods for removal are very similar as for an embolism.

PRACTICE EXERCISE 5-20

Code the following procedures.

1. Thrombectomy, with catheter; vena cava, iliac vein by abdominal incision

Code(s) _____

2. Embolectomy, without catheter; innominate, subclavian artery, by thoracic incision

Code(s) _____

3. Thrombectomy, direct; axillary, and subclavian vein, by arm incision

Code(s) _____

Endovascular Repair of Abdominal Aortic and Iliac Aneurysm

An **aneurysm** is the abnormal dilation of a blood vessel due to a weakening of the wall of a vessel. The most common causes are atherosclerosis, infections, and trauma. Aneurysms are localized; they most often involve the iliac arteries, but may involve the renal arteries. Procedures considered extensive involve repair, interventional. Guide wires and catheters should be reported separately. You should report bilateral procedures with modifier 50, and procedures that are staged must be reported with modifier 58. If grafting is performed, report this separately.

PRACTICE EXERCISE 5-21

Code the following procedures.

1. Open brachial artery exposure to assist in the deployment of aortic endovascular prosthesis by arm incision, bilateral

Code(s) _____

2. Open femoral artery exposure for delivery of endovascular prosthesis, by groin incision unilateral

Code(s) _____

3. Endovascular graft placement for repair of iliac artery

Code(s) _____

Direct Repair of Aneurysm or Excision and Graft Insertion for Aneurysm, Pseudoaneurysm, Ruptured Aneurysm, and Associated Occlusive Disease

When reporting a repair procedure for this section, you must remember that the preparation of the artery is included within the code for all anastomosis and endarterectomies. The codes are based on procedure, then site.

PRACTICE EXERCISE 5-22

Code the following procedures.

1. Direct repair of ruptured aneurysm, axillary-brachial artery, by arm incision

Code(s) _____

2. Total excision and graft insertion for aneurysm, popliteal artery

Code(s) _____

3. Direct repair pseudoaneurysm without patch graft, by neck incision

Code(s) _____

Repair Blood Vessel Other Than for Fistula

Codes within this section may or may not include a patch angioplasty. Report them by anatomical site.

PRACTICE EXERCISE 5-23

Code the following procedures.

1. Direct repair of a lower extremity blood vessel

Code(s) _____

2. Repair of an intra-abdominal blood vessel with graft and bypass

Code(s) _____

3. Repair of a lower extremity blood vessel with vein graft

Code(s) _____

Thromboendarterectomy

A **thromboendarterectomy** is the surgical removal of a blood clot from an artery. This may be an initial procedure or a reoperation. In the case of a reoperation, you must report the primary procedure. These codes do not include any of the coronary arteries.

ⓅPRACTICE EXERCISE 5-24

Code the following procedures.

1. Thromboendarterectomy with patch graft of the renal artery

   Code(s) _____

2. Thromboendarterectomy without patch graft of the deep femoral

   Code(s) _____

3. Thromboendarterectomy with patch graft of the carotid artery by neck incision, with reoperation 45 days later

   Code(s) _____

Transluminal Angioplasty/Atherectomy

Procedures in this section are performed as open or percutaneous procedures. When they are performed in conjunction with other procedures, you may append modifier 51 (multiple procedure) or modifier 52 (reduced service). You should also report any radiologic supervision and interpretation or catheter placements.

ⓅPRACTICE EXERCISE 5-25

Code the following procedures.

1. Transluminal peripheral atherectomy, tibioperoneal trunk and branches, open procedure

   Code(s) _____

2. Transluminal balloon angioplasty, open procedure, on the femoropopliteal artery

   Code(s) _____

3. Transluminal peripheral atherectomy, percutaneous, on the renal artery

   Code(s) _____

Bypass Graft

Procedures including a bypass graft always include the procurement of the saphenous vein as well. But when a vein is harvested from the femoropopliteal, you should report the procedure using code 35572. Bilateral procedures must be reported with modifier 50.

PRACTICE EXERCISE 5-26

Code the following procedures.

1. Bypass graft, with vein; axillary-axillary

   Code(s) _____

2. Bypass graft with other than vein; iliofemoral

   Code(s) _____

3. In situ vein bypass, femoropopliteal

   Code(s) _____

VASCULAR INJECTION PROCEDURES

When coding vascular injection procedures, it is important to remember these codes are performed by first, second, and third order.

PRACTICE EXERCISE 5-27

Code the following procedures.

1. Introduction of catheter into the inferior vena cava

   Code(s) _____

2. Revision of implanted intra-arterial infusion pump

   Code(s) _____

3. Introduction of a needle into a vein

   Code(s) _____

Central Venous Access Procedures

A central venous access line is used to access a vein that may collapse or be difficult to enter. Access lines are inserted into the vena cava, jugular, femoral, cephalic, or subclavian veins. Central lines are used to infuse fluids, medications, or even to measure the venous circulation; they can also be used as a catheter to obtain blood or give nutrition. These codes are based on procedure first, which includes insertion, repair, partial or complete replacement, and removal. When reporting the removal of an old central venous access line and the insertion of a new access line, you should report both procedures.

PRACTICE EXERCISE 5-28

Code the following procedures.

1. Insertion of tunneled centrally inserted central venous access device, with subcutaneous pump

   Code(s) _____

2. Catheterization, umbilical artery, newborn, for therapy

   Code(s) _____

3. Complete replacement of tunneled centrally inserted central venous catheter, without subcutaneous port through same venous access

   Code(s) _____

4. Mechanical removal of pericatheter obstructive material from central venous device via separate venous access

   Code(s) _____

5. Arterial puncture, withdrawal of blood for diagnosis

   Code(s) _____

Hemodialysis Access, Intervascular Cannulation for Extracorporeal Circulation, or Shunt Insertion

Hemodialysis is the cleansing of the blood, and is used in patients with ESRD (end-stage renal disease). Patients are connected to an artificial kidney, which circulates the blood to cleanse it of waste products, toxins, and excess fluids. Intravascular cannulation is when a tube enclosing a **trocar** (a sharp instrument contained in a cannula for the use of extracting fluids) is inserted into a large vein to administer drugs or to replace or remove fluids. Extracorporeal simply means outside the body. All of these procedures use cleansing methods outside the body. When bilateral procedures are performed, report modifier 50, or 59 if it is a distinct procedural service.

PRACTICE EXERCISE 5-29

Code the following procedures.

1. Insertion of a Thomas shunt with the plastic repair of an arteriovenous aneurysm

   Code(s) _____

2. Creation of arteriovenous fistula by other than direct arteriovenous anastomosis; nonautogenous graft

   Code(s) _____

3. Insertion of cannula for hemodialysis, vein to vein

Code(s) _____

4. Mechanical thrombectomy for dialysis fistula

Code(s) _____

Transcatheter Procedures and Other Procedures

"Trans-" is a medical prefix that means across, over, through, or beyond. Codes associated with a transcatheter are considered therapeutic, not diagnostic. They are performed with radiologic supervision and interpretation (see Chapter 8), which you should report separately. When a thrombolytic agent is used, it is considered part of the service and should not be reported separately. But, if the thrombolytic agent is administered as a continuous agent or as a subsequent procedure, you may report it separately.

PRACTICE EXERCISE 5-30

Code the following procedures.

1. Transcatheter biopsy, with radiologic supervision and interpretation

Code(s) _____

2. Percutaneous transluminal mechanical thrombectomy, vein, including intraprocedural pharmacological thrombolytic injection and fluoroscopic guidance, repeat treatment on a subsequent day during the course of the therapy

Code(s) _____

3. Primary percutaneous transluminal mechanical thrombectomy, noncoronary, including fluoroscopic guidance and intraprocedural pharmacological thrombolytic injections into an initial vessel, with the addition of a second vessel of the same vessel family

Code(s) _____

Ligation

Ligation is a procedure in which the vessel is tied with nylon, catgut, silk, or cotton in order to stop blood flow. Such procedures are used for varicose veins, ruptured vessels, and trauma. These codes do not include phleborrhaphy or arteriorrhaphy, which should be reported using codes 35201–35286.

PRACTICE EXERCISE 5-31

Code the following procedures.

1. Ligation of a femoral vein

   Code(s) _____

2. Ligation of the common carotid artery

   Code(s) _____

3. Stab phlebectomy of varicose veins, both extremities, 22 incisions per leg

   Code(s) _____

4. Interruption, complete, of inferior vena cava by ligation, with radiologic supervision and interpretation

   Code(s) _____

5. Ligation and excision of varicose vein cluster, bilaterally

   Code(s) _____

Bone Marrow or Stem Cell Services and Procedures

Codes within this section refer to the preservation, preparation, and purification of bone marrow or stem cells prior to transplantation. You may only report these codes once per day. The procedures usually need to be reported initially with a compatibility study (86812–86822), diagnostic thawing and expansion of cells (88241), or diagnostic cryopreservation and storage (88240).

PRACTICE EXERCISE 5-32

Code the following procedures.

1. Bone marrow peripheral stem cell transplantation; allogenic

   Code(s) _____

2. Bone marrow aspiration only

   Code(s) _____

3. Transplant preparation of hematopoietic progenitor cells, cryopreservation, and storage

   Code(s) _____

4. Bone marrow harvesting for transplantation

   Code(s) _____

LYMPH NODES AND LYMPHATIC CHANNELS

Lymph nodes are small kidney-shaped organs that lie at intervals along the lymphatic vessels (see Figure 5–6). The lymph is tissue fluid, which is mostly water. As the lymph flows through the channels, it destroys microorganisms and abnormal cells. Codes within this section deal with incision, excision, laparoscopy, introduction, and resection of the lymph nodes.

PRACTICE EXERCISE 5-33

Code the following procedures.

1. Injection procedure for the identification of sentinel node

   Code(s) _____

2. Biopsy of a lymph node, open, superficial

   Code(s) _____

3. Bilateral cervical lymphadenectomy, complete

   Code(s) _____

4. Dissection of deep jugular node

   Code(s) _____

5. Drainage of lymph node abscess; extensive

   Code(s) _____

Mediastinum and Diaphragm

The mediastinum is the middle portion between two cavities. The diaphragm separates the abdominal cavity from the thoracic cavity. Codes that deal with this section include the incision, excision, repair, and endoscopy codes. The codes dealing with the mediastinum consist only of incision, excision, and endoscopy, and the codes relating to the diaphragm only consist of repair codes.

PRACTICE EXERCISE 5-34

Code the following procedures.

1. Resection of the diaphragm with simple repair

   Code(s) _____

2. Excision of a mediastinal cyst

   Code(s) _____

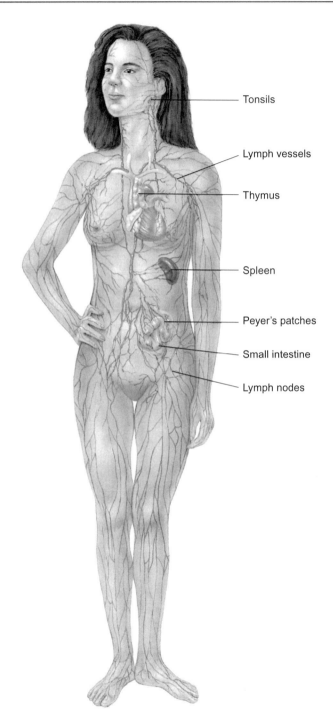

Tonsils

Lymph vessels

Thymus

Spleen

Peyer's patches

Small intestine

Lymph nodes

Figure 5-6 Lymphatic system

3. Unlisted procedure of the diaphragm

   Code(s) _____

4. Repair of a neonatal diaphragmatic hernia, without chest tube and without creation of ventral hernia

   Code(s) _____

CHAPTER 5 REVIEW

I. True/False

Indicate whether the sentence or statement is true or false.

___ **1.** The word "trans-" is a medical prefix that means across, over, through, or beyond.

___ **2.** Hemodialysis is the cleaning of the blood.

___ **3.** An aneurysm is the abnormal dilation of a blood vessel.

___ **4.** Only the ethmoid bone is included in the accessory sinuses.

___ **5.** Staged procedures must be reported with modifier 58.

___ **6.** Tetra means four.

___ **7.** When a biopsy of the upper airway is obtained, you should code the procedure twice.

___ **8.** The lymph is tissue fluid.

___ **9.** When a thrombolytic agent is used, it is never considered part of the service.

___ **10.** The triscupid is a heart valve.

II. Multiple Choice

Identify the letter of the code that best fits the procedure.

___ **11.** Bypass graft, with vein; aortobi-iliac.

   a. 35537   c. 35538

   b. 35302   d. 35303

___ **12.** Repair choanal atresia; intranasal

   a. 30540   c. 30630

   b. 30310   d. 30120

___ **13.** Pericardiocentesis; subsequent

   a. 33010   c. 33011

   b. 33020   d. 33010

___ **14.** Push transfusion, blood, one-year-old patient

   a. 36470   c. 36440

   b. 36425   d. 36450

___ **15.** Repair of a cardiac wound; without bypass

   a. 33404   c. 33330

   b. 33300   d. 33321

___ **16.** Insertion of epicardial electrode; endoscopic approach

   a. 33202   c. 33211

   b. 33201   d. 33203

III. Coding Exercises

Code the following procedures.

17. Excision of cystic hygroma, cervical, without deep neurovascular dissection

   Code(s) _____

18. Emergency tracheostomy; transtracheal

   Code(s) _____

19. Reoperation, coronary artery bypass, 45 days after the original coronary artery bypass, vein only; two coronary venous grafts

   Code(s) _____

IV. Coding Cases

Code the following cases.

20. A 59-year-old male was admitted into the hospital due to an abnormal chest x-ray. A CT scan was ordered, which showed a 2.5 cm mass located at the mitral valve. A valvuloplasty, mitral valve, with cardiopulmonary bypass and a prosthetic ring was performed.

   Code(s) _____

21. Jamie presented to the emergency department with a severe nose bleed. Dr. Carson performed a cauterization to the posterior nasal cavity with inserted nasal packs.

   Code(s) _____

22. A 42-year-old male was admitted into the hospital for removal of a lesion on the vocal cords. Using an operating microscope, Dr. Berg performed a direct laryngoscopy with submucosal removal of a non-neoplastic lesion, and then performed reconstruction with a local tissue flap.

   Code(s) _____

23. Carol was admitted into the hospital due to an abnormal chest x-ray. Dr. Kellerman performed a limited thoracotomy and biopsy of the lung and inserted a drainage tube to prevent Carol's lung from collapsing. Code only the thoracotomy and biopsy.

   Code(s) _____

Chapter 6
The Digestive System

KEY TERMS

dentoalveolar	esophagus	uvula
duodenum	pharynx	

LEARNING OBJECTIVES

After completing this chapter, the learner should be able to:

- Identify structures associated with the digestive system
- Demonstrate the application of modifiers
- Comprehend medical terminology associated with the digestive system
- Apply guidelines to coding
- Differentiate between simple and complex procedures

DIGESTIVE SYSTEM

Codes within the Digestive System section include the mouth, pharynx, adenoids, tonsils, esophagus, stomach and intestines, appendix, liver, pancreas, rectum, and anus (see Figure 6–1). As in previous chapters, these codes are first divided by anatomic site, then by procedure. These procedures include excision, repair incision laparoscopy, and endoscopy. The pancreas, liver, and gallbladder are not usually considered a part of the digestive system, but their codes are included in the section on the digestive system because they aid in the digestion process. You should include diagnostic endoscopies with a surgical endoscopy. To correctly report the endoscopy, you must choose the farthest extent to which the scope was passed.

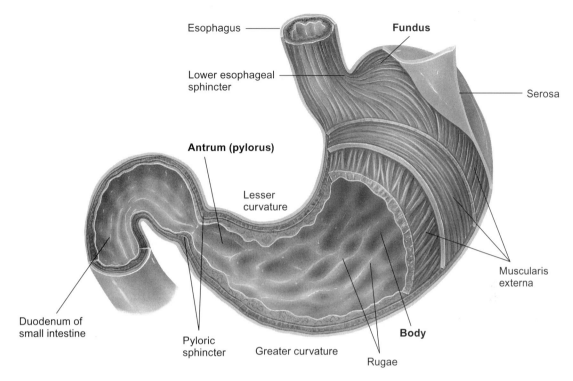

Figure 6-1 Digestive system

Lips

The section on coding for procedures involving the lips only includes the excision and repair codes. To report a procedure performed on the skin of the lips, you must code from the Integumentary System section. In coding for reconstruction of the lip, check the codes within the Integumentary System section to ensure you have coded the procedure correctly.

PRACTICE EXERCISE 6-1

Code the following procedures.

1. Plastic repair of cleft lip/nasal deformity; primary bilateral one stage procedure

   Code(s) _____

2. Excision of lip; transverse wedge excision with primary closure

   Code(s) _____

3. Plastic repair of cleft lip/nasal deformity; secondary, by recreation of defects and reclosure, bilateral

   Code(s) _____

4. Biopsy of the lip

   Code(s) _____

5. Unlisted procedure of the lips

   Code(s) _____

Vestibule of Mouth

Codes within this section include the mucosal and submucosal tissue of the lips and cheeks (see Figure 6–2). Some codes within this section include simple or complex repairs, and may be unilateral or bilateral. When coding for repairs, you should be aware that a skin graft may also be part of the procedure. In these cases, you must report the skin grafts from the Integumentary System. Procedures within this section include only incision, excision or destruction, and repair.

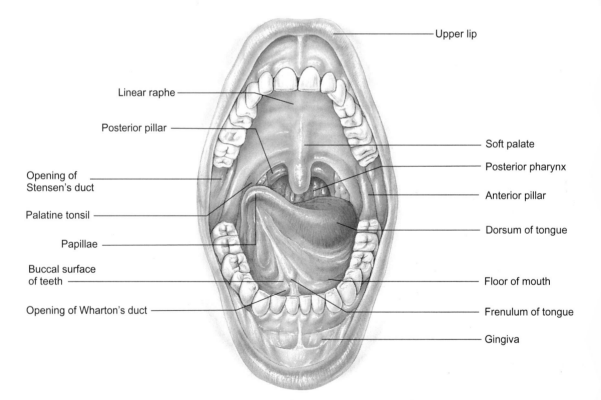

Figure 6-2 Structures of the mouth

PRACTICE EXERCISE 6-2

Code the following procedures.

1. Simple drainage of a hematoma

   Code(s) _____

2. Complex closure of a laceration, 3.0 cm

   Code(s) _____

3. Frenectomy

   Code(s) _____

4. Vestibuloplasty; entire arch

   Code(s) _____

5. Removal of an embedded object from the vestibule of the mouth; complicated

   Code(s) _____

Tongue and Floor of Mouth

The tongue is a muscular organ that aids in the digestion of food. Anatomically, it lies partly on the floor of the mouth and partly in the pharynx (refer to Figure 6–2). It is attached by a muscle to the hyoid bone. The floor of the mouth is the space that is the lowest limit of the cavity. It is important to remember that the coding of procedures involving the tongue is based on the location of the procedure.

PRACTICE EXERCISE 6-3

Code the following procedures.

1. Glossectomy; one-fourth of the tongue

   Code(s) _____

2. Repair of a laceration, 2.0 cm, floor of the mouth and the posterior one-third of the tongue

   Code(s) _____

3. Biopsy of the floor of the mouth

   Code(s) _____

4. Mechanical fixation of the tongue with a K-wire

   Code(s) _____

5. Extraoral incision and drainage of a cyst on the floor of the mouth; submandibular

   Code(s) _____

Dentoalveolar Structures

Although **dentoalveolar** pertains to the alveolus of the tooth and the tooth itself (see Figure 6–3), these codes do not include the removal of the teeth. Codes within this section include procedures for incision, excision, and construction. Some codes require that you report each quadrant separately.

PRACTICE EXERCISE 6-4

Code the following procedures.

1. Excision of fibrous tuberosities, dentoalveolar structures

    Code(s) _____

2. Periodontal mucosal grafting

    Code(s) _____

3. Destruction of a lesion, dentoalveolar structures

    Code(s) _____

4. Gingivoplasty, first quadrant

    Code(s) _____

5. Drainage of a cyst from the dentoalveolar structures

    Code(s) _____

Palate and Uvula

When you visualize the palate of the mouth, you probably think of the roof of the mouth, but the palate actually separates the mouth from the nasal cavity. The **uvula** is a small muscle that hangs at the back of the throat above the root of the tongue. Procedures within this section include excision and destruction, incision, and repair. Some procedures that require a graft may or may not include obtaining of the graft. When a skin graft is required, you must use codes from the Integumentary System section. Report a mucosal graft by using code 40818. Reconstruction of the palate with extraoral tissue must also be coded from the Integumentary System section.

PRACTICE EXERCISE 6-5

Code the following procedures.

1. Complex repair of a laceration of the palate

    Code(s) _____

2. Excision of a lesion of the palate and uvula, with a simple primary closure

    Code(s) _____

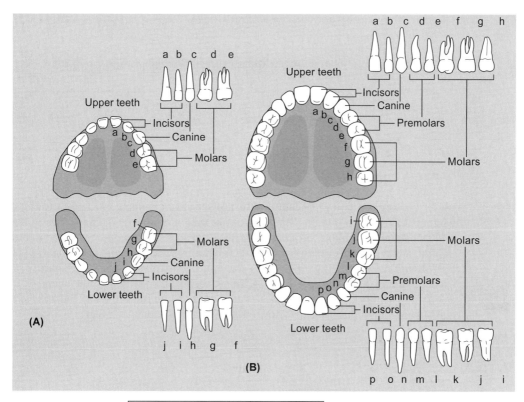

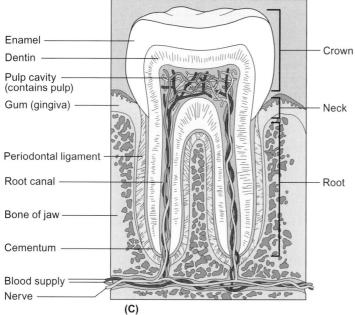

Figure 6-3 Structures of a tooth

3. Maxillary impression for a palatal prosthesis

   Code(s) _____

4. Palatoplasty for cleft palate, with bone graft to alveolar ridge

   Code(s) _____

5. Repair of nasolabial fistula

   Code(s) _____

Salivary Gland and Ducts

When you are reporting procedures for the salivary glands, you need to understand what gland you are reporting. There are major salivary glands—the parotid, sublingual, and the submandibular—and minor salivary glands—the lingual, sublingual, buccal, palatal, labial, and the glosspharyngeal. The major salivary glands may need to be reported with nerve grafting procedures. Procedures within this section include incision, excision, repair, and other procedures. Remember that within the excision codes, imaging guidance may be necessary. These codes are covered in Chapter 8. These codes may also include procedures for suturing and grafting of the facial nerves.

PRACTICE EXERCISE 6-6

Code the following procedures.

1. Excision of parotid gland; lateral lobe, without nerve dissection

   Code(s) _____

2. Closure of the salivary fistula

   Code(s) _____

3. Marsupialization of sublingual salivary cyst

   Code(s) _____

4. Dilation and catheterization of salivary duct, with injection

   Code(s) _____

5. Plastic repair of salivary duct, sialodochoplasty; primary

   Code(s) _____

Pharynx, Adenoids, and Tonsils

The **pharynx** is the passageway for air traveling from the nose to the larynx. It extends from the base of the skull to the sixth cervical vertebra. The nasopharynx is located above the soft palate of the mouth. The adenoids are located in the soft recesses of the nasopharynx. Tonsils, however, are located at the base of the tongue in the membranes of the pharynx. To correctly report the removal of the tonsils or adenoids, you should base the codes on the age of the patient. These codes may be either primary or secondary. The primary codes are used for the removal of the tonsils or adenoids the first time. If the tonsils or adenoids have grown back, then the second removal would be considered secondary. When both tonsils are removed, you must remember to append modifier 50 for the bilateral procedure.

PRACTICE EXERCISE 6-7

Code the following procedures.

1. Destruction of a lesion of the pharynx using cryotherapy

   Code(s) _____

2. Primary adenoidectomy; patient 15 years of age

   Code(s) _____

3. Limited pharyngectomy

   Code(s) _____

4. Tonsillectomy and adenoidectomy; patient 5 years of age

   Code(s) _____

5. Excision of tonsil, three tags

   Code(s) _____

Esophagus

The **esophagus** is a hollow muscular tube that carries food from the mouth to the stomach. Physicians performing endoscopies use the esophagus to view the internal esophagus and stomach. In order to observe these structures they may or may not use radiological supervision and interpretation. They may or may not obtain biopsies, which you should report as one biopsy even if multiple biopsies are obtained. However, if a lesion is biopsied and a different lesion is removed, both codes may be reported if the code does not include "with or without biopsy." It is also important to remember that most codes within this section are modifier 51 exempt.

PRACTICE EXERCISE 6-8

Code the following procedures.

1. Esophagoplasty, thoracic approach, with repair of tracheoesophageal fistula

   Code(s) _____

2. Partial esophagectomy, distal two-thirds, with thoracotomy only, without proximal gastrectomy, with thoracic esophagogastrostomy, with pyloroplasty

   Code(s) _____

3. Endoscopic retrograde cholangiopancreatography; diagnostic, with collection of specimen by brushing, separate procedure

Code(s) _____

4. Diverticulectomy of hypopharynx without myotomy; thoracic approach

Code(s) _____

5. Closure of fistula; transthoracic approach

Code(s) _____

Stomach

Procedures included in this section are incision, excision, introduction and laparoscopy, bariatric surgery, and other procedures. As always, surgical laparoscopy includes the diagnostic laparoscopy. When the patient receives bariatric surgery, it may involve the stomach, the duodenum, the jejunum, and the ileum (see Figure 6–4). The **duodenum** is the lower opening of the stomach, and the esophagus is the top opening of the stomach.

PRACTICE EXERCISE 6-9

Code the following procedures.

1. Closure of gastrostomy; surgical

Code(s) _____

2. Laparoscopy, surgical; transection of vagus nerves, truncal

Code(s) _____

3. Percutaneous placement of gastrostomy tube

Code(s) _____

4. Gastrostomy, open; neonatal, for feeding

Code(s) _____

5. Laparoscopy, surgical, gastric restrictive procedure; revision of adjustable gastric band component only

Code(s) _____

Intestines

The intestines extend from the stomach to the anus. They include the ascending, descending, and transverse colon, which are considered the large intestines (see Figure 6–5). The small intestines are the duodenum, jejunum, and ileum. Procedures within

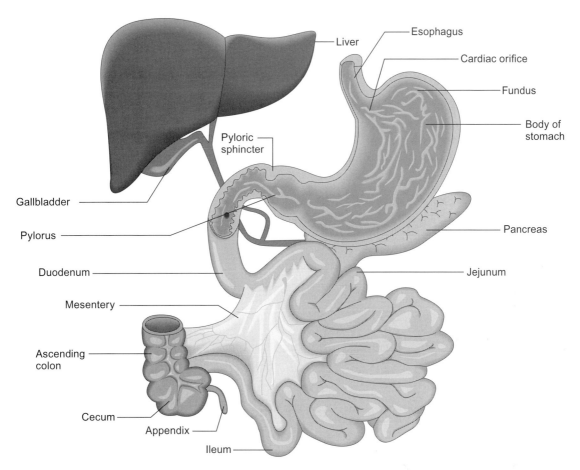

Figure 6-4 Structures of the digestive system

this section include transplant procedures from a cadaver of both the large and small intestines. To report these codes correctly, you must recognize that transplantation involves three distinct components of the physician's work. The first component is the code regarding the cadaver donor, the second component includes the standard preparation of the allograft, and the last component is the allotransplantation.

PRACTICE EXERCISE 6-10

Code the following procedures.

1. Duodenotomy, for exploration

   Code(s) _____

2. Suture repair of the small intestine for perforated ulcer

   Code(s) _____

3. Enterectomy, small intestines; single resection and anastomosis

   Code(s) _____

4. Enterostomy tube for feeding

   Code(s) _____

5. Laparoscopy, surgical; jejunostomy for decompression

   Code(s) _____

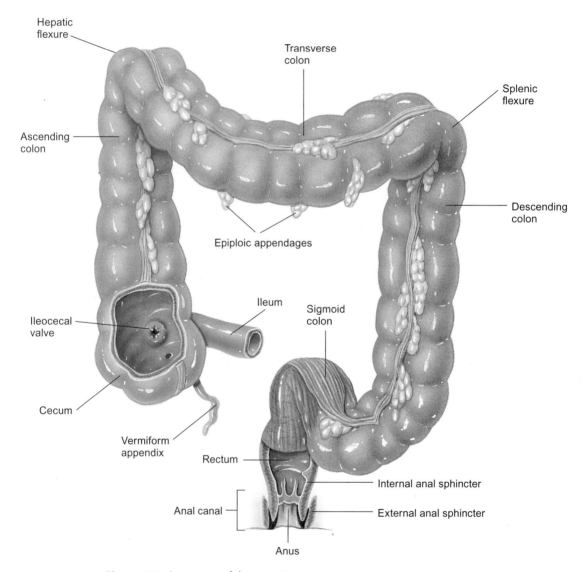

Figure 6-5 Structures of the intestines

Rectum

The rectum is located between the sigmoid colon and the anal canal, and it is divided into four sacral segments. However, these segments are not individually identified in the procedural codes. To ensure correct coding of endoscopic procedures within this section, you must carefully read the medical record. Physician may use different approaches to examine individual sections of the colon. The scope they use may be flexible or rigid. When procedures are performed in which the patient needs anesthesia, you must report the anesthesia if more than a local anesthesia was given. These codes are located in Chapter 3. Codes within this section include diagnostic procedures when surgical procedures are performed.

PRACTICE EXERCISE 6-11

Code the following procedures.

1. Laparoscopy, surgical; open procedure, proctopexy

    Code(s) _____

2. Biopsy of anorectal wall, anal approach

    Code(s) _____

3. Sigmoidoscopy, flexible; diagnostic, with single biopsy

    Code(s) _____

4. Excision of rectal tumor, transanal approach

    Code(s) _____

5. Diagnostic anorectal exam, surgical, requiring anesthesia with removal of fecal impaction

    Code(s) _____

Anus

Codes that deal with the anus are mostly for the removal of hemorrhoids and fistulas, which are usually performed in the physician's office. The removal of hemorrhoids may be performed by excision, destruction, or injection. They can be either internal or external. The physician may use one or more methods at the same time. In these cases, report the codes separately, appending modifier 51.

PRACTICE EXERCISE 6-12

Code the following procedures.

1. Closure of anal fistula with rectal advancement flap

    Code(s) _____

2. Anoplasty on an infant, plastic operation

Code(s) _____

3. Cryosurgery of rectal tumor; benign

Code(s) _____

4. Hemorrhoidectomy by simple ligature

Code(s) _____

5. Injection of sclerosing solution, hemorrhoids

Code(s) _____

LIVER

The liver is the largest solid organ, and it is divided into lobes or segments. When coding for procedures of the liver, you must remember several points. In the incision codes, imaging guidance or fine needle aspiration may be included. This section also includes liver transplantation procedures; therefore, the three distinct components of the physician's work must be coded. It is important that you read the medical record carefully to determine which segments are being transplanted. The left lobe contains the second to the fourth segments and the right lobe contains the fifth to the eighth segments.

PRACTICE EXERCISE 6-13

Code the following procedures.

1. Biopsy of the liver, needle; percutaneous

Code(s) _____

2. Management of liver hemorrhage; exploration of hepatic wound, with hepatic artery ligation

Code(s) _____

3. Hepatotomy; for open drainage of abscess, one stage

Code(s) _____

4. Unlisted procedure of the liver

Code(s) _____

5. Total liver transplant from cadaver

Code(s) _____

Biliary Tract

Procedures for the Biliary Tract section include incision, introduction, endoscopy, laparoscopy, excision, and repair. Some procedures require imaging guidance or radiological supervision and interpretation. We will discuss codes for these in Chapter 8.

PRACTICE EXERCISE 6-14

Code the following procedures.

1. Cholecystectomy with cholangiography

   Code(s) _____

2. Percutaneous cholecystostomy

   Code(s) _____

3. Exploration for congenital atresia of bile ducts, without repair, with liver biopsy, with cholangiography

   Code(s) _____

4. Laparoscopy, surgical; cholecystectomy with exploration of common bile duct

   Code(s) _____

5. Introduction of percutaneous transhepatic catheter for biliary drainage

   Code(s) _____

Pancreas

The pancreas is located behind the stomach (see Figure 6-4). The enzymes it produces help in the digestion of foods. Procedures located within this section include incision, excision, introduction, repair, and transplantation. You should report procedures for peroral pancreatic endoscopy using codes 43260–43272. Diabetic patients may require transplantation of both the pancreas and kidney. Once again, you need to report transplantation codes using the three components of the physician's work.

PRACTICE EXERCISE 6-15

Code the following procedures.

1. Marsupialization of pancreatic cyst

   Code(s) _____

2. Removal of pancreatic calculus

   Code(s) _____

3. Placement of drains, peripancreatic, for acute pancreatitis; with cholecystostomy, gastrostomy, and jejunostomy

   Code(s) _____

4. Pancreaticojejunostomy, Puestow-type operation

   Code(s) _____

5. Pancreatorrhaphy for injury

   Code(s) _____

Abdomen, Peritoneum, and Omentum

Procedures within this section include incision, excision and destruction, introduction, repair, laparoscopy, and suture. Procedures that include an exploratory laparotomy are always included in the larger procedure; never report them separately. Codes within the repair section are primarily used for the repair of hernias. These codes are first categorized by type, then based on an initial or recurrent hernia. Note that these codes are also reported based on the age of the patient.

PRACTICE EXERCISE 6-16

Code the following procedures.

1. Excision of presacral tumor

   Code(s) _____

2. Repair of an umbilical hernia of an infant; reducible

   Code(s) _____

3. Secondary suture of the abdominal wall for dehiscence

   Code(s) _____

4. Ligation of peritoneal-venous shunt

   Code(s) _____

5. Laparoscopy, surgical, with multiple biopsies

   Code(s) _____

URINARY SYSTEM

The urinary system consists of two kidneys, two ureters, the bladder and urethra (see Figure 6-6). When you code the Urinary System section, first report by the anatomic site, then by procedure. Also report by the approach the physician is using. Most procedures include the minor procedures with the major procedures.

Kidney

The kidneys are located under the back muscles, behind the parietal peritoneum, just above the waistline (refer to Figure 6-6). The right kidney is usually a little lower than the left. In coding for kidney stones removal, you must determine which approach the physician is using. Methods for the removal of a stone include a percutaneous method, lithotripsy, open incision, or endoscopic. Remember, you must use modifier 50 for procedures that are performed bilaterally.

Also within this section are the codes for kidney transplant. In order to code this correctly, you must remember that the renal allotransplant involves the components of the

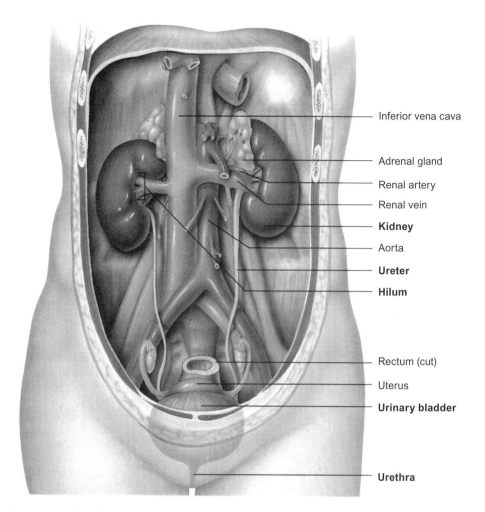

Figure 6-6 The urinary system

physician's work. Renal autotransplantation includes reimplantation of the autograft as the primary procedure. The secondary procedures, which include the nephrectomy, should be reported with the modifier 51.

PRACTICE EXERCISE 6-17

Code the following procedures.

1. Nephrectomy, including partial ureterectomy, open procedure, including rib resection; complicated because of previous surgery on this same kidney

    Code(s) _____

2. Aspiration and injection of renal cyst by needle, percutaneous

   Code(s) _____

3. Lithotripsy, extracorporeal shock wave

   Code(s) _____

4. Removal and replacement of internally dwelling ureteral stent via percutaneous approach, including radiological supervision and interpretation bilaterally

   Code(s) _____

5. Suture of a kidney wound

   Code(s) _____

Ureter

Ureters are narrow, long tubes with an expanded upper end (renal pelvis) located inside the kidney and lined with a mucous membrane. Ureters drain urine from the renal pelvis to the urinary bladder (see Figure 6–6). Physicians who perform procedures on the ureter may perform the procedure in various ways, including endoscopic, laparoscopic, and open procedures. Some procedures may be bilateral, which you need to report with modifier 50. In order for you to code the removal of stones correctly, the physician needs to have documented which portion of the ureter was incised. For coding purposes, these codes have been divided into the upper third, middle third, and lower third of the ureter.

PRACTICE EXERCISE 6-18

Code the following procedures.

1. Ureteroureterostomy

   Code(s) _____

2. Closure of ureterocutaneous fistula

   Code(s) _____

3. Ureterolithotomy; middle one third of ureter

   Code(s) _____

4. Surgical laparoscopy, ureterolithotomy

   Code(s) _____

5. Bilateral ureteroenterostomy, direct anastomosis of ureter to the intestine

   Code(s) _____

Bladder

The bladder is an elastic, muscular organ that has the capability to expand greatly. The walls of the bladder permit the storage of urine with little increase in pressure. Correct documentation by the physician should include whether the removal of the bladder was partial or complete. You may require codes for imaging guidance or radiological supervision and interpretation. You must append modifier 50 for bilateral procedures.

PRACTICE EXERECISE 6-19

Code the following procedures.

1. Cystectomy, complete; with bilateral pelvic lymphadenectomy, including external iliac hypogastric and obturator nodes

   Code(s) _____

2. Injection procedure for retrograde urethrocystography

   Code(s) _____

3. Injection procedure for cystography

   Code(s) _____

4. Aspiration of the bladder by trocar, with insertion of suprapubic catheter

   Code(s) _____

5. Bladder irrigation, simple lavage and installation

   Code(s) _____

Urodynamics

Urodynamics is the study of the storage of urine in the bladder. Within the Urodynamics section codes, these procedures may be reported separately or in combination with each other. Procedures within this section are under the direct supervision of the physician; therefore, the physician must supply all materials, including equipment. If the physician interprets the results and/or operates the equipment, you must report this with modifier 26 to identify the professional component. When combinations of procedures are performed within the same session, append modifier 51 to the procedure code.

PRACTICE EXERCISE 6-20

Code the following procedures.

1. Voiding pressures studies; with measurement of post-voiding residual urine and bladder capacity by ultrasound, non-imaging

   Code(s) _____

2. Cystourethroplasty with bilateral ureteroneocystostomy

   Code(s) _____

3. Simple cystometrogram with urethral pressure profile studies of anal sphincter, with physician operating the cystometrogram

   Code(s) _____

4. Cutaneous vesicostomy

   Code(s) _____

5. Closure of vesicouterine fistula

   Code(s) _____

Transurethral Surgery

Codes within this section include urethra and bladder, and the ureter and pelvis. When coding for the ureter and pelvis, here are a few points you should remember. First, surgical cystourethroscopy always includes the diagnostic cystourethroscopy. Second, when the insertion and removal of the temporary stent takes place during a diagnostic procedure, it should not be reported separately. Third, when the procedure calls for an insertion of a self-containing stent during a diagnostic or therapeutic procedure, it is necessary to report code 52332 in addition to the primary procedure. You must append this code with modifier 51. If the procedure is bilateral, then append modifier 50. This type of bilateral procedure is a staged procedure. It must be reported with modifier 58.

PRACTICE EXERCISE 6-21

Code the following procedures.

1. Litholapaxy: fragmentation of calculus in the bladder with removal of fragments measuring 3.0 cm

   Code(s) _____

2. Cystourethroscopy with insertion of radioactive material, with biopsy

   Code(s) _____

3. Diagnostic cystourethroscopy, with ureteroscopy and pyeloscopy

   Code(s) _____

4. Cystourethroscopy, with dilation of bladder for interstitial cystitis; local anesthesia

   Code(s) _____

5. Cystourethroscopy with manipulation, without removal of ureteral calculus

   Code(s) _____

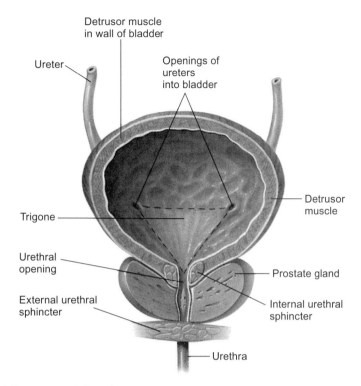

Detrusor muscle
in wall of bladder

Ureter

Openings of
ureters
into bladder

Detrusor
muscle

Trigone

Urethral
opening

Prostate gland

External urethral
sphincter

Internal urethral
sphincter

Urethra

Figure 6-7 Structures of the urinary system

Urethra

The urethra is a long tube extending from the urinary bladder to the exterior of the body. It functions as a passage for urine to the exterior and, in males, for the passage of the male reproductive fluid (see Figure 6–7). Some codes within this section are specific to the patient being male or female; other codes are for reporting procedures on infants. Other codes identify a first or second stage procedure or whether the procedure is an initial or subsequent procedure.

When coding these procedures, be careful not to confuse the urethra with the ureter.

PRACTICE EXERCISE 6-22

Code the following procedures.

1. Drainage of eight deep periurethral abscesses

   Code(s) _____

2. Sling operation for correction of male urinary incontinence

   Code(s) _____

3. Meatotomy, separate procedure on an infant

Code(s) _____

4. Urethrorrhaphy, suture of urethral injury, female

Code(s) _____

5. Dilation of female urethra, general anesthesia

Code(s) _____

6. Marsupialization of urethral diverticulum, male

Code(s) _____

CHAPTER REVIEW

I. True/False

Indicate whether the sentence or statement is true or false.

___ **1.** The tongue is considered a muscular organ.

___ **2.** The parotid gland is a minor salivary gland.

___ **3.** The duodenum is the upper opening of the stomach.

___ **4.** The pancreas is located in front of the stomach.

___ **5.** Ureters are long narrow tubes.

II. Multiple Choice

Identify the letter of the code that best describes the procedure.

___ **6.** Delayed creation of exit site from embedded subcutaneous segment of intraperitoneal cannula

a. 49402   c. 49436

b. 49422   d. 49423

___ **7.** Removal of peritoneal foreign body from peritoneal cavity

a. 49402   c. 49555

b. 49425   d. 49422

___ **8.** Cystourethroscopy, with ureteroscopy and pyeloscopy; diagnostic

a. 52344   c. 52341

b. 52351   d. 52352

___ **9.** Dilation of female urethra, including suppository and instillation; initial

a. 53600   c. 53620

b. 53660   d. 53605

___ **10.** Repair of initial incisional hernia; reducible

    a. 49585   c. 49550

    b. 49565   d. 49560

III. Coding Exercises

Use an encoder or coding manuals to code the following procedures.

11. Diagnostic colonoscopy through a stoma, with multiple biopsies

    Code(s) _____

12. Revision of the parotid duct with excision of both submandibular glands

    Code(s) _____

13. A pancreatorrhaphy performed for an injury

    Code(s) _____

14. Cricopharyngeal myotomy

    Code(s) _____

15. Transurethral resection performed after the postoperative period because of residual obstructive tissue

    Code(s) _____

16. Surgical laparoscopy repair for a recurrent inguinal hernia

    Code(s) _____

17. Complicated procedure for the removal of an embedded object from the vestibule of the mouth

    Code(s) _____

18. Physician interpretation of an electromyography study of an anal sphincter

    Code(s) _____

19. Ureterocolon conduit including intestine anastomosis, bilaterally

    Code(s) _____

20. Removal of the appendix due to rupture with generalized peritonitis

    Code(s) _____

IV. Coding Cases

Code the following cases.

21. Jamie presented to Dr. Tann's office with a complaint of weight loss and stomach pain. Upon examination and test review, Jamie was diagnosed with gastric adenocarcinoma. Dr. Tann scheduled Jamie for a distal partial gastric resection with gastrojejunostomy. (Code the procedure.)

    Code(s) _____

22. Jenny presented to her family physician with complaints of bloody diarrhea, nausea, and vomiting. She denied having fever or chills, had moderate use of alcohol, and smoked half a pack of cigarettes per day. Her physician scheduled her for a colonoscopy of the transverse colon.

Code(s) _____

23. Peter was diagnosed three years ago with hiatal hernia. Today, he presented to Dr. Saunder with a complaint of difficulty breathing, heartburn, and a slight cough. Dr. Saunder performed the usual examination and scheduled Peter for an endoscopy of the stomach. (Code the stomach endoscopy.)

Code(s) _____

Chapter 7
The Reproductive, Endocrine, and Nervous Systems

KEY TERMS

adrenal glands	introitus	vagina
carotid body	oviduct	vas deferens
cervix uterus	parathyroid gland	vulva
corpus uterus	prostate	
epididymis	thymus gland	

LEARNING OBJECTIVES

After completing this chapter, the learner should be able to:

- Identify anatomic structures
- Apply multiple codes to procedures
- Identify staged procedures
- Apply correct modifiers to surgical procedures

MALE GENITAL SYSTEM

The male reproductive system consists of the testes and the ducts and glands that contribute to the formation of semen (see Figure 7–1). These include the penis, testis, epididymis, scrotum, vas deferens, spermatic cord, and the prostate. Codes within these sections are determined by the approach of the procedure.

Penis

The penis is composed of erectile tissue that has three columns (one that contains the urethra) and is completely covered in skin. It is suspended from the front and sides of the male pubic arch. Procedure codes include incision, destruction, excision, introduction, and repair. To ensure correct coding of an incision for drainage, you must code from the Integumentary System section unless the procedure involves a deep incision. Within the

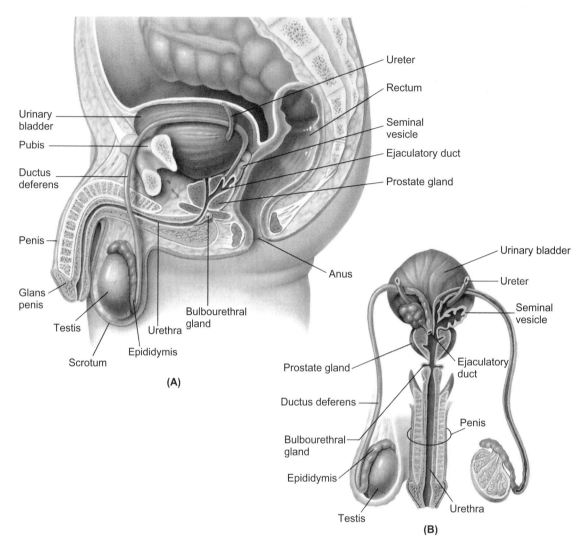

Figure 7-1 Male genital system

destruction codes, physicians who perform a simple destruction may code the method of destruction. However, if the destruction was extensive, the code will include all methods of destruction. Excision codes differ when it comes to circumcision. To correctly report these codes, read the medical record carefully. Circumcision for a newborn is different than circumcision for an infant a few days old. The latter is considered an E/M code.

PRACTICE EXERCISE 7-1

Code the following procedures.

1. Insertion of a semi-rigid penile prosthesis; non-inflatable

   Code(s) _____

2. Destruction of lesion, extensive

   Code(s) _____

3. Urethroplasty for second stage hypospadias, 4 cm

   Code(s) _____

4. Circumcision, surgical excision using clamp, on newborn, with injection of corpora cavernosa with pharmacologic agent

   Code(s) _____

5. Plastic operation of penis for injury

   Code(s) _____

Testis

The testes are located in the scrotum and suspended from the spermatic cord. They are one of the two male reproductive glands. Procedures include excision, repair, and laparoscopy. These procedures may be unilateral or bilateral. If bilateral procedures are performed, you must append modifier 50 to the procedure code.

PRACTICE EXERCISE 7-2

Code the following procedures.

1. Exploration for undescended testis with abdominal exploration, bilateral

   Code(s) _____

2. Excision of extraparenchymal lesion of testis

   Code(s) _____

3. Partial orchiectomy with surgical laparoscopy

   Code(s) _____

4. Suture repair of testicular injury

   Code(s) _____

5. Needle biopsy of the testis, bilateral

   Code(s) _____

Epididymis, Scrotum, Vas Deferens, and Spermatic Cord

The **epididymis** is a long coiled tube on the posterior surface of each testis, and the scrotum is the pouch that contains the testicles and part of the spermatic cord. The **vas deferens,** also known as the ductus deferens, extends from the epididymis into the abdominal cavity through the inguinal canal, behind the urinary bladder. It then joins the ejaculatory duct. Procedures in this section may or may not include bilateral procedures. They may distinguish the approach the physician chooses to use, such as abdominal or laparoscopic. The code for a vasectomy includes both unilateral and bilateral procedures.

PRACTICE EXERCISE 7-3

Code the following procedures.

1. Complicated scrotoplasty

    Code(s) _____

2. Incision and drainage of epididymis, testis, and scrotal space

    Code(s) _____

3. Resection of scrotum

    Code(s) _____

4. Vasectomy

    Code(s) _____

5. Exploration of epididymis, with biopsy

    Code(s) _____

Prostate

The **prostate** is a single gland located below the urinary bladder (refer to Figure 7–1). Procedures within this section may be performed as one total procedure or performed on different days. For this reason, it is important for you to read the medical record carefully to ensure proper coding.

PRACTICE EXERCISE 7-4

Code the following procedures.

1. Laparoscopy, surgical prostatectomy, retropubic radical, including nerve sparing

    Code(s) _____

2. Prostatotomy, external drainage of prostatic abscess, abdominal approach; simple

    Code(s) _____

3. Exposure of prostate, any approach, for insertion of radioactive substance

    Code(s) _____

4. Cryosurgical ablation of the prostate with ultrasonic guidance for interstitial cryosurgical probe placement

    Code(s) _____

5. Biopsy, prostate, punch, multiple

Code(s) _____

FEMALE GENITAL SYSTEM

The female reproductive system, or genital system, consists of the ovaries, fallopian tubes, uterus, vagina, and external genitals (see Figure 7–2). Coding for this section may involve a little more reading on your part. Some procedures within this section refer to other subsections, depending on their diagnosis. For example, a benign or malignant tumor of the genitals would be coded from the Integumentary System section. These codes are also intended for procedures on females who are not pregnant. (There is a subsection for pregnancy.) For procedures that require regional anesthesia, you must code the anesthesia in addition to the primary code. Anesthesia codes are located in Chapter 3 of this workbook.

Vulva, Perineum, and Introitus

The **vulva** is the external portion of the female genitals, which is posterior to the mons veneris, whereas the perineum is the area between the vulva and anus. The opening into

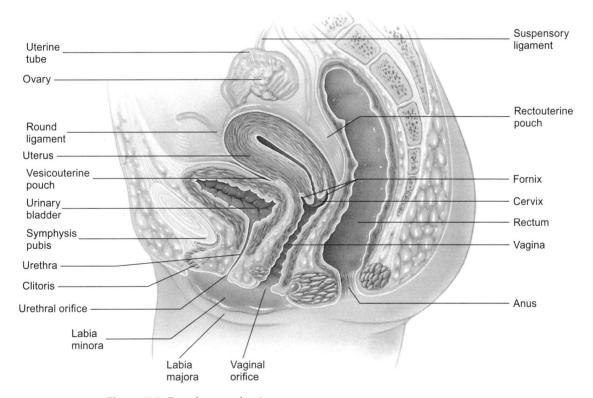

Figure 7-2 Female reproductive system

the vaginal canal is called the **introitus.** Procedures that involve wound repair should be reported from the Integumentary System section; however, injuries to the vagina and perineum that have been newly acquired should be reported within that subsection. When procedures involve a vulvectomy, there are a few points to remember. Removal of skin and superficial subcutaneous tissue is considered a simple procedure. A radical procedure involves removal of skin and deep subcutaneous tissue. Partial procedures are the removal of less than 80 percent of the vulvar area; more than 80 percent is considered a complete removal procedure.

PRACTICE EXERCISE 7-5

Code the following procedures.

1. Plastic repair of introitus

    Code(s) _____

2. Destruction of a lesion, vulva; simple, using chemosurgery

    Code(s) _____

3. Vulvectomy, radical, complete with unilateral inguinofemoral lymphadenectomy

    Code(s) _____

4. Biopsy of perineum; three lesions

    Code(s) _____

5. Revision of hymenal ring

    Code(s) _____

Vagina

The **vagina** extends from the cervix to the vaginal orifice and serves as the birth canal. However, procedure codes within this section do not cover pregnancy or delivery and may state "non-obstetrical." You may find some procedure codes within the Urinary System section, but read the code carefully. The code for a paravaginal defect repair (57284) includes stress urinary incontinence, but a laparoscopy for stress incontinence (51990) is listed in the Urinary System section.

PRACTICE EXERCISE 7-6

Code the following procedures.

1. Fitting and insertion of an intravaginal support device, with dilation of vagina under anesthesia

    Code(s) _____

2. Closure of rectovaginal fistula; abdominal approach

    Code(s) _____

3. Colposcopy of the entire vagina with cervix, with biopsy of vagina and cervix

    Code(s) _____

4. Vaginectomy, complete, with removal of vaginal wall

    Code(s) _____

5. Excision of vaginal tumor

    Code(s) _____

Cervix Uteri

The **cervix uterus** is the neck of the uterus. This portion of the uterus may become torn during childbirth. The lacerations may be single or bilateral, and they are sutured to prevent hemorrhage.

PRACTICE EXERCISE 7-7

Code the following procedures.

1. Dilation and curettage of cervical stump

    Code(s) _____

2. Colposcopy of the cervix, including upper/adjacent vagina

    Code(s) _____

3. Excision of cervical stump; with pelvic floor repair

    Code(s) _____

4. Endocervical curettage

    Code(s) _____

5. Trachelorrhaphy, plastic repair of uterine cervix, vaginal approach

    Code(s) _____

Corpus Uteri

The **corpus uterus** is the main body of the uterus, which is located above the cervix. Here you will find, within the excision codes, the procedure codes for vaginal hysterectomy. These procedures may be performed using various methods; therefore, they are divided by the method of approach, with abdominal first, then vaginal. Within the introduction section, you will find the codes for both the insertion and removal of an intrauterine device.

PRACTICE EXERCISE 7-8

Code the following procedures.

1. Nonobstretical repair of a ruptured uterus

   Code(s) _____

2. Endometrial sampling performed in conjunction with colposcopy

   Code(s) _____

3. Radical hysterectomy, vaginal, Schauta type operation

   Code(s) _____

4. Insertion of an IUD

   Code(s) _____

5. Diagnostic dilation and curettage, nonobstretical

   Code(s) _____

Oviduct and Ovary

The **oviduct** is the medical term used for the fallopian tube. Codes for the Oviduct and Ovary section are considered unilateral and bilateral procedures; therefore, modifier 50 is not necessary. When coding for a tubal ligation, you must read the medical record carefully. This procedure may be performed separately or at the time of a cesarean delivery.

PRACTICE EXERCISE 7-9

Code the following procedures.

1. Drainage of ovarian abscess; vaginal approach, open

   Code(s) _____

2. Fimbrioplasty

   Code(s) _____

3. Ovarian cystectomy, bilateral

   Code(s) _____

4. Laparoscopy, surgical; with lysis of adhesions (separate procedure)

   Code(s) _____

5. Ligation of fallopian tubes, abdominal approach, bilateral

   Code(s) _____

Maternity Care and Delivery

Codes within the Maternity Care and Delivery section are considered normal maternity and delivery, without complications. These include the antepartum care, delivery, and postpartum care. Antepartum care includes the initial assessment, physical examinations, blood pressure, fetal heart tones, routine urinalysis, and weekly visits up to the time of delivery. The delivery includes admission to the hospital, a history, and physical examination; the management of the uncomplicated labor includes the vaginal or cesarean delivery. Postpartum codes include follow-up care in the hospital as well as outpatient office visits. Any medical problem resulting from the complication of the pregnancy, such as diabetes or hypertension, should be reported from the E/M section or the Medicine section. Complications of the pregnancy requiring any surgical procedure, such as an ovarian cyst, should be reported from the Surgery section. Abortion procedures are also found here within this subsection.

PRACTICE EXERCISE 7-10

Code the following procedures.

1. Diagnostic amniocentesis

   Code(s) _____

2. Routine obstetric care including antepartum care, cesarean delivery, and postpartum care

   Code(s) _____

3. Treatment of septic abortion, completed surgically

   Code(s) _____

4. Cesarean delivery only, following attempted vaginal delivery after previous cesarean delivery

   Code(s) _____

5. Unlisted fetal invasive procedure, including ultrasound guidance

   Code(s) _____

ENDOCRINE SYSTEM

If you remember your anatomy and physiology, you should know that the endocrine system consists of a number of glands located throughout the body (see Figure 7–3). Their function is to release hormones into the bloodstream and provide homeostasis. But this coding section does not include all glands. For example, the pituitary and pineal glands are located within in the Nervous System section because they are located within the

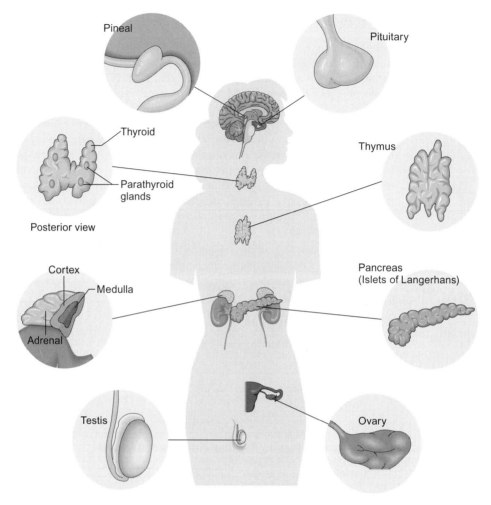

Figure 7–3 The endocrine system

brain. Ovaries and testes are located in the Reproductive System section, and the pancreas is located within the Digestive System section.

Thyroid Gland

The thyroid gland is located at the base of the neck. It sits on both sides of the upper portion of the trachea and the lower portion of the larynx. The isthmus connects these two lateral lobes. The thyroidectomy codes include a partial removal or subtotal removal—either way, it is not a complete or total removal of the thyroid. Codes within this section include the incision and excision codes. If a fine needle aspiration is performed, code this from the Integumentary System section. You should report imaging guidance and ultrasound procedures from the Radiology section.

PRACTICE EXERCISE 7-11

Code the following procedures.

1. Transection of the isthmus

   Code(s) _____

2. Excision of a recurrent thyroglossal duct cyst

   Code(s) _____

3. Biopsy of the thyroid, percutaneous core needle

   Code(s) _____

4. Thyroidectomy, including substernal thyroid, cervical approach

   Code(s) _____

5. Partial thyroid lobectomy, unilateral; with contralateral subtotal lobectomy, including isthmusectomy

   Code(s) _____

Parathyroid, Thymus, Adrenal Glands, and Carotid Body

The **parathyroid gland** is located on the back of the thyroid gland. These little glands regulate calcium and phosphorus metabolism. The **thymus gland** is located in the mediastinal cavity and above the heart. It continues to grow until puberty and then begins to shrink. The **adrenal glands** are located above the surface of each kidney. They function by regulating electrolyte balance and the metabolism of proteins, fat, and glucose. The **carotid body** refers to the body of the adrenal gland. Codes within this section include excision and laparoscopy.

PRACTICE EXERCISE 7-12

Code the following procedures.

1. Laparoscopy, surgical, with adrenalectomy, partial, lumbar approach

   Code(s) _____

2. Thymectomy, total; transcervical approach

   Code(s) _____

3. Exploration of parathyroids

   Code(s) _____

4. Thymectomy, total; sternal split with radical mediastinal dissection (separate procedure)

   Code(s) _____

5. Parathyroidectomy with mediastinal exploration, transthoracic approach

Code(s) _____

NERVOUS SYSTEM

The Nervous System section includes the brain, skull, spinal column, and nerves of the central nervous system, along with the peripheral and autonomic nerves (see Figures 7–4 and 7–6). These nerves act as the reflex center, and they control messages to and from the body. Although this section does not list each nerve independently, it does in fact base the reporting of codes on the anatomic site, then the procedure. Many of these codes are used in conjunction with one another; other codes are used as a totally separate procedure. Make certain you report the radiologic supervision, bilateral procedures, and the closure of the wound.

Skull, Meninges, and Brain

The codes for reporting the injection procedures for cerebral angiography are located in the sections for the cardiovascular system (36100–36218), ventriculography (61026–61120), and pneumoencephalography (61055). Use these codes in addition to the primary procedure. Within the injection codes, you will notice that some of the codes deal with the cervical nerves only. Physicians who perform procedures on the brain may sometimes have to relieve pressure within the skull or to implant or inject radioactive material. These procedures are performed by a twist drill, burr hole, or trephine. When you are coding for craniectomy or craniotomy, be sure to read the procedure and the annotations carefully: these procedures may be bundled. It may also be necessary for physicians who perform these procedures to remove part of the skull. In these instances, another procedure to graft the bones that were removed will be performed. When the grafting is performed, you must report the grafting procedure in addition to the primary procedure. Once again, read the medical record carefully, add the correct modifier for bilateral procedures, and check to make sure the procedure is not bundled (see Figure 7–5).

PRACTICE EXERCISE 7-13

Code the following procedures.

1. Subtemporal decompression

   Code(s) _____

2. Cisternal puncture, without injection

   Code(s) _____

3. Craniectomy, posterior fossa; for excision of brain abscess

   Code(s) _____

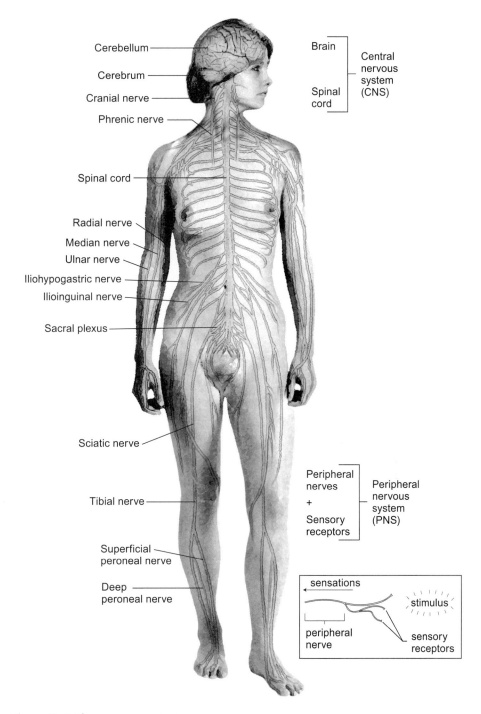

Cerebellum

Cerebrum

Cranial nerve

Phrenic nerve

Spinal cord

Radial nerve

Median nerve

Ulnar nerve

Iliohypogastric nerve

Ilioinguinal nerve

Sacral plexus

Sciatic nerve

Tibial nerve

Superficial peroneal nerve

Deep peroneal nerve

Brain

Spinal cord

Central nervous system (CNS)

Peripheral nerves

+

Sensory receptors

Peripheral nervous system (PNS)

sensations

stimulus

peripheral nerve

sensory receptors

Figure 7–4 The nervous system

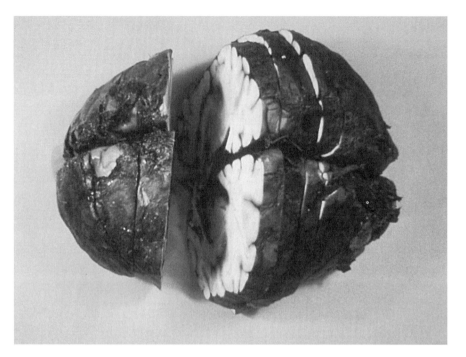

Figure 7–5 Hemorrhagic meningitis due to inhalation anthrax (Image courtesy of the Centers for Disease Control and Prevention)

4. Craniectomy, with excision of foreign body from brain

   Code(s) _____

5. Puncture of shunt tubing for aspiration

   Code(s) _____

Surgery of Skull Base

Codes within this section are divided by the approach (adequate exposure), definitive procedure (treatment), and the repair and reconstruction. The approach procedure is the anatomic site in which the procedure is performed. The definitive procedures are the repairs, resections, and so forth along with the closure of the wound. Repair and reconstruction are reported separately when needed: you should only report these procedures if grafts, flaps, or cranioplasty were performed. Surgeons who perform these procedures may require another surgeon. One surgeon will perform the approach procedure and the second surgeon will perform the definitive procedure. If one surgeon performs both the approach and definitive procedure, you must report both codes and append modifier 51 to the secondary procedure. If there is extensive repair or reconstruction, more surgeons may be involved in the care of the patient. In these instances, each surgeon would report only the procedure they performed. Surgeries performed on the skull are always performed and closed at the same session because of the high risk of infection. Primary closure of the skull must be coded from the Integumentary System section. (See Figure 7–6.)

PRACTICE EXERCISE 7-14

Code the following procedures.

1. Craniofacial approach to anterior fossa; extradural, including lateral rhinotomy, orbital exenteration, ethmoidectomy, sphenoidectomy, and maxillectomy with excision of neoplastic lesion of base of anterior cranial fossa; extradural

   Code(s) _____

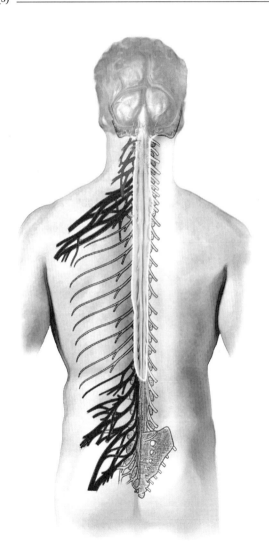

Figure 7–6 Spinal column with associated nerves

2. Surgery of intracranial arteriovenous malformation; infratentorial, complex

Code(s) _____

3. Transcochlear approach to posterior cranial fossa, including labyrinthectomy, with mobilization of facial nerve and petrous carotid artery

Code(s) _____

4. Resection of neoplastic lesion of infratemporal fossa, parapharyngeal space, petrous apex; extradural with ligation, carotid in petrous canal; without repair

Code(s) _____

5. Orbitocranial approach to anterior cranial fossa, extradural, including supraorbital ridge osteotomy and elevation of frontal and temporal lobes, with orbital exenteration

Code(s) _____

Surgery for Aneurysm, Arteriovenous Malformation, or Vascular Disease

Physicians who perform procedures on an aneurysm or for any vascular disease may need the use of a surgical microscope. These codes are located in the Medicine section. An aneurysm is a localized weakness in the wall of an artery or blood vessel. Other procedures performed may need to be reported from the Cardiovascular System section, so you must read the procedure very carefully. Report aneurysms larger than 15 mm using code 61697 or 61698.

PRACTICE EXERCISE 7-15

Code the following procedures.

1. Surgery of aneurysm, cervical approach, by application of occluding clamp to cervical carotid artery

Code(s) _____

2. Surgery of intracranial arteriovenous malformation; dural, complex

Code(s) _____

3. Anastomosis, arterial, extracranial–intracranial

Code(s) _____

4. Surgery of intracranial arteriovenous malformation supratentorial; simple

Code(s) _____

5. Surgery of simple intracranial aneurysm, intracranial approach; carotid circulation

Code(s) _____

Stereotaxis

Stereotaxis is a procedure in which precise measurements are used in order to perform specific procedures. Stereotaxis provides the surgeon the precise location in three-dimensional space when identifying and excising tissue. If radiosurgery is performed, you must report its codes in addition to the primary code. These codes include the delivery plan and treatment.

PRACTICE EXERCISE 7-16

Code the following procedures.

1. Stereotactic biopsy, including burr hole for intracranial lesion

   Code(s) _____

2. Creation of lesion by stereotactic method, percutaneous, by neurolytic agent; gasserian ganglion

   Code(s) _____

3. Creation of lesion by stereotactic method, including burr hole and localizing and recording techniques, single stage; globus pallidus

   Code(s) _____

4. Stereotactic radiosurgery, one session

   Code(s) _____

5. Stereotactic implantation of depth electrodes into the cerebrum for long-term seizure monitoring

   Code(s) _____

Neurostimulators (Intracranial)

Codes within this section include the neurostimulators, repair, and neuroendoscopy. Neuroendoscopy includes simple and complex procedures. You must also include the electronic analysis and programming of the neurostimulators' pulse generators from the Medicine section.

PRACTICE EXERCISE 7-17

Code the following procedures.

1. Replacement of bone flap of skull

   Code(s) _____

2. Elevation of depressed skull fracture; simple, extradural

   Code(s) _____

3. Twist drill for implantation of neurostimulator electrodes, cortical

   Code(s) _____

4. Cranioplasty with autograft, 5 cm

   Code(s) _____

5. Repair of encephalocele, skull vault, including cranioplasty

   Code(s) _____

Cerebrospinal Fluid (CSF) Shunt

Codes within this section are for the placement, removal, and creation of the shunt. These procedures are performed to relieve pressure on the brain by removing fluid. Procedures that require intracranial neuroendoscopic ventricular catheters should be reported in addition to the primary code. To report irrigation or aspiration of the shunt reservoir, use code 61070 for the percutaneous procedure. To report the programmable CSF or the reprogramming, use code 62252.

PRACTICE EXERCISE 7-18

Code the following procedures.

1. Replacement of irrigation, subarachnoid/subdural catheter

   Code(s) _____

2. Removal of programmable cerebrospinal fluid shunt

   Code(s) _____

3. Ventriculocisternostomy, third ventricle

   Code(s) _____

4. Ventriculocisternostomy

   Code(s) _____

5. Creation of shunt; ventriculoatrial

   Code(s) _____

Spine and Spinal Cord

Codes within this section include injection, drainage and aspiration, excision, laminectomy, repairs, and shunting procedures. In coding for these services, be aware that fluoroscopic guidance, radiologic supervision and interpretation, and contrast material may be needed to perform these procedures. Two primary surgeons may work together to perform them; in these cases, you must append modifier 62 to the procedure code. The codes in this section are not only based on the condition, but on the approach, so read the medical record carefully to determine the exact approach performed.

PRACTICE EXERCISE 7-19

Code the following procedures.

1. Laminectomy with rhizotomy; two segments

    Code(s) _____

2. Repair of meningocele, 3 cm

    Code(s) _____

3. Percutaneous aspiration, spinal cord cyst

    Code(s) _____

4. Injection procedure, arterial, for occlusion of arteriovenous malformation, spinal

    Code(s) _____

5. Laminectomy for biopsy and excision of intraspinal neoplasm; extradural, sacral

    Code(s) _____

Extracranial Nerves, Peripheral Nerves, and Autonomic Nervous System

This section includes introduction, stimulators, destruction, transection, excision, and repair. More than one surgeon may perform the procedures, and codes may include both simple and complex procedures. Some procedures may need to be reported with instrumentation and grafting procedures. When bilateral procedures are performed, you must append modifier 50 to the primary code.

PRACTICE EXERCISE 7-20

Code the following procedures.

1. Suture of posterior tibial nerve

    Code(s) _____

2. Transection of avulsion of infraorbital nerve

    Code(s) _____

3. Chemodenervation of eccrine glands; both axillae

Code(s) _____

4. Injection, anesthetic agent; carotid sinus

Code(s) _____

5. Neuroplasty; ulnar nerve at wrist

Code(s) _____

EYE AND OCULAR ADNEXA

You should report codes within this section first by anatomic site, then by procedure. Procedures include incision, excision, removal, repair, and destruction. When coding for implants, remember that the ocular implant is inside the muscular cone, whereas the orbital implant is outside the muscular cone. When reporting cataract procedures, include pharmacologic agents with the removal procedure (see Figure 7-7). Although most people think cataract removal is performed in one session, that may not be the case. If an intraocular lens prosthesis is inserted in a separate session, then report it separately. For procedures that are performed on the eyelid, you must append the correct modifier. These include modifiers E1–E4, which differentiate the right or left eyelid and the upper and lower eyelids. When bilateral procedures are performed, use the correct modifier.

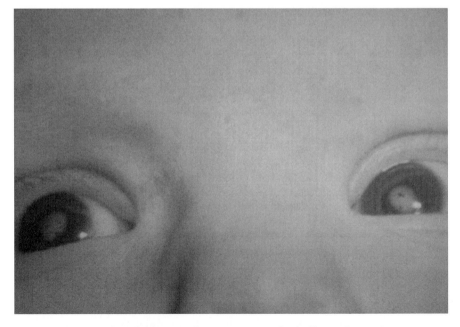

Figure 7-7 Cataracts in a child's eyes due to congenital rubella syndrome (Image courtesy of the Centers for Disease Control and Prevention)

Sutures may be used and may be adjustable: in these cases, the procedure code 67335 for the adjustable sutures is used only once, no matter how many sutures were placed.

PRACTICE EXERCISE 7-21

Code the following procedures.

1. Blepharotomy, drainage of the left lower eyelid

Code(s) _____

2. Orbital implant; insertion (implant outside muscle cone)

Code(s) _____

3. Repair of brow ptosis; coronal approach

Code(s) _____

4. Repair of entropion; thermocauterization

Code(s) _____

5. Evisceration of ocular contents; without implant

Code(s) _____

Conjunctiva

Procedures involving the conjunctiva include incision, excision, and repair. This section also includes the lacrimal system. When reporting a conjunctivoplasty procedure, you must include the wound repair, using codes 65273–65273.

PRACTICE EXERCISE 7-22

Code the following procedures.

1. Snip incision of lacrimal punctum

Code(s) _____

2. Probing of lacrimal canaliculi, with irrigation

Code(s) _____

3. Destruction of lesion, conjunctiva

Code(s) _____

4. Bilateral dilation of lacrimal punctum; by laser surgery

Code(s) _____

5. Harvesting conjunctival allograft, living donor

Code(s) _____

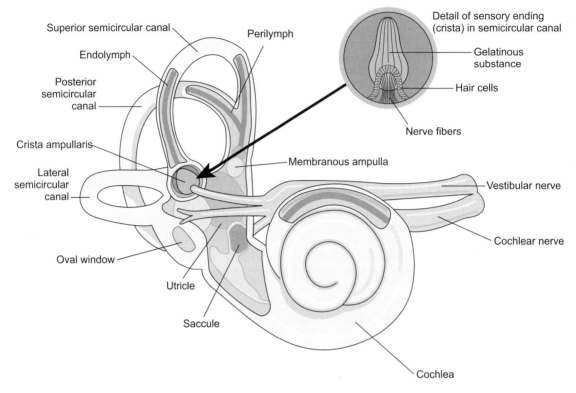

Figure 7-8 Structures of the ear

AUDITORY SYSTEM

The Auditory System section consists of the external, middle, and inner ear (see Figure 7-8). Sections are divided by anatomic site, then procedure, as in most cases throughout this book. Coding may include bilateral procedures, grafting, reconstruction, and the use of an operating microscope. Most of the procedures are considered unilateral, although when a physician performs the removal of cerumen in both ears, you should not append with modifier 50. It is also important to remember that if the closure of a wound on the external ear is performed, it must be reported from the Integumentary System section.

PRACTICE EXERCISE 7-23

Code the following procedures.

1. Cochlear device implantation, without mastoidectomy

   Code(s) _____

2. Stapes mobilization

   Code(s) _____

3. Eustachian tube inflation, transnasal; with catheterization

   Code(s) _____

4. Ear piercing

   Code(s) _____

5. Endolymphatic sac operation, with shunt

   Code(s) _____

CHAPTER REVIEW

I. True/False

Indicate whether the sentence or statement is true or false.

___ 1. In reporting a conjunctivoplasty procedure, you must include the wound repair.

___ 2. Procedures performed on the eyelid must include a modifier.

___ 3. An aneurysm is the same as a blood clot.

___ 4. The approach procedure is the anatomic site in which the procedure is performed.

___ 5. The carotid body refers to the adrenal gland.

II. Multiple Choice

Identify the letter of the code that best describes the procedure.

___ 6. Temporary closure of the eyelids by suturing, bilateral

   a. 67715   c. 67911

   b. 67875   d. 67875-50

___ 7. Hysterotomy, abdominal, with tubal ligation

   a. 59110   c. 59100, 58611

   b. 59121   d. 59121, 59300

___ 8. Exploration of the scrotum, with excision of a complicated lesion of the skin, measuring 3.0 cm

   a. 55110   c. 55100, 11423

   b. 11423   d. 55100, 11423-23

___ 9. Surgical treatment of a spontaneous abortion

   a. 59820   c. 59855

   b. 59812   d. 59830

___ **10.** Biopsy of the spinal cord by fine needle aspiration

a. 62269

c. 6228

b. 62269, 10021

d. 62269, 10022

III. Coding Exercises

Use an encoder or coding manuals to code the following procedures.

11. Removal of epithelial downgrowth of the anterior chamber of the eye, under anesthesia, on a normal healthy female, aged 72 years

Code(s) _____

12. Suture of three digital nerves of the foot, with anesthesia

Code(s) _____

13. Removal of an entire lumbosubarachnoid shunt system

Code(s) _____

14. Reexploration of the parathyroid gland

Code(s) _____

15. Partial vulvectomy, using local intravenous anesthesia

Code(s) _____

16. Craniotomy for evacuation of hematoma; subdural, followed by a burr hole

Code(s) _____

17. Enucleation of the eye without implant, with conjunctivoplasty

Code(s) _____

18. Right ear tympanic neurectomy

Code(s) _____

19. Bilateral size reduction of the ears

Code(s) _____

20. Myomectomy, for the removal of four fibroid tumors of the uterus; abdominal, with anesthesia

Code(s) _____

IV. Coding Cases

Use an encoder or coding manuals to code the following.

21. Jennifer was referred to Dr. Adams for a low back pain. Upon her first visit, she informed Dr. Adams that she was experiencing a burning sensation in her leg, with low back pain that traveled to the back of her thigh and leg. While examining Jennifer, Dr. Adams also discovered a decrease in the flexibility of the knee. After Dr. Adams and Jennifer discussed her options to treat her sciatic nerve, Jennifer decided upon a less invasive procedure. Dr. Adams scheduled Jennifer for single nerve block of the sciatic nerve.

Code(s) _____

22. Manuel presented to the emergency department as a result of an accident at work: while working, he received a retinal detachment of the left eye. After examination, Dr. Caruthers repaired the detached retina by pneumatic retinopexy under local anesthetic.

Code(s) _____

23. Diane suffered from endometriomas two years ago. Today she presented to the outpatient surgery for a laparoscopic biopsy of the ovaries. During the procedure, Dr. Brinkman discovered adhesions on Janet's ovaries. Dr. Brinkman performed a surgical laparoscopy with ovariolysis.

Code(s) _____

24. Theresa had an appointment with Dr. Zimmerman today for a removal of wax from her ears. While performing the procedure, Dr. Zimmerman discovered a small lesion in the external auditory canal of the left ear, took a biopsy of the lesion, and removed it.

Code(s) _____

Chapter 8
Radiology

LEARNING OBJECTIVES

After completing this chapter, the learner should be able to:

- Identify radiology positions
- Comprehend the use of modifiers
- Identify different types of imaging
- Comprehend the introduction of contrast material
- Identify the different types of guidance
- Comprehend the difference between diagnostic and therapeutic radiology
- Identify the different techniques used in radiology

RADIOLOGY

Radiology is a specific division within the medical field that uses various types of imaging techniques (see Figure 8–1). The **radiologist** is a licensed physician who specializes in radiology. **Diagnostic radiology** is the use of any imaging device to obtain a diagnosis. It includes but is not limited to the use of ultrasound, CT scan, and MRI, to name a few. The views that are taken during a CT scan or MRI are the sagittal, transverse, or coronal planes. Diagnostic radiology may be used with or without **guidance,** which is the use of any device that will assist the physician during a specific radiologic

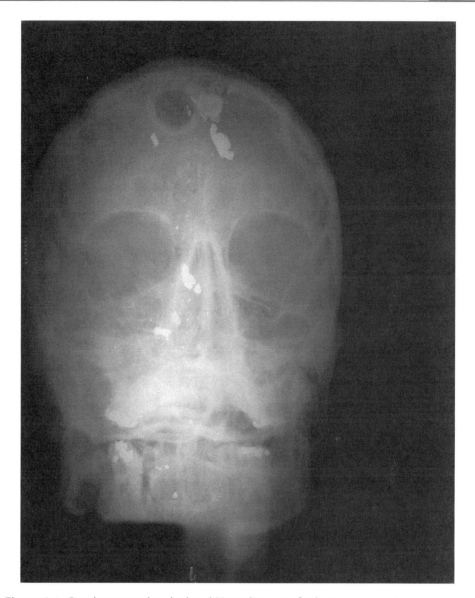

Figure 8-1 Gunshot wound to the head (Compliments of John Lampignano)

procedure. In some cases, more than one body system must be examined; for instance, patients who have multiple injuries may require a series of radiologic examinations. In these instances, you should add modifier 59 to the code for the separate area of injury. You should also add it if a completely separate body system or organ is viewed, incised, excised, or is considered a component of the total procedure being performed. In order to assist correct coding, the Radiological Society of North America (RSNA) has defined these body systems and their parts:

- Abdomen—digestive, intestines, kidneys, liver, stomach, urinary

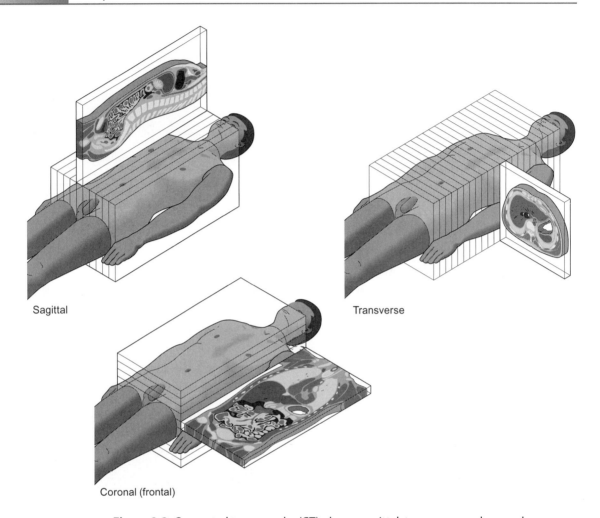

Sagittal

Transverse

Coronal (frontal)

Figure 8-2 Computed tomography (CT) planes: sagittal, transverse, and coronal

- Central nervous system—brain, spine
- Face and neck—sinuses, carotid arteries
- Heart and vascular system—heart, blood vessels
- Musculoskeletal system—bone, muscles, joints, back, spine, neck

Other additive modifiers include:

- **Technical component** (TC)—used only when the radiologist performed a procedure but did not read the end results
- **Professional component** (26)—used if the radiologist performed or supervised the procedure and completed the interpretation, followed by a written report
- **Global**—the technical component and professional component together

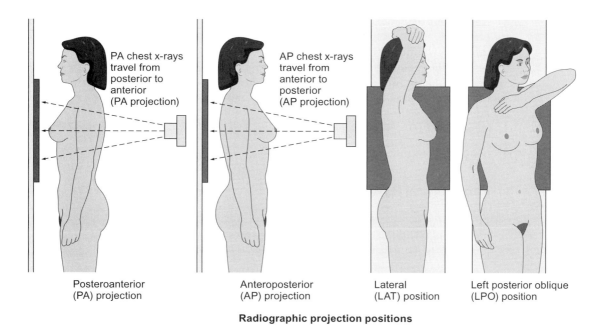

Radiographic projection positions

Figure 8-3 Radiographic projection position for x-ray

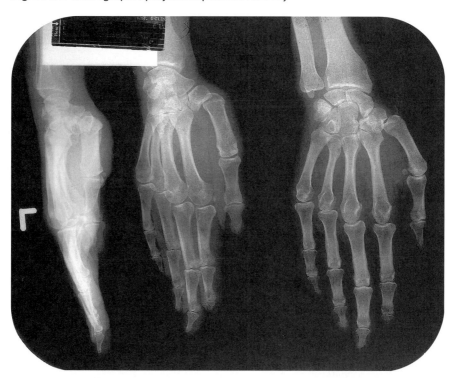

Figure 8-4 X-ray of the hand: three views

New coders tend to become confused while trying to remember when to use the modifiers. So, let's take an example. A technical component modifier should be used when a radiology technician uses equipment that belongs to the hospital and does not read the results. The professional component modifier should be used when the radiologist supervises the technician and interprets the x-ray with a written report. The global modifier should be used when the radiologist actually takes the x-ray, interprets the x-ray, and writes a written report.

Radiological Positions

In order for the radiologist to obtain an organ or structure image, the patient must be placed in a certain position (see Figure 8–2). This allows the electromagnetic waves to penetrate the patient at the exact location for a proper viewing position. This may be a Fowler's position, a prone position, or an oblique position. The most common positions used for a chest x-ray are the posteroanterior (PA) projection, anteroposterior (AP) projection, lateral (LAT) projection, and the left posterior oblique (LPO) or right posterior oblique (RPO) position (see Figure 8–3). When taking an x-ray of the hand, the radiologist may require a single x-ray or multiple views (see Figure 8–4).

PRACTICE EXERCISE 8-1

Using an encoder, code the following x-ray procedures.

1. X-ray examination of the mastoids; one view

   Code(s) _____

2. X-ray examination of the lumbosacral spine; five views

   Code(s) _____

3. Bilateral x-ray of the ribs, including posteroanterior chest; four views

   Code(s) _____

4. Complete x-ray examination of the ankle

   Code(s) _____

5. X-ray examination of the shoulder; one view

   Code(s) _____

6. X-ray examination of the elbow; two views

   Code(s) _____

7. X-ray examination of the cervical esophagus

   Code(s) _____

8. X-ray examination of the lower extremity of an infant; two views

   Code(s) _____

Contrast

Contrast is any substance that is administered orally or rectally in order to view the body's internal organs or their structures. Radiological procedures may be viewed without contrast, followed by the same procedure using contrast. Some codes are designated "with contrast"; this is considered part of the procedure and is not coded separately. This includes contrast being administered intravascularly, intrathecally, or intra-articularly during a CT scan, CTA, MRI, or MRA procedure.

Diagnostic Ultrasound

Diagnostic ultrasound is a technique used to view the internal structures of the body by the application of sound waves. Ultrasound procedures require a written report, with the permanent recorded image being placed in the patient's medical record. There are also different techniques used to view an anatomical structure or region that are classified by the use of various dimensions.

- **A-mode** is a one-dimensional view of the body structure
- **M-mode** is a one-dimensional view that records movement (Doppler)
- **B-scan** is a two-dimensional view of a structure with two dimensional displays (non-invasive vascular studies)
- **Real-time scan** is a two-dimensional view that records movement of a structure (ultrasound guidance)

These techniques are not only used for specific views of a structure, but also for the quality of the view. A request for A-mode imaging lets the radiologist know the physician wants amplitude ("A" stands for amplitude). This mode is most frequently used to diagnose bone fractures, for example.

Technicians may use the aid of a fluoroscope. This is a device in which the image is interposed between the x-ray and a fluorescent computer screen. The image is called a **fluoroscopy.** Although it has been replaced by an image intensifier, you would still code it as a fluoroscopy. Ordering an M-mode indicates that the physician wants to see motion or movement of the body structure ("M" stands for motion). This type is often used to evaluate the movement of the heart. Ordering a B-scan indicates the physician wants to see the organs projected onto a television screen as black and gray images (B stands for brightness). This type is scan is frequently used when ordering an ultrasound of the abdominal area. Physicians who order a real-time scan are often surgeons who need ultrasonic guidance while performing specific procedures. Real-time scans are also used to evaluate the performance of an organ along with its size and shape. Learn to always read carefully to ensure that you code the proper method of ultrasound performed.

PRACTICE EXERCISE 8-2

Using an encoder, code the following procedures.

1. Ultrasound follow-up study

   Code(s) _____

2. Magnetic resonance imaging; brain, during open intracranial procedure to assess for residual tumor without contrast, followed by contrast material and further sequence

   Code(s) _____

3. Ultrasound; abdomen, B-scan complete

   Code(s) _____

4. Intravascular ultrasound on a non-coronary vessel with radiological supervision and interpretation; two vessels

   Code(s) _____

5. Computed tomography guidance for stereotactic localization.

   Code(s) _____

Obstetrical

Obstetrical ultrasound is used for various purposes: to determine the number of fetuses, evaluate the fetus, or evaluate the amniotic fluid. It is also used in non-obstetrical evaluation in both males and females. Only one code is used for the imaging of the male pelvic girdle: it includes evaluation and management of the urinary bladder, prostate, and seminal vesicles.

PRACTICE EXERCISE 8-3

Using an encoder, code the following procedures.

1. Fetal biophysical profile without non-stress testing

   Code(s) _____

2. Repeat study of a Doppler echocardiography, fetal, pulsed wave; complete

   Code(s) _____

3. First trimester ultrasound, pregnant uterus with real-time image, transabdominal approach

   Code(s) _____

4. Transvaginal ultrasound

   Code(s) _____

5. Ultrasound of the scrotum and contents

Code(s) _____

RADIATION ONCOLOGY

Therapeutic radiology is the application of radiation administered on a timely basis for the treatment of cancer. The Radiation Oncology section includes the clinical management and treatment, modality (type of treatment), and the radiation treatment delivery and management. For the initial patient encounter, the use of an E/M is required. For example, the plan of treatment might include the initial consultation, clinical treatment and management, and follow-up care of the patient for three months after treatment has been rendered. Before any treatment begins, the physician must assess the patient to determine the route and dosage of administration, if any special services must be rendered, and how many ports and devices are to be used in the procedure. The oncologist will determine the size and location of the tumor and provide interpretation of any special testing. As in the E/M section, there are three levels of clinical treatment plans.

- Simple—requires a single treatment area of interest that is encompassed in a single port or in simple parallel opposed ports with simple or no blocking
- Intermediate—requires three or more converging ports, two separate treatment areas, multiple blocks, or special time–dose constraints
- Complex—requires highly complex blocking, custom shielding blocks, tangential blocks, special wedges or compensators, three or more separate treatment areas, rotational or special beams considerations, combination of therapeutic modalities

A radiation oncologist will also develop a treatment plan by using a simulator. This helps the oncologist to develop the best treatment option to be administered to the patient. There are four levels of simulator service:

- Simple—simulation AV, single treatment area, with either a single port or parallel opposed ports, simple or no blocking
- Intermediate—simulation of three or more converging ports, two separate treatment areas, multiple blocks
- Complex—simulation of tangential portals, three or more treatment areas, rotation or arc therapy, complex blocking, custom shielding blocks, brachytherapy source verification, hyperthermia probe verification, any use of contrast materials
- Three-dimensional—computer-generated reconstructions of tumor volume and surrounding critical normal tissue structures from direct CT scans and or MRI data in preparation for non-coplanar or coplanar therapy. This type of simulation utilizes documented three-dimensional beam's-eye view volume dose displays of multiple or moving beams. Documentation with three-dimensional volume reconstruction and dose distribution is required. Simulations must be billed on the initial simulation and each time a new plan of treatment is implemented.

Radiation Physics, Dosimetry, Treatment Devices, and Special Services

Codes within this section deal with the modality of radiation and the amount of dosage the patient is to receive. **Dosimetry** is the calculation section of radiology. This section also deals with special services such as treatment devices, design and construction (code 77332), and continuing medical physics consultation (77226).

PRACTICE EXERCISE 8-4

Code the following procedures.

1. Simple block treatment device, design and construction

   Code(s) _____

2. Complex therapeutic radiology, simulation-aided field setting

   Code(s) _____

3. Special teletherapy port plan, total body

   Code(s) _____

4. Special medical radiation physics consultation

   Code(s) _____

5. Ultrasonic guidance for placement of radiation therapy

   Code(s) _____

Radiation Treatment Delivery

Radiation delivery deals with the actual administration of the various energy levels (MeV) of radiation. The technical component (TC) modifier may be added to the primary code to indicate the radiologist has only administered, not interpreted, the radiation. In order to code correctly, you must code the amount of energy level, the number of ports (site of entry into the body), and how many blocks (an obstruction used to stop the flow of radiation) were used.

Radiation Treatment Management

Radiation management includes examination of the patient (E/M), assessment, coordination of care, and review of imaging. It also includes the review of the port films, the patient treatment set-up, review of dosimetry, the dose delivery, and treatment parameters. Management codes are reported in units of five fractions (treatment sessions), regardless of the actual time during which the services were furnished. The fractions must be of the same character, usually furnished on different days. The services do not need to be on consecutive days. The patient may have one treatment per day for two days and then resume treatment on the fourth or fifth day. The patient may have two fractions on the same day that are coded as two separate sections, as long as there is sufficient time between each session. Remember, radiation may not be the same dosage for every treatment. If there are three or four fractions beyond a multiple of five fractions at the end of a treatment course, then you should use code 77427 to report the extra fractions. If only one or two fractions are used beyond a multiple of five at the end of the treatment course, then do not report them separately. (In order to code this portion of radiation correctly, you need to place modifier 26 to signify the professional component of the service.)

PRACTICE EXERCISE 8-5

Code the following procedures.

1. Radiation treatment management, five treatments

   Code(s) _____

2. Radiation treatment delivery, superficial ortho voltage

   Code(s) _____

3. Unlisted procedure of medical radiation physics, dosimetry, treatment devices, and special services

   Code(s) _____

4. Therapeutic radiology port films

   Code(s) _____

5. Complex inverted Y, teletherapy, isodose plan by computer

   Code(s) _____

Proton Beam Treatment Delivery

The proton beam is a type of delivery for radiation. It is also coded by the type complexity, as follows.

- Simple—delivered to a single treatment area, with a custom block: with compensation (77522) or without compensation (77520)
- Intermediate—delivered to one or more areas using two or more ports, with custom blocks and compensators
- Complex—delivered to one or more areas using two or more ports, with matching fields and/or multiple isomers, and with custom block and compensators

Hyperthermia

Hyperthermia is a type of treatment that is used in conjunction with radiation. It may be introduced in various ways and from a variety of different methods. Hyperthermia can be given by the application of probes, microwave, ultrasound, or low energy radiation. It may also be external, interstitial, or intracavitary. Once hyperthermia has been given, the radiologist must include the follow-up care for the patient for three months, although the initial consultation may be billed. The physics planning, temperature sensors, and heat generating sources are included in the treatment and may not be billed separately.

Clinical Brachytherapy

Brachytherapy is the introduction of radioactive material (gold, radium, cesium) into or around the site of treatment. It is performed only by the radiologist and includes the admission into the hospital. The application may be interstitial (temporary) or intracavity (permanent) placement. The ribbon (so named because it is long and thin like a ribbon) may be simple, intermediate or complex; it is a kind of temporary interstitial placement.

- Simple—one to four applications
- Intermediate—five to ten applications
- Complex—greater than ten applications

In order to code correctly, remember to code for the supervision and handling of the material by using code 77790. You may also code for the insertion of the materials by using code 58346 (Heyman capsule) or 57155 (Tandems). A **tandem** is a stainless steel tube that is inserted into the uterus during brachytherapy to restrict the radioactive material from exiting the body.

PRACTICE EXERCISE 8-6

Code the following procedures.

1. Complex interstitial radiation source application

   Code(s) _____

2. Proton treatment delivery; intermediate

   Code(s) _____

3. Complex intracavitary radiation source application with deep hyperthermia, externally generated.

   Code(s) _____

4. Supervision, handling, loading of radiation source

   Code(s) _____

5. Hyperthermia generated by five interstitial applicators, under conscious sedation

   Code(s) _____

NUCLEAR MEDICINE

Nuclear medicine deals with the placement of atoms that disintegrate by emitting electromagnetic rays known as gamma rays. They are used to assess and diagnose certain body organs. The codes for this section are grouped into systems, such as the Endocrine System section (78000–78099), and include diagnostic testing of the thyroid (thyroid uptake, thyroid imaging, and adrenal imaging). The Lymphatic System section includes the Hematopoietic and Reticuloendothelial sections and range and codes (78102–78199). Diagnostic testing includes bone marrow imaging, red cell volumes, and platelet survival studies. The Gastrointestinal System section (78201–78299) deals with the imaging of the liver, esophageal, gastrointestinal, and vitamin B-12 absorption. The Musculoskeletal System section (78300–78399) deals solely with the imaging of the bones and joints. It should not be confused with the imaging of the bone marrow. Codes within the Cardiovascular System section (78414–78499) deal with imaging of the heart and veins to diagnose blood pooling and clots, assess cardiac function, and perform shunt detection. The imaging may be acquired while the patient is at rest or during exercise. In the latter case, you need to code using the Stress Testing codes (93015–93018) in addition to the imaging code studies. The Respiratory System section (78580–78599) deals only with the imaging of pulmonary ventilation and perfusion. The Genitourinary System section (78700–78799) deals with the imaging of the kidneys. It also includes the imaging and vascular studies of the testicles. The Other Procedures section (78800–78999) deals primarily with identification and imaging of tumors. This is done by a PET or SPECT scan.

PRACTICE EXERCISE 8-7

Code the following procedures.

1. Gastroesophageal reflux study

   Code(s) _____

2. Thyroid imaging with vascular flow

   Code(s) _____

3. SPECT imaging of the brain, complete study

   Code(s) _____

4. Kidney function study, non-imaging radioisotopic study

   Code(s) _____

5. Cerebrospinal fluid leakage detection and localization

   Code(s) _____

Therapeutic Nuclear Medicine

The Therapeutic Nuclear Medicine section (79005–79999) deals only with the administration of radiopharmaceuticals. The route of administration includes oral, intravenous, intra-articular, intra-cavitary, and interstitial. Any route of administration other than oral and intravenous must include the Procedure Injection code of 90783.

PRACTICE EXERCISE 8-8

Code the following procedures.

1. Intravenous administration of a radiopharmaceutical; therapy

   Code(s) _____

2. Kidney imaging (SPECT), with oral administration of a radiopharmaceutical

   Code(s) _____

3. Whole body tumor imaging (PET), with administration of intravenous radiopharmaceutical

   Code(s) _____

4. Bone marrow imaging; limited, with administration of oral radiopharmaceutical

   Code(s) _____

CHAPTER REVIEW

I. True/ False

Indicate whether the sentence or statement is true or false.

___ 1. A ribbon is a temporary interstitial placement.

___ 2. B-scan is one dimensional with a two-dimensional display.

___ 3. Oral and rectal administration of contrast qualifies as a study "with contrast."

___ 4. Diagnostic ultrasound requires a written report.

___ 5. Contrast can only be administered orally.

___ 6. "Guidance" is the use of any device to assist the physician during a procedure.

___ 7. A global modifier is used when the radiologist reads the x-ray.

II. Multiple Choice

Identify the letter of the code that best describes the procedure.

___ 8. Transcatheter biopsy, radiological supervision and interpretation

   a. 75961   c. 75960

   b. 79570   d. 75978

___ **9.** Ultrasound guidance

   a. 76400   c. 76529

   b. 76775   d. 76998

___ **10.** Bone age studies

   a. 77261   c. 77072

   b. 77077   d. 72220

___ **11.** Bilateral mammography

   a. 77002   c. 77056

   b. 77013   d. 73630

___ **12.** Sialography, radiological supervision and interpretation

   a. 78011   c. 70390

   b. 76827   d. 74210

III. Coding Exercises

Use an encoder or coding manuals to code the following.

13. X-ray of the ribs; bilateral; three views

   Code(s) _____

14. Swallowing function, with videoradiography

   Code(s) _____

15. Consultation on an x-ray exam made elsewhere, with written report

   Code(s) _____

16. Cardiac shunt detection

   Code(s) _____

17. Adrenal imaging, cortex and medulla

   Code(s) _____

18. Percutaneous transhepatic portography with hemodynamic evaluation, radiological supervision and interpretation

   Code(s) _____

19. X-ray of the colon; barium enema with KUB

   Code(s) _____

20. Complete x-ray of the teeth

   Code(s) _____

21. MRI of the spinal canal and contents, with contrast

   Code(s) _____

22. X-ray of the chest, two views, frontal and lateral; with oblique projection

Code(s) _____

IV. Coding Cases

Code the following cases.

23. Dr. McMillen, a radiologist, was called into the ER to assist Dr. Homes with the radiological guidance and placement of a catheter and percutaneous drainage of an abscess on Joe's chest cavity. After completing the procedure, Dr. McMillen prepared the interpretation of the procedure. (Code the procedure.)

Code(s) _____

24. Celeste presented to San Salvador Medical Center for a loss of hearing after being struck with a ball while playing soccer. Upon examination, Dr. Fields could see no apparent damage, and ordered a CT scan of the inner ear, without contrast.

Code(s) _____

25. Susie broke her shoulder four weeks ago in an auto accident. Today, she presents to her orthopedic surgeon with complaints of severe joint pain in her shoulder. Upon examination, her physician decides to schedule her for an MRI, without contrast, of her shoulder joint to determine the cause of her pain. (Code the MRI of the upper extremity.)

Code(s) _____

Chapter 9
Pathology and Laboratory

LEARNING OBJECTIVES

After completing this chapter, the learner should be able to:

- Identify drug panels versus individual drug tests
- Understand the use of clinical pathology codes
- Understand codes associated with microbiology
- Correctly use the pathology codes

ORGAN- OR DISEASE-ORIENTED PANELS

When new coders think about pathology and laboratory, they can only imagine the amount of codes that might be used alone or in conjunction with one another. But, to make it easier for the new or experienced coder, this section is broken down according to a specific test (single) or **panel** (multiple tests) when coding for laboratory. A good example of this is a basic metabolic panel (80048). Based on this code, you must include eight different laboratory tests. This panel must include blood tests for calcium (82310), carbon dioxide (82374), chloride (82435), creatinine (82565), glucose (82947), potassium (84132), sodium (84295), and urea nitrogen (84520) (also known as a BUN). In coding for a panel, you cannot break up the panel by not reporting one of the tests listed in that panel, but you may add a test to that panel as long as you report the additional test separately, in addition to the panel code. So, if a physician ordered a basic metabolic panel and a total bilirubin (which is not included in the metabolic panel), the codes would be 80048 and 82247. The code for the total bilirubin is considered a single test in addition to the metabolic panel.

PRACTICE EXERCISE 9-1

Code the following procedures.

1. Electrolyte panel

   Code(s) _____

2. Renal function panel and bilirubin

   Code(s) _____

3. Hepatic function panel and automated complete blood count

   Code(s) _____

4. Basic metabolic panel and thyroid stimulating hormone

   Code(s) _____

5. Obstetric panel

   Code(s) _____

Drug Testing and Therapeutic Assays

Codes for drug testing are grouped by the classification of the drug. They include, but are not limited to, opiates, barbiturates, and methadones. It is also possible to detect three or four drugs using a single sample, by a procedure known as **chromatography.** This procedure is a separation of at least two or more chemical compounds such as opiates and methadones. Drug testing also is **qualitative** or **quantitative.** Qualitative testing determines that a drug is or is not present, and quantitative determines that the drug is present and provides results based on numeric values.

Although this may seem overwhelming, it's actually very easy. In order to code correctly, let's start with a basic example. First, we run a simple drug test to establish if any drugs are present (qualitative), using code 80100. The results are positive for one classification of drugs. Second, we confirm (quantitative) there is one classification of drugs, using code 80102. When testing for multiple classifications, use code 80101 for each drug class and then confirm each drug by using code 80102.

Therapeutic drug assays are always quantitative because you know for certain the drug is present. These drugs, such as digoxin (used for cardiac patients), are essential to maintain quality of life for the patient. Therefore, a certain drug level (therapeutic) must be maintained in order for the drug to be effective. These **therapeutic drugs** are more commonly known as maintenance drugs.

PRACTICE EXERCISE 9-2

Code the following procedures.

1. Drug test for lithium

   Code(s) _____

2. Drug test for amphetamines

Code(s) _____

3. Drug test for alcohol and opiates

Code(s) _____

4. Drug test for tobramycin and gold

Code(s) _____

5. Drug test for lithium, with confirmation

Code(s) _____

Evocative/Suppression Testing

Codes within this section also refer to a panel test. These tests may be administered by a physician and should be reported separately by using the appropriate administration codes, E/M codes, and supplies codes. When coding for the E/M portion, you may use the prolonged service code if required, as long as the physician is not using a prolonged infusion code (90769–90761). Each one of these panels uses a particular analyte, such as renin or cortisol, followed by a number (Renin $\times$ 2 or Cortisol $\times$ 6). This number refers to how many times the analyte test must be performed for that particular panel. This is done to establish an initial baseline to compare with a subsequent measurement of their effects.

PRACTICE EXERCISE 9-3

Code the following procedures.

1. Renal vein renin stimulation panel

Code(s) _____

2. TRH stimulation panel

Code(s) _____

3. ACTH stimulation panel; for adrenal insufficiency

Code(s) _____

4. CRH stimulation panel

Code(s) _____

5. Dexamethasone suppression panel, 48 hr timed collection

Code(s) _____

URINALYSIS

A urinalysis may be performed and evaluated by several different methods. It may or may not be automated, with or without microscopy. A dipstick or tablet reagent may test

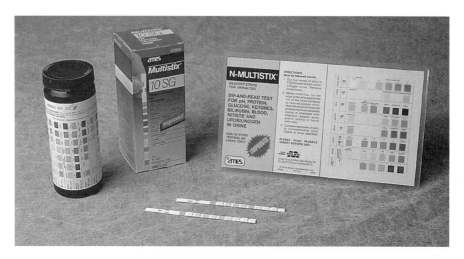

Figure 9-1 Reagent method urinalysis test

urinalysis (see Figure 9-1). In order to code correctly, you must know which method is being used.

PRACTICE EXERCISE 9-4

Code the following procedures.

1. Urine pregnancy test, by visual color comparison

   Code(s) _____

2. Urinalysis, by dipstick, automated, without microscopy

   Code(s) _____

3. Unlisted urinalysis procedure

   Code(s) _____

4. Semiquantitative urinalysis, except immunoassays

   Code(s) _____

5. Volume measurement for timed collection

   Code(s) _____

Chemistry

Within the Chemistry section, all codes are listed alphabetically. These codes represent specimens that can be obtained from any body fluid, and examination is considered quantitative unless specified within the code itself. Some of these codes refer to the measurement of multiple analytes, which may require up to several procedures. In these cases, each procedure is coded separately, especially if they are obtained at different times. When the exact test is repeated on the same day on two different specimens, you should report this code with modifier 91 to indicate this was a repeat laboratory procedure. When laboratory data is mathematically calculated, it is always considered a part of the procedure and not reported separately. It is always important to remember that these codes are quantitative; therefore, if a qualitative analysis is required, you must report codes from 80100 to 80103.

PRACTICE EXERCISE 9-5

Code the following procedures.

1. Calcium; obtained from urine, quantitative; time released

   Code(s) _____

2. Triglycerides, obtained at 10:00 a.m. and 4:00 p.m.

   Code(s) _____

3. Iron

   Code(s) _____

4. Red blood count

   Code(s) _____

5. Amino acids, three amino acids, quantitative specimen

   Code(s) _____

HEMATOLOGY AND COAGULATION

Hematology and Coagulation section tests deal solely with the blood. Blood specimens can be obtained in various ways, which determines the appropriate code to be used. Be sure to read the code before reporting to determine whether the method of testing is manual or automated. If you the coder are not sure of the code, it is always best to check with the laboratory prior to choosing a code. Blood that is being used for transfusion purposes is not coded from this section. You must refer to the Transfusion Medicine section in order to report these codes. It is also important to remember that certain codes within this section must include physician's interpretation and/or a written report.

PRACTICE EXERCISE 9-6

Code the following procedures.

1. Clotting factor VIII, related antigen

   Code(s) _____

2. Automated reticulocyte

   Code(s) _____

3. Sedimentation rate, erythrocyte; automated

   Code(s) _____

4. PTT; partial from whole blood

   Code(s) _____

5. Bleeding time

   Code(s) _____

Immunology

Codes within this section deal with the patient's immune system. They include codes for reporting STDs (sexually transmitted disease), hepatitis, and even the influenza virus. Some codes must deal with multiple-step procedures required to detect certain infectious disease and antibodies. These codes should be reported separately when multiple steps are being performed. In coding for viruses, you must code in the order of the virus first, then family, and last the genus type or species; code as precisely as possible. Single-step detection may use a regent strip, which is usually read as positive or negative.

PRACTICE EXERCISE 9-7

Code the following procedures.

1. Hepatitis C antibody with confirmatory test

   Code(s) _____

2. LHR (leukocyte histamine release) test

   Code(s) _____

3. Coxsackie test

   Code(s) _____

4. Immunoelectrophoresis from cerebrospinal fluid

   Code(s) _____

5. Antinuclear antibodies (ANA)

   Code(s) _____

Transfusion Medicine

Codes within this section deal with blood and its products, such as serum or blood cells. These codes are used for blood typing, antibody screening, and transfusion. Different methods and techniques may be used in specific procedures.

PRACTICE EXERCISE 9-8

Code the following procedures.

1. Compatibility test on three units, using incubation technique

   Code(s) _____

2. Leukocyte transfusion

   Code(s) _____

3. Antibody screen, RBC; serum technique

   Code(s) _____

4. Splitting of blood products; two units

   Code(s) _____

5. Unlisted transfusion medicine procedure

   Code(s) _____

Microbiology

Microbiology deals with microorganisms. These procedures detect and identify bacteria, fungus (mold, yeast), and parasites. Different techniques are used for detection and identification, such as cultures, probes, and special stains. These codes may be qualitative or quantitative. When coding in this section, it is important to remember that separate assays that are performed for different organisms are reported separately.

PRACTICE EXERCISE 9-9

Code the following procedures.

1. Pinworm examination using tape preparation

   Code(s) _____

2. Chlamydia culture

   Code(s) _____

3. Borrelia burgdorferi, direct probe technique

   Code(s) _____

4. Streptococcus, group A, quantification

   Code(s) _____

5. Infectious agent phenotype analysis by nucleic acid (RNA) with drug resistant tissue culture; 12 analysis

   Code(s) _____

ANATOMIC PATHOLOGY

Codes within this section deal solely with the physician's services. These codes are strictly used for autopsy and may or may not include microscopic examination. Remember to include modifier 90 on all outside laboratory services that are performed.

PRACTICE EXERCISE 9-10

Code the following procedures.

1. Necropsy; forensic examination

   Code(s) _____

2. Necropsy, gross examination only, without CNS

   Code(s) _____

3. Necropsy, gross and microscopic, with brain

   Code(s) _____

4. Limited autopsy; gross and microscopic exam of a single organ

   Code(s) _____

5. Unlisted necropsy procedure

   Code(s) _____

Cytopathology

Cytopathology is the study of cell disease. Most codes within this section deal with the collection and testing of vaginal and cervical specimens. They may or may not be based on a reporting system called the Bethesda System. This is a system used to report the cellular changes within a specimen. Specimens can be collected and preserved by various methods until examination. Some codes include a manual screening then a rescreening under physician supervision.

PRACTICE EXERCISE 9-11

Code the following procedures.

1. Forensic cytopathology

   Code(s) _____

2. Flow cytometry, interpretation; 10 markers

   Code(s) _____

3. Cytopathology slides, vaginal; manual, under physician supervision

Code(s) _____

4. Cytopathology slides, vaginal; manual, under physician supervision; Bethesda System

Code(s) _____

5. Cytopathology, cervical requiring physician interpretation

Code(s) _____

Cytogenetic Studies

Cytogenic studies involve the production of cells. Cytogenic studies are performed for inherited or oncologic disorders. They are performed on chromosomes (DNA) and tissue cultures. When coding from this section, be sure to use the appropriate modifiers to specify any type of probe used or condition being tested for if used with cytogenic procedures or molecular diagnostics.

PRACTICE EXERCISE 9-12

Code the following procedures.

1. Tissue culture for non-neoplastic disorders; skin tissue

Code(s) _____

2. Thawing and expansion of frozen cells; one aliquot

Code(s) _____

3. Unlisted cytogenetic study

Code(s) _____

4. Chromosome analysis; five cell count, one karyocyte with banding

Code(s) _____

5. Tissue culture for neoplastic disorder; solid tumor

Code(s) _____

Surgical Pathology

The level of examination divides codes within the Surgical Pathology section. These codes are based on the degree of probability of disease and are reported from Level I through Level VI. A Level I pathology code indicates a gross examination only and does not require the use of a microscope, whereas Level VI requires a more complex examination of the neoplastic tissue. When two tissue samples are taken from the patient in the same area and examined, each tissue sample should be coded separately. One tissue sample may be examined in two different areas; when this occurs, the code should only be reported once. Codes within this section also include consultation, specialized stains, and instruments used.

PRACTICE EXERCISE 9-13

Code the following procedures.

1. Pathology consultation during surgery, first tissue block with the frozen section; single section

   Code(s) _____

2. Level V, surgical pathology, gross and microscopic examination

   Code(s) _____

3. Microdissection; mechanical

   Code(s) _____

4. Diagnostic electron microscopy

   Code(s) _____

5. Level VI, surgical pathology, gross and microscopic examination

   Code(s) _____

Reproductive Medicine Procedures

The Reproductive Medicine Procedures section codes deal with the evaluation, collection, fertilization, and storage of reproductive sperm and oocytes.

PRACTICE EXERCISE 9-14

Code the following procedures.

1. Cryopreservation; embryo

   Code(s) _____

2. Semen analysis; presence and motility of sperm, including Huhner test

   Code(s) _____

3. Culture of oocyte embryo, less than four days

   Code(s) _____

4. Sperm identification from testis tissue; fresh

   Code(s) _____

5. Insemination of oocytes

   Code(s) _____

CHAPTER REVIEW

I. True/False

Indicate whether the sentence or statement is true or false.

___ 1. You cannot break up a laboratory panel test.

___ **2.** The dipstick method only performs a urine test.

___ **3.** Codes within the evocative/suppression testing codes are panel codes and may not be reported separately.

___ **4.** Codes for transfusions deal only with plasma.

___ **5.** Anatomic pathology codes are used strictly for autopsies.

___ **6.** Cytogenic studies are performed on DNA and tissue cultures.

___ **7.** Cultures are a method used to detect and identify microorganisms.

___ **8.** When coding viruses, you must code the genus species first, then the family.

___ **9.** When laboratory data is mathematically calculated, it is always considered a part of the procedure.

___ **10.** Reproductive medicine procedure codes deal only with the storage of oocytes.

II. Multiple Choice

Identify the letter of the code that best describes the procedure.

___ **11.** Urine pregnancy test, by visual color

a. 81000   c. 81025

b. 81003   d. 81099

___ **12.** Total bilirubin

a. 82247   c. 84578

b. 82248   d. 86622

___ **13.** ACTH stimulation panel for adrenal insufficiency

a. 82533   c. 80400, 82533

b. 85233 ×2   d. 80400, 82533 × 2

___ **14.** Extended oocyte culture, four to seven days

a. 89250   c. 89272

b. 89254   d. 89258

___ **15.** Irradiation of blood products, two units

a. 86890 × 2   c. 86945 × 1

b. 86945 × 2   d. 86999

___ **16.** HIV-1 antigen

a. 86701   c. 87390

b. 86702   d. 86391

III. Coding Exercises

Use an encoder or coding manuals to code the following.

17. Lipid panel

Code(s) _____

18. LDL cholesterol

Code(s) _____

19. Flow cytometry, DNA analysis

Code(s) _____

20. Level V surgical pathology, gross and microscopic examination

Code(s) _____

21. Chemistry test for aluminum, copper, and quinine

Code(s) _____

22. Blood bank physician services for difficult cross match and evaluation of irregular antibody, with interpretation and written report.

Code(s) _____

23. Streptokinase antibody

Code(s) _____

24. Tissue culture for neoplastic disorders; solid tumor

Code(s) _____

IV. Coding Cases

Code the following cases.

25. Jimmy, aged 73, presents to his family physician for his yearly examination. He has no complaints but wants to get his regular blood tests. After performing a brief examination, the physician gives Jimmy a prescription for a general health panel to be performed by the laboratory. (Code the general health panel.)

Code(s) _____

26. Carol has been in surgery for the past two hours for the removal of a breast lesion. During the procedure, a frozen section has been sent to the laboratory for analysis of the tissue. Code the consultation on a frozen block of tissue specimen.

Code(s) _____

27. Timmy presents to his physician with a fever, sore throat, and general malaise. Upon examination, his physician discovers pustules on Timmy's tonsils. He decides to swab Timmy's throat and send the sample to the laboratory for Group A streptococcus identification.

Code(s) _____

Chapter 10
Medicine

KEY TERMS

cardiography	echocardiography	neurostimulators
dialysis	infusion	nystagmus
Doppler	modality	

LEARNING OBJECTIVES

After completing this chapter, the learner should be able to:

- Understand diagnostic and therapeutic drug administration
- Correctly code the administration of vaccines and toxoids
- Identify prophylactic and therapeutic injections and infusions
- Identify therapeutic diagnostic services
- Correctly code for chemotherapy administration
- Understand conscious sedation

IMMUNE GLOBULINS

Immunoglobulin is mostly known by the common name of immune globulin. It is a human-donated solution obtained from plasma, and it contains antibodies used for a specific purpose. It is given intramuscularly or intravenously to fight against various allergies and respiratory viruses for which patients have no or little antibodies of their own. Procedures that deal with any type of injection must be reported with an administration code. This rule applies to all immune globulins, vaccines, toxoids, or any type of therapeutic service. Injection administration codes are found later in this chapter. These codes are modifier 51 exempt.

PRACTICE EXERCISE 10-1

Code the following procedures.

1. Tetanus immune globulin (Tig), human, intramuscular

Code(s) _____

2. Immune globulin (Ig), human, intramuscular use

Code(s) _____

3. Rabies immune globulin, heat-treated (Rib-HT), human, for subcutaneous use

Code(s) _____

4. Diphtheria antitoxin, equine, intravenous

Code(s) _____

5. Botulism immune globulin, human, intravenous use

Code(s) _____

Immunization Administration for Vaccines and Toxoids

When coding for the administration of a vaccine or toxoids (see Figure 10–1), you must be careful in choosing the correct code. These codes are age related and the services depend on face-to-face encounters with the physician. For correct coding, a separately identifiable E/M service must be performed with the addition of some of these codes. Services that are not face-to-face with the physician should be reported by using codes 90741–90474. When a physician provides face-to-face services during the administra-

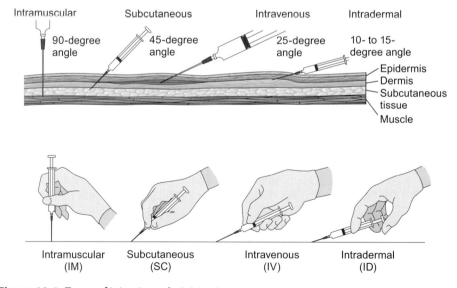

Figure 10-1 Types of injection administration

tion, you should report codes 90465–90468. Do not forget to report codes 90465–90474 in addition to the vaccine and toxoids codes 90476–90749.

PRACTICE EXERCISE 10-2

Code the following procedures.

1. Oral administration of immunization by a single toxoid

   Code(s) _____

2. Immunization administration of a first injection of toxoids with physician counseling, intradermal

   Code(s) _____

3. Subcutaneous injection administration of a single vaccine

   Code(s) _____

Vaccines and Toxoids

Codes within this section are for the reporting of the vaccine or toxoids only. In order to correctly report these vaccines and toxoids, you must report the administration of the product in addition to the vaccine or toxoids. Some of the codes are, once again, age related. When vaccines are grouped together and used as a single injection (90707), you must report it as the MMR; do not report each component of that code separately. Individual codes are assigned for measles (90705), mumps (90704), and rubella (90706). These codes are modifier 51 exempt.

PRACTICE EXERCISE 10-3

Code the following procedures.

1. Plague vaccine, intramuscular use

   Code(s) _____

2. Lyme disease vaccine, adult dosage, intramuscular use

   Code(s) _____

3. Typhoid vaccine, live, oral

   Code(s) _____

4. Unlisted vaccine or toxoids

   Code(s) _____

5. Diphtheria toxoids, intramuscular use

   Code(s) _____

Hydration, Therapeutic, Prophylactic, and Diagnostic Injections and Infusions

When coding for **infusion** (fluids introduced into the body), you should be aware that physicians are most likely in direct supervision of the procedures. These infusions are for the administration of drugs, and the fluids are not reported separately. They must have the supervision of a physician. Codes for infusions are based on time; therefore, if an antibiotic was given over a period of 2 hours and 10 minutes, you would report the codes for the 2 hours. Any infusion less than 15 minutes is not reported.

PRACTICE EXERCISE 10-4

Code the following procedures.

1. Therapeutic injection; subcutaneous

   Code(s) _____

2. Intravenous infusion, for therapy, 2 hr

   Code(s) _____

3. Unlisted infusion

   Code(s) _____

4. Intravenous infusion; initial, 45 min

   Code(s) _____

PSYCHIATRY

Most patients who require psychiatric care have been seen as an inpatient, and the codes must reflect an inpatient hospital code. If the patient has received additional care such as psychotherapy, then the additional procedure is coded separately. In such cases, the psychotherapy is coded along with the medical evaluation and management. Interactive psychotherapy is usually provided to children. When reporting psychotherapy, the code is based on the type of psychotherapy and on the time spent with the patient. This section of codes includes the psychiatric evaluation, therapeutic procedures, outpatient services, inpatient services, and psychotherapy services or procedures.

PRACTICE EXERCISE 10-5

Code the following procedures.

1. Psychoanalysis

   Code(s) _____

2. Individual psychotherapy, insight oriented, behavior modifying, outpatient, session 45 min, with evaluation of hospital records and projective tests

   Code(s) _____

3. Pharmacologic management and review of medication, with more than minimal medical psychotherapy

   Code(s) _____

4. Inpatient psychotherapy, insight oriented, with medical evaluation and management

   Code(s) _____

5. Family psychotherapy with the patient present

   Code(s) _____

DIALYSIS

Dialysis is a type of cleansing (see Figure 10-2). Patients who are diagnosed with end-stage renal disease (ESRD) require this procedure to remove toxins from their body. The procedure is performed once a month and is coded as such. The codes are based on the age of the patient and can be performed on either an outpatient or inpatient basis. For patients who have not received dialysis for an entire month (because of hospitalization, for example), you must report these services using codes 90922–90925. Hemodialysis is a procedure whereby the blood is routed outside the body and cleansed; these codes are based on the number of times the patient is evaluated during the procedure. Codes within the dialysis section include ESRD services, hemodialysis, and miscellaneous dialysis procedures.

PRACTICE EXERCISE 10-6

Code the following procedures.

1. Hemodialysis procedure, with single physician evaluation

   Code(s) _____

2. Dialysis training, patient, including helper where applicable, course completed

   Code(s) _____

3. Hemoperfusion

   Code(s) _____

4. ESRD-related services, full month, for patient 25 years old

   Code(s) _____

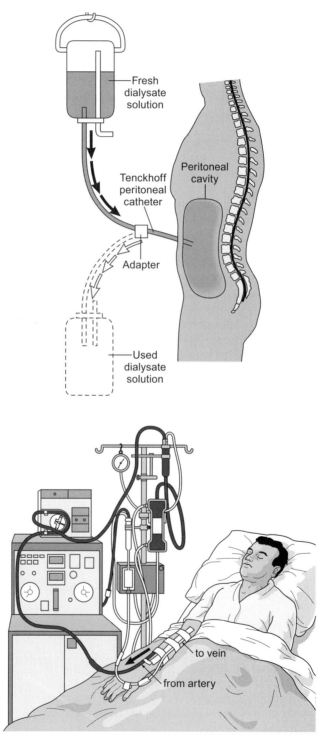

Figure 10-2 Dialysis

5. Hemodialysis access flow study to determine blood flow in grafts and arteriovenous fistulae by indicator method

Code(s) _____

GASTROENTEROLOGY

Codes within this section include nonsurgical procedures; therefore, any procedure that requires the use of a scope must be reported from the Surgery section. Laboratory procedures must be reported from the Laboratory section.

PRACTICE EXERCISE 10-7

Code the following procedures.

1. Bernstein test for esophagitis

    Code(s) _____

2. Pulsed irrigation of fecal impaction

    Code(s) _____

3. Esophageal balloon distension provocation study

    Code(s) _____

4. Gastric intubation and aspiration treatment

    Code(s) _____

5. Electrogastrography, diagnostic, transcutaneous; with provocative testing

    Code(s) _____

OPHTHALMOLOGY

Codes within this section include both General Ophthalmological Services and Special Ophthalmological Services. General Ophthalmologic Services are reported for new and established patients. These services are considered to be face-to-face encounters with the physician. Special Ophthalmological Services are considered diagnostic treatment and may be reported separately in addition to the E/M codes. Reading a Snellen's Chart (see Figure 10–3) is considered a diagnostic service.

PRACTICE EXERCISE 10-8

Code the following procedures.

1. Tonography with water provocation

    Code(s) _____

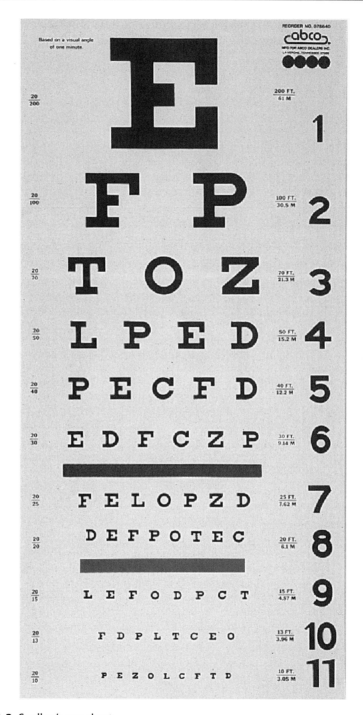

Figure 10-3 Snellen's eye chart

2. Comprehensive E/M, new patient

   Code(s) _____

3. Fitting for contact lens for treatment of disease, including supply
   of lens

   Code(s) _____

4. Determination of refractive state

   Code(s) _____

5. Provocative test for glaucoma, with interpretation and report without tonography

   Code(s) _____

Ophthalmoscopy and Specialized Services

A routine ophthalmoscopy is considered a part of the general services except when an extended service is provided; only then can the procedure be reported separately. The codes in this section are considered bilateral procedures, so modifier 50 must not be appended. However, if the procedure is performed on only one eye, then modifier 52 must be appended to show the reduced service.

PRACTICE EXERCISE 10-9

Code the following procedures.

   1. Fundus photography on left eye only, with interpretation and report

      Code(s) _____

   2. Color vision examination, extended, anomaloscope

      Code(s) _____

   3. Ophthalmodynamometry

      Code(s) _____

   4. Fluorescein angioscopy, with interpretation and report

      Code(s) _____

Contact Lens and Spectacles

The provision of contact lenses is not part of the general eye examination. The fitting of the lens always includes the training and general instructions to the patient. If the lenses need to be revised during the training period, this is considered part of the service. The supply of the contact lenses may or may not be reported separately. When coding for the fitting of glasses (spectacles), you should consider it a separate procedure when provided by a physician. Therefore, it may be reported separately. You may also report the supply of materials.

PRACTICE EXERCISE 10-10

Code the following procedures.

1. Replacement of contact lens

   Code(s) _____

2. Repair and refitting spectacles; except for aphakia

   Code(s) _____

3. Prescription of optical and physical characteristics of and fitting of contact lens, with medical supervision of adaptation; corneal lens, one eye, except for aphakia

   Code(s) _____

4. Fitting for spectacle prosthesis for aphakia; multifocal

   Code(s) _____

5. Modification of contact lens, with medical supervision of adaptation

   Code(s) _____

Special Otorhinolaryngologic Services

Services performed within this section are not usually included in an evaluation within an office setting. Procedures within this section are reported separately and include the diagnostic evaluation.

PRACTICE EXERCISE 10-11

Code the following procedures.

1. Otolaryngologic examination, under general anesthesia

   Code(s) _____

2. Treatment of swallowing dysfunction for feeding

   Code(s) _____

3. Nasopharyngoscopy with endoscope

   Code(s) _____

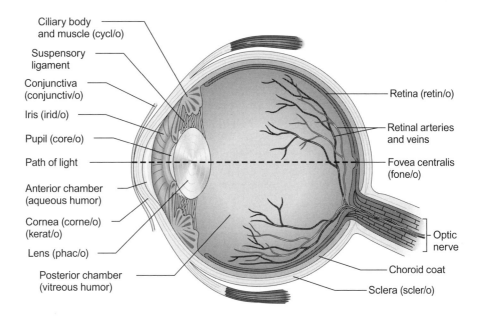

Ciliary body and muscle (cycl/o)

Suspensory ligament

Conjunctiva (conjunctiv/o)

Iris (irid/o)

Pupil (core/o)

Path of light

Anterior chamber (aqueous humor)

Cornea (corne/o) (kerat/o)

Lens (phac/o)

Posterior chamber (vitreous humor)

Retina (retin/o)

Retinal arteries and veins

Fovea centralis (fone/o)

Optic nerve

Choroid coat

Sclera (scler/o)

Lateral view of eyeball interior

Figure 10-4 Anatomy of the eye

Vestibular Function Tests

Codes within this section deal with the testing for **nystagmus.** Nystagmus is a disease of the eyes that causes the eye to move back and forth involuntarily. The movements may be horizontal, vertical, or rotational, and are primarily caused by lesions. (Refer to Figure 10–4 for the parts of the eye.)

PRACTICE EXERCISE 10-12

Code the following procedures.

1. Positional nystagmus test

   Code(s) _____

2. Spontaneous nystagmus test, including gaze and fixation nystagmus, with recording, with the use of vertical electrodes

   Code(s) _____

3. Computerized dynamic posturography

   Code(s) _____

AUDIOLOGIC FUNCTIONS TEST WITH MEDICAL DIAGNOSTIC EVALUATION

Audiologic tests deal with the testing of hearing and speech. Except for tuning fork and whispered voice tests, most of these tests use calibrated electronic equipment, which is considered part of the services. These codes are considered bilateral procedures (unless specified), so the use of modifier 50 is unnecessary. However, if procedures are performed unilaterally, you must append modifier 52 for the reduced services. These services may be performed on a group of individuals; this would require the use of code 92599 and listing of the individual tests.

PRACTICE EXERCISE 10-13

Code the following procedures.

1. Hearing aid check; monoaural

   Code(s) _____

2. Stenger test, pure tone

   Code(s) _____

3. Speech audiometry threshold; with speech recognition

   Code(s) _____

4. Electrocochleography

   Code(s) _____

5. Evaluation for use and fitting of voice prosthetic device to supplement oral speech

   Code(s) _____

Evaluative and Therapeutic Services

Codes within this section deal mostly with postoperative placement of devices and stimulators for hearing and speech. Some codes are based on the age of the patient, others on time spent with the family face-to-face. When endoscopic evaluations are performed without video recording or cine, it must be reported using the unlisted procedure code. If this is the case, you must submit a written report.

PRACTICE EXERCISE 10-14

Code the following procedures.

1. Evaluation of oral and pharyngeal swallowing function

   Code(s) _____

2. Evaluation of auditory rehabilitation status; 1 hr 30 min

   Code(s) _____

3. Diagnostic analysis of cochlear implant with programming, in patient aged three years

   Code(s) _____

4. Therapeutic services for the use of speech-generating device, including programming and modification

   Code(s) _____

5. Auditory rehabilitation; prelingual hearing loss

   Code(s) _____

CARDIOVASCULAR AND THERAPEUTIC SERVICES

Codes within the cardiovascular section include those for Therapeutic Services, Cardiography, Echocardiography, and Cardiac Catheterization, to name a few.

PRACTICE EXERCISE 10-15

Code the following procedures.

1. Cardio-assist method of circulatory assist; internal

   Code(s) _____

2. Percutaneous transluminal coronary balloon angioplasty; three vessels

   Code(s) _____

3. CPR

   Code(s) _____

4. Thrombolysis, coronary; by intracoronary infusion, including selective coronary angiography

   Code(s) _____

5. Percutaneous balloon valvuloplasty; pulmonary valve

   Code(s) _____

Cardiography

Cardiography is the recording of the electrical functions within the heart muscle (see Figure 10–5). This procedure can be performed in one setting or over a 24-hour period. When the recording is completed, it produces the data for analysis. This analysis must be interpreted by a physician and accompanied by a written report.

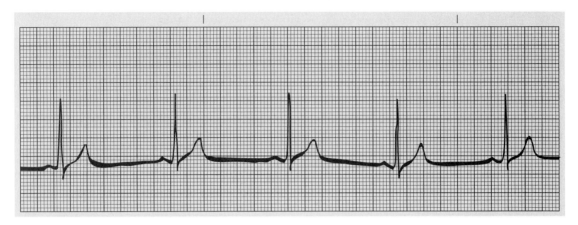

Bradycardia < 60 bpm

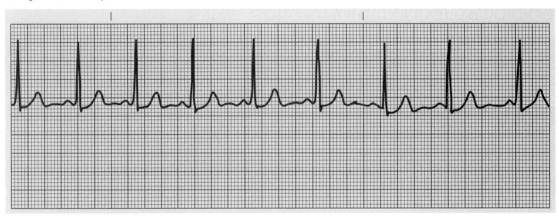

Tachycardia > 100 bpm

Figure 10-5 Rhythm strip electrocardiograph

PRACTICE EXERCISE 10-16

Code the following procedures.

1. Rhythm ECG, three leads; with interpretation and report

    Code(s) _____

2. Routine ECG, 12 leads, with interpretation and report

    Code(s) _____

3. Signal-averaged electrocardiography, without ECG interpretation, report only

    Code(s) _____

4. Cardiovascular stress test using maximal treadmill exercise, continuous ECG monitoring and pharmacological stress; with interpretation and report

    Code(s) _____

5. ECG monitoring for 24 hours by continuous original ECG waveform recording and storage, with visual superimposition scanning and physician review, interpretation, and report.

Code(s) _____

Echocardiography

Echocardiography produces an ultrasound image of the heart, including the cardiac valves, chambers, great vessels, and the pericardium. This procedure can produce what is called a **Doppler,** or a two-dimensional image. The procedure includes the written report and interpretation by the physician. If the interpretation is performed separately, modifier 26 must be appended to the code.

PRACTICE EXERCISE 10-17

Code the following procedures.

1. Transesophageal echocardiography for congenital cardiac anomalies; including probe placement, image acquisition, and interpretation and report

   Code(s) _____

2. Transthoracic echocardiography for congenital cardiac anomalies; complete study

   Code(s) _____

3. Echocardiography, transthoracic, real-time with image documentation (2-D), without M-mode recording, during rest and cardiovascular stress test using treadmill and pharmacologically induced stress, with interpretation.

   Code(s) _____

Cardiac Catheterization

Cardiac catheterization is considered a diagnostic procedure. The catheter is placed into a chamber of the heart and used for the assessment of abnormalities, treatment, and evaluation of the great vessels and heart muscle itself. This procedure measures the intracardiac pressure and also the motion of the cardiac walls. The procedure includes the introduction, positioning, repositioning, and obtaining of blood samples and cardiac output. All of the codes within this section are modifier 51 exempt.

PRACTICE EXERCISE 10-18

Code the following procedures.

1. Right heart catheterization, for congenital cardiac anomalies

   Code(s) _____

2. Right heart catheterization

   Code(s) _____

3. Left heart catheterization, retrograde, from the brachial artery, percutaneous

   Code(s) _____

4. Injection procedure during cardiac catheterization; for selective opacification of arterial conduits for bypass

   Code(s) _____

5. Imaging supervision, interpretation and report for injection procedure during cardiac catheterization; atrial angiography

   Code(s) _____

Intracardiac Electrophysiological Procedures and Studies

Physicians who perform electrophysiological studies usually perform them on patients with cardiac arrhythmias. The complete procedure may or may not be performed on the same day. This type of procedure requires mapping and ablation (ablation is the removal or destruction of tissue by electrocautery or radiofrequency). In most cases, the procedure is performed with two or more electrodes. These electrodes may be placed in one or more locations to map (record) the procedure. Mapping is considered a separate procedure, so be sure to report this portion of the study. It may also be performed by different techniques and moved from one point to another. The ablation portion of the procedure should be reported once only, even though several ablations may have been performed. This procedure may also be performed on the same day or at a later date. Either way, these procedures are reported separately, without the use of modifier 51.

PRACTICE EXERCISE 10-19

Code the following procedures.

1. Intraventricular mapping of tachycardia site with catheter manipulation to record from multiple sites to identify origin of tachycardia, with intracardiac catheter ablation of arrhythmogenic focus; for treatment of ventricular tachycardia

   Code(s) _____

2. Bundle of His recording

   Code(s) _____

3. Comprehensive electrophysiologic evaluation with right atrial pacing and recording, right ventricle pacing and recording, His bundle recording, including insertion and repositioning of multiple electrode catheters, with induction of arrhythmia and programmed stimulation and pacing after intravenous drug infusion

   Code(s) _____

4. Evaluation of cardiovascular function with tilt table evaluation, with continuous ECG monitoring and intermittent blood pressure monitoring, without pharmacological intervention

   Code(s) _____

5. Electrophysiologic follow-up study with pacing and recording to test effectiveness of therapy, including induction of arrhythmia

   Code(s) _____

Other Vascular Studies

Codes within this section are for electronic analysis of either a pacemaker or implantable loop recorder. But they also include the initial set-up, venous pressure, and temperature gradient studies. When reporting codes from this section, remember that it is vascular studies, so it includes not only the heart but also the head and peripheral studies. When cannulation is used, report these codes from the Cardiac System section.

PRACTICE EXERCISE 10-20

Code the following procedures.

1. Temperature gradient studies

   Code(s) _____

2. Bioimpedance, thoracic, electrical

   Code(s) _____

3. Therogram; cephalic

   Code(s) _____

4. Electronic analysis of single chamber pacemaker system, with reprogramming, with interpretation and report

   Code(s) _____

5. Determination of venous pressure

   Code(s) _____

Non-Invasive Vascular Diagnostic Studies

Codes within this section include cerebrovascular studies, studies of the extremity (arterial and venous), visceral and penile vascular and arteriovenous studies. They are performed by either a Doppler or duplex scan. Some of these codes are used for the evaluation and some for the actual diagnostic study. Physicians who perform these procedures must include a hard copy analysis, supervision and interpretation of the study, and patient care. If a hard copy of the study is not produced, then the procedure is considered a part of the evaluation and cannot be reported separately.

PRACTICE EXERCISE 10-21

Code the following procedures.

1. Duplex scan of upper extremity arteries; complete bilateral study

   Code(s) _____

2. Transcranial Doppler study of the intracranial arteries; emboli detection with intravenous microbubble injection

   Code(s) _____

3. Duplex scan of aorta, inferior vena cava, iliac vasculature; complete study

   Code(s) _____

4. Limited duplex scan of extracranial arteries

   Code(s) _____

5. Non-invasive physiologic studies of extracranial arteries; complete bilateral study

   Code(s) _____

PULMONARY

The pulmonary codes seem easier to deal with than those for the cardiac system. All the codes throughout this section include the laboratory procedures and the interpretation of the reports. Codes that require a nebulizer (J code) should be coded from the HCPCS section, which is included later in the book. If you need to code for ventilation, report the first day (94656) then each subsequent day (94657), in addition to the initial ventilation. Any additional procedures, such as biopsies, arterial catheterizations, and so forth must be reported separately from the surgery section. To report bronchodilator supply, use the supply code of 99070 in addition to the primary code.

PRACTICE EXERCISE 10-22

Code the following procedures.

1. Prolonged exercise test for bronchospasm, with pre- and post-spirometry

   Code(s) _____

2. Noninvasive pulse oximetry for oxygen saturation; single determination

   Code(s) _____

3. Determination of airway closing volume; single breath test

   Code(s) _____

4. Maximum breathing capacity; maximal voluntary ventilation

   Code(s) _____

5. Continuous positive airway pressure ventilation, initiation and management

   Code(s) _____

ALLERGY AND CLINICAL IMMUNOLOGY

Codes that are included in this section are for the testing for allergies. Tests are performed a number of ways, such as scratch, intradermal, and injection testing. Therefore, the type of test groups the codes.

Allergy Testing

Percutaneous tests for allergens can be accomplished by several methods. These include the scratch test, prick test, and puncture test. Other types of testing include photo test, intradermal test inhalation, and ingestion testing. When physicians test for more than one allergy, such as both ragweed and dust, you must code two procedures. Another example of this would be a scratch test with allergenic extracts for immediate type reaction (95004), which would be coded as 95004 × 2 to indicate the number of allergens being tested.

PRACTICE EXERCISE 10-23

Code the following procedures.

1. Ophthalmic mucous membrane test

   Code(s) _____

2. Application of six patch tests

   Code(s) _____

3. Intradermal test, sequential and incremental, with allergenic extracts for airborne allergens, immediate type reaction, three allergens

   Code(s) _____

4. Photo test, one

   Code(s) _____

5. Rinkel test

   Code(s) _____

Allergen Immunotherapy

Immunotherapy deals with the desensitization of the patient to a particular allergen. The procedures may be performed within an office setting or sent home with the patient. To distinguish between the two, be sure to read the codes carefully. It is also necessary to determine if the code is prescription and injection or only injection.

PRACTICE EXERCISE 10-24

Code the following procedures.

1. Unlisted allergy/clinical immunologic procedure

   Code(s) _____

2. Professional services for allergen immunotherapy, not including provision of allergenic extracts; three injections

   Code(s) _____

3. Professional services for the supervision, preparation, and provision of antigens for allergen immunotherapy; four single stinging insect venoms

   Code(s) _____

4. Professional services for allergen immunotherapy prescribing, physician office, including provision of allergenic extract; single injection

   Code(s) _____

5. Rapid desensitization procedure, three hours

   Code(s) _____

NEUROLOGY AND NEUROMUSCULAR PROCEDURES

Patients who need to see a neurologist would normally do so as a consultation. Therefore, the use of an E/M consultation code should be reported with the appropriate level of service. Procedures would include sleep studies, EEG, range of motion, and nerve conduction tests, to name a few. Codes within these sections may also need the correct modifiers. When the physician who performs the procedure does not own the equipment, remember to append modifier TC or, for interpretation only, append modifier 26.

Sleep Testing

Physicians who perform sleep studies may or may not be in attendance. These studies are based on certain parameters of sleep and must be measured for six or more hours. The physician must review, interpret, and give a written report. Parameters might include snoring, muscle activity, ventilation and respiratory effort, and body positions, to name a few. Physicians may conduct a polysomnogram, which is a type of sleep staging that includes an EEG, an EMG, and an ECG. If the procedure is not recorded and staged, it is not considered a polysomnogram.

PRACTICE EXERCISE 10-25

Code the following procedures.

1. Sleep study, simultaneous recording of ventilation, respiratory effect, ECG, and oxygen saturation, unattended by technologist

   Code(s) _____

2. Polysomnography; sleep staging with three additional parameters of sleep; attended by a physician

   Code(s) _____

Routine Electroencephalography (EEG)

Routine EEGs usually are conducted for approximately 20 to 40 minutes. They include photic stimulation and hyperventilation if needed. When these procedures are performed during surgery, they must be reported from the Special EEG Test section, covered later in this book. When reporting a digital analysis, use code 95957.

PRACTICE EXERCISE 10-26

Code the following procedures.

1. Insertion by physician of sphenoidal electrodes for EEG recording

   Code(s) _____

2. EEG lasting 90 min

   Code(s) _____

3. All night recording, including awake and drowsy EEG

   Code(s) _____

Electromyography and Nerve Conduction Tests

An electromyogram is the graphic record of muscle activity during rest and voluntary movements as a result of electrical stimulation. It provides the physician with information as to the severity of any abnormalities as well as helping to develop a treatment plan for the patient. These codes include the interpretation by the physician. When coding nerve conduction studies, it is important to report the correct nerves that are involved with each study. These nerves are each reported according to sensory, motor, and mixed (sensory and motor), then further divided into upper and lower extremity, cranial, and nerve roots. Each nerve within the study is considered one unit of service. These nerves consist of:

MOTOR NERVES

Upper Extremity, Cervical Plexus/Brachial Plexus

1. Axillary motor nerve to the deltoid
2. Long thoracic motor nerve to the serratus anterior
3. Median nerve
   a. Median motor nerve to the abductor pollicis brevis
   b. Median motor nerve, anterior interosseous branch, to the pollicis longus
   c. Median motor nerve, anterior interosseous branch, to the pronator quadratus
   d. Median motor nerve to the first lumbrical
   e. Median motor nerve to the second lumbrical
4. Musculocutaneous motor nerve to the biceps brachii
5. Radial nerve
   a. Radial motor nerve to the extensor carpi ulnaris
   b. Radial motor nerve to the extensor digitorum communis
   c. Radial motor nerve to the extensor indicis proprius
   d. Radial motor nerve to the brachioradialis
6. Supracapular nerve
   a. Supracapular motor nerve to the supraspinatus
   b. Supracapular motor nerve to the infraspinatus
7. Thoracodorsal motor nerve to the latissimus dorsi
8. Ulnar nerve
   a. Ulnar motor nerve to the abductor digiti minimi
   b. Ulnar motor nerve to the palmar interosseous
   c. Ulnar motor nerve to the first dorsal interosseous
   d. Ulnar motor nerve to the flexor carpi ulnaris
9. Other

Lower Extremity Motor Nerves

1. Femoral motor nerve to the quadriceps
   a. Femoral motor nerve to vastus medialis
   b. Femoral motor nerve to vastus lateralis
   c. Femoral motor nerve to vastus intermedialis
   d. Femoral motor nerve to rectus femoris
2. Ilioinguinal motor nerve

3. Peroneal (fibular) nerve
   a. Peroneal motor nerve to the extensor digitorum brevis
   b. Peroneal motor nerve to the peroneus brevis
   c. Peroneal motor nerve to the peroneus longus
   d. Peroneal motor nerve to the tibialis anterior
4. Plantar motor nerve
5. Sciatic nerve
6. Tibial nerve
   a. Tibial motor nerve, inferior calcaneal branch, to the abductor digiti minimi
   b. Tibial motor nerve, medial plantar branch, to the abductor hallucis
   c. Tibial motor nerve, lateral plantar branch, to the flexor digiti minimi brevis
7. Other

CRANIAL NERVES AND TRUNK

1. Cranial nerve VII (facial motor nerve)
   a. Facial nerve to the frontalis
   b. Facial nerve to the nasalis
   c. Facial nerve to the orbicularis oculi
   d. Facial nerve to the orbicularis oris
2. Cranial nerve XI (spinal accessory motor nerve)
3. Cranial nerve XII (hypoglossal motor nerve)
4. Intercostal motor nerve
5. Phrenic motor nerve to the diaphragm
6. Recurrent laryngeal nerve
7. Other

Nerve Roots

1. Cervical nerve root stimulation
   a. Cervical level 5 (C5)
   b. Cervical level 6 (C6)
   c. Cervical level 7 (C7)
   d. Cervical level 8 (C8)
2. Thoracic nerve root stimulation
   a. Thoracic level 1 (T1)
   b. Thoracic level 2 (T2)
   c. Thoracic level 3 (T3)
   d. Thoracic level 4 (T4)
   e. Thoracic level 5 (T5)
   f. Thoracic level 6 (T6)

   g. Thoracic level 7 (T7)

   h. Thoracic level 8 (T8)

   i. Thoracic level 9 (T9)

   j. Thoracic level 10 (T10)

   k. Thoracic level 11 (T11)

   l. Thoracic level 12 (T12)

3. Lumbar nerve root stimulation

   a. Lumbar level 1 (L1)

   b. Lumbar level 2 (L2)

   c. Lumbar level 3 (L3)

   d. Lumbar level 4 (L4)

   e. Lumbar level 5 (L5)

4. Sacral nerve root stimulation

   a. Sacral level 1 (S1)

   b. Sacral level 2 (S2)

   c. Sacral level 3 (S3)

   d. Sacral level 4 (S4)

SENSORY AND MIXED NERVES

Upper Extremity Sensory and Mixed Nerves

  1. Lateral antebrachial cutaneous sensory nerve

  2. Medial antebrachial cutaneous sensory nerve

  3. Medial brachial cutaneous sensory nerve

  4. Median nerve

   a. Median sensory nerve to the first digit

   b. Median sensory nerve to the second digit

   c. Median sensory nerve to the third digit

   d. Median sensory nerve to the fourth digit

   e. Median palmar cutaneous sensory nerve

   f. Median palmar mixed nerve

  5. Posterior antebrachial cutaneous sensory nerve

  6. Radial sensory nerve

   a. Radial sensory nerve to the base of the thumb

   b. Radial sensory nerve to digit 1

  7. Ulnar nerve

   a. Ulnar dorsal cutaneous sensory nerve

   b. Ulnar sensory nerve to the fourth digit

    c. Ulnar sensory nerve to the fifth digit

    d. Ulnar palmar mixed nerve

8. Intercostal sensory nerve

9. Other

Lower Extremity Sensory and Mixed Nerves

1. Lateral femoral cutaneous sensory nerve

2. Medial calcaneal sensory nerve

3. Medial femoral cutaneous sensory nerve

4. Peroneal nerve

    a. Deep peroneal sensory nerve

    b. Superficial peroneal sensory nerve, medial dorsal cutaneous branch

    c. Superficial peroneal sensory nerve, intermediate dorsal cutaneous branch

5. Posterior femoral cutaneous sensory nerve

6. Saphenous nerve

    a. Saphenous sensory nerve (distal technique)

    b. Saphenous sensory nerve (proximal technique)

7. Sural nerve

    a. Sural sensory nerve, lateral dorsal cutaneous branch

    b. Sural sensory nerve

8. Tibial sensory nerve (digital nerve to toe one)

9. Tibial sensory nerve (medial plantar nerve)

10. Tibial sensory nerve (lateral plantar nerve)

11. Other

Head and Trunk Sensory Nerves

1. Dorsal nerve of the penis

2. Greater auricular nerve

3. Ophthalmic branch of the trigeminal nerve

4. Pudendal sensory nerve

5. Suprascapular sensory nerves

6. Other

PRACTICE EXERCISE 10-27

Code the following procedures.

    1. Nerve conduction amplitude and latency/velocity study, each nerve; sensory

        Code(s) _____

2. Needle electromyography; four extremities, with related paraspinal areas

Code(s) _____

3. Needle electromyography using single fiber electrode, with quantitative measurement of jitter, blocking, and fiber density of the gastrocnemius muscle

Code(s) _____

4. Nerve conduction, amplitude, and latency motor, with F-wave study of sciatic nerve and femoral motor nerve to the quadriceps

Code(s) _____

Evoked Potentials and Special EEG Tests

The evoked potentials and reflex tests are performed by the stimulation of the nerves. The test is recorded and interpreted. To ensure proper coding, you must read the description carefully. Some codes are considered bilateral or unilateral, so they must be reported either with modifier 50 in addition to the unilateral code or with modifier 52 for a bilateral code. Special EEG tests within this section are performed on patients with a seizure disorder. These codes may or may not be used in conjunction with other procedures; if this is the case, the use of additional modifiers is warranted.

PRACTICE EXERCISE 10-28

Code the following procedures.

1. Digital analysis of EEG, for epileptic spike

Code(s) _____

2. Blink reflex by electrodiagnostic testing

Code(s) _____

3. EEG during nonintracranial surgery

Code(s) _____

4. Short-latency somatosensory evoked potential study, stimulation of all peripheral nerves, recording from the CNS in the lower legs

Code(s) _____

5. EMG recording and analysis for spontaneous brain magnetic activity

Code(s) _____

Neurostimulators and Motion Analysis

Neurostimulators for the purpose of motion analysis use a pulse generator to transmit electricity to the nerves of the muscles. They are considered simple or complex pulse, which is implanted into the spinal column or brain. A pulse generator can contain as many as eight or more electrodes. You should code the insertion and removal of the pulse generator from the Nervous System section in the Surgery section.

Motion analysis can be performed as a diagnostic or as a therapeutic procedure. These procedures must be performed in a dedicated laboratory where videotaping allows for the viewing of the front, back and both sides.

PRACTICE EXERCISE 10-29

Code the following procedures.

1. Electronic analysis of implanted neurostimulator pulse generator system; complex spinal cord, with intraoperative programming, 2 hr

   Code(s) _____

2. Dynamic fine wire electromyography, during walking, one muscle

   Code(s) _____

3. Unlisted neuromuscular diagnostic procedure

   Code(s) _____

4. Comprehensive computer-based motion analysis by videotaping and 3-D kinematics

   Code(s) _____

Central Nervous System Assessments and Tests

Testing of the central nervous system (CNS) mostly consists of psychological testing. The tests may be conducted face-to-face with the physician or conducted through a computerized system. They are conducted to assess speech and language, intellectual abilities, memory, and reasoning and judgment. Testing may involve a single test or a combination of tests and assessments. Physicians who perform a mini test should report codes from the E/M section.

PRACTICE EXERCISE 10-30

Code the following procedures.

1. Neuropsychological testing administered by a computer, with interpretation and report

   Code(s) _____

2. Developmental testing; limited, with interpretation and report

   Code(s) _____

3. Face-to-face psychological testing administered by a technician; 1 hr, with interpretation and report

Code(s) _____

CHEMOTHERAPY

Chemotherapy is used for the treatment of cancer. It can be administered by injection, intravenously, and arterially. Codes for chemotherapy are bundled, so include the anesthesia, IV start, catheter, port, preparation, and so forth. Chemotherapy may also be either "regional" or "isolation." Placement of the intra-arterial catheter is coded from the Cardiovascular System in the Surgery section. Report the procedure code for chemotherapy first by the method of administration, then by technique. As a coder, be sure to code for the administration of the drug or substance that is provided, in addition to the primary code.

PRACTICE EXERCISE 10-31

Code the following procedures.

1. Administration of chemotherapy into peritoneal cavity; including peritoneocentesis.

   Code(s) _____

2. Chemotherapy administration, infusion technique, 6 hr

   Code(s) _____

3. Chemotherapy administration, subcutaneous; non-hormonal anti-neoplastic

   Code(s) _____

Dermatological Procedures

Most dermatological procedures are performed on a consultative basis. Therefore, you may report E/M codes in addition to the procedures performed.

PRACTICE EXERCISE 10-32

Code the following procedures.

1. Laser treatment for inflammatory skin disease, 200 sq cm

   Code(s) _____

   2. Actinotherapy (ultraviolet light)

   Code(s) _____

   3. Photochemotherapy; tar and ultraviolet B

   Code(s) _____

Physical Medicine and Rehabilitation

Physical medicine includes evaluation and treatment through the application of therapeutic modalities. A **modality** is an application of a therapeutic agent (ultrasound) or regimen (exercise). The procedures include the application of ultrasound, mechanical traction, and electrical stimulation, among a few others. This section of codes includes therapeutic procedures, wound care, and orthotic and prosthetic management. Unless otherwise specified, these codes require one-on-one contact with the provider, and are coded in increments of 15 minutes. You should report an evaluation procedure in addition to the primary procedure; this is modifier 51 exempt.

PRACTICE EXERCISE 10-33

Code the following procedures.

   1. Prosthetic training for the lower extremity; 30 min

   Code(s) _____

   2. Application of manual electrical stimulation; 60 min

   Code(s) _____

   3. Therapeutic activities, direct patient contact by provider; 15 min

   Code(s) _____

   4. Negative pressure wound therapy, including topical application, wound assessment, and instruction for ongoing care, surface area 40 sq cm

   Code(s) _____

OTHER PROCEDURES

The last section of the CPT-4 manual deals with acupuncture, osteopathic manipulative treatment, chiropractic manipulative treatment, and training for patient self-management. There are only a few codes listed in each individual section. They should be reported by time and body region. Acupuncture is based on a 15-minute increment, not the actual duration of acupuncture needle placement; only one code may be reported for each 15-minute increment and only one initial code is reported per day.

Osteopathic manipulative treatment (OMT) is a manual treatment used to eliminate or alleviate somatic dysfunctions. Chiropractic manipulative treatment (CMT) is a manual treatment used to influence joints and neurophysiological functions. There are five spinal regions of CMT, which are cervical (atlanto-occipital joint); thoracic region (costovertebral and costotransverse joints); lumbar region; sacral region; and pelvic (sacroiliac joint) region. The five extraspinal regions are the head (temporomandibular joint), lower extremities, upper extremities; rib cage, and abdomen. In order to correctly report these codes, read the annotations to ensure correct reporting. Some of these codes may be reported in addition to E/M codes.

PRACTICE EXERCISE 10-34

Code the following procedures.

1. Osteopathic manipulative treatment; six body regions

   Code(s) _____

2. Acupuncture, 15 needles; without electrical stimulation; 15 min

   Code(s) _____

3. Educational training for patient self-management; face-to-face with patient, 30 min

   Code(s) _____

4. Chiropractic manipulative treatment; spinal, five regions

   Code(s) _____

CHAPTER REVIEW

I. True/False

Indicate whether the sentence or statement is true or false.

____ 1. A code for chemotherapy is bundled.

____ 2. Cardiac catheterization is a diagnostic procedure.

____ 3. Nystagmus is primarily caused by an inflammatory disease.

____ 4. A pulse generator can contain up to five electrodes only.

____ 5. Dopplers produce a three-dimensional image.

____ 6. A puncture test is a method used in allergy testing.

____ 7. Immunoglobulin is a human-donated solution obtained from plasma.

____ 8. Procedures that deal with any type of injection must be reported with an administration code.

___ **9.** Interactive psychotherapy is usually performed on adults.

___ **10.** Infusions must have physician supervision.

II. Multiple Choice

Identify the letter of the code that best describes the procedure.

___ **11.** Continuous inhalation treatment with aerosol medication, for acute airway obstruction; 1 hr

    a. 94644   c. 92326

    b. 92512   d. 92340

___ **12.** Nitric oxide expired gas determination

    a. 90918   c. 90940

    b. 91105   d. 95012

___ **13.** Spontaneous nystagmus, including gaze

    a. 92502   c. 92531

    b. 92563   d. 92548

___ **14.** Ophthalmic mucous membrane tests

    a. 92370   c. 92543

    b. 92506   d. 95060

___ **15.** Physical therapy reevaluation

    a. 97001   c. 97602

    b. 97761   d. 97139

III. Coding Exercises

Use an encoder or coding manuals to code the following.

16. Physical therapy training evaluation

    Code(s) _____

17. Digital analysis of an electroencephalogram

    Code(s) _____

18. Anogenital examination with colposcopic magnification, in child, for suspected trauma

    Code(s) _____

19. Transcranial Doppler study of the intracranial arteries; complete study

    Code(s) _____

20. Tone decay test

    Code(s) _____

21. Diphtheria toxoids, intramuscular administration

Code(s) _____

22. Gastric saline load test

Code(s) _____

23. Respiratory flow volume loop

Code(s) _____

24. Chiropractic manipulation treatment on three spinal regions

Code(s) _____

25. Medical testimony

Code(s) _____

IV. Coding Cases

Code the following cases.

26. Heather brought her infant to Dr. Schantz for an MMR vaccine. Dr. Schantz gave the infant a 10-minute examination and the MMR vaccine.

Code(s) _____

27. Carlos has been an inpatient at the Riverview Psychiatric Treatment Center for the past five years. He has been treated with various types of drugs that have not been effective. Today, his physician is trying electroconvulsive therapy. Dr. Timmons applies and monitors the therapy for a total of 15 minutes.

Code(s) _____

28. Julianna has had trouble with her vision since she reached the age of 70. Today she is being seen by her regular ophthalmologist, Dr. C. J. Martin, for her vision problems. Dr. Martin performs a medical examination and a test with interpretation and report for glaucoma.

Code(s) _____

29. Joe has a follow-up today for a duplex scan of the arterial inflow and venous outflow of the penile vessels.

Code(s) _____

30. D. A. Cusso, R.N., is performing a home visit to check the effects of the hemodialysis Bryant is receiving. The visit with Bryant lasts 30 minutes, and no other procedures are performed.

Code(s) _____

Chapter 11
ICD-9 CM Coding

KEY TERMS

bacterial	infectious	puerperium
bacterium	late effects code	viral
Ghon's lesion	morphology	zoonotic

LEARNING OBJECTIVES

After completing this chapter, the learner should be able to:

- Understand thse use of symbols
- Code to the highest degree
- Correctly code for underlying disease
- Know the correct use of V codes
- Know the correct use of modifiers
- Code for neoplasms

LEARNING TO CODE FOR THE DIAGNOSIS

When starting to code for the diagnosis, new coders can become very apprehensive because of the multitude of diagnoses. But if you take it one step at a time, it becomes increasingly easy. There are also web sites for ICD-9 that will help you in coding, including web site of the AHA Central Office for ICD-9 (http://www.icd-9-cm.org).

First, let's understand what ICD-9 is and why we use it. The acronym ICD-9 stands for the International Classification of Diseases (ICD), Ninth Revision. This manual is used to report diseases. Computers cannot understand terms, but they can understand numbers; therefore, all diseases have been transformed into a number so that computers may read the claims.

So, let's get started. As with the CPT-4, symbols are used to signify new codes, revisions, deletions, and so forth. The same holds true within the ICD-9 CM, only the symbols are different and have different meanings. In order to report the IDC-9 codes, let's learn the new symbols, what they mean, and why they are used. Listed below are the symbols used throughout the ICD-9 CM manual, with their definitions. When using Encoder Pro, refer to the Color Coding Legend.

◄►   Addition to the previous addition

☐   Nonspecific code

•   Use additional digits (colored red)

⇐⇒   Revised from the previous edition

✖   Valid operating room procedure

•   Not a principle diagnosis

❋   Special coverage instructions

These symbols will help you to report codes accurately and to the highest degree. To correctly report a diagnosis when using the ICD-9 manual, there are a few steps you must take. First, identify the main term (such as disease). Second, locate the type of disease (such as lung), and then locate the type of lung disease (black). Enter *black lung disease* into the Search box of Encoder Pro. The diagnosis code for black lung disease is 500. Now that you have completed the step of locating the disease, you must make sure it has been coded to the highest degree. The 500-code range is now listed in the Tabular Results box. Click on the code range and check if black lung disease (code 500) is the highest level of service. You will see that this particular disease is listed under code 500 (along with miner's asthma, coal worker's lung, etc.) and does not require a fourth or fifth digit. Therefore, black lung disease has been correctly coded to the highest degree. (Refer to Figure 11–1 to 11–6)

Infectious and Parasitic Disease

Diseases covered by the diagnosis codes within this section are considered transmittable (communicable). They are classified as infectious, bacterial, or viral. **Infectious** means transmittable with or without skin contact. **Bacterial** is the actual development of a disease caused by a specific bacterium, while **viral** pertains to a specific virus (see Figure 11–1). This section includes diseases that are transmitted from human to human and animal to human. Most of the codes listed must have additional digits to signify a more specific diagnosis, as with code 001. A code that appears in red in the Code Detail box signifies that a more specific code must be reported. Also, at the bottom of the code detail box, Encoder Pro reminds you that a fourth digit is to be reported ("Fourth digit required"). Codes that are nonspecific, such as paratyphoid fever (002.9) are not colored, but are stated within the code ("Unspecified paratyphoid fever"). **Late effects codes** are used to signify an additional problem that is the result of the primary code, but happens after the initial episode. Consider this example: a patient is diagnosed with botulism because, although the patient shows no sign of an active botulism, there is still evidence of a specific problem because of the botulism in the past. Therefore, you must code the botulism (primary) then code the late effects (secondary) of the botulism.

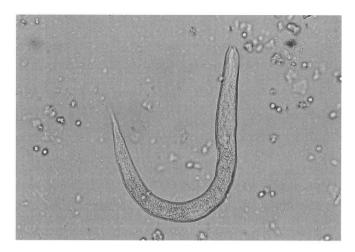

Figure 11-1 *Strongyloids stercoralis* in lung tissue

Tuberculosis is caused by the *Mycobacterium tuberculosis* bacterium. There are actually three types of tubercle bacillus: bovine, avian, and human. The disease mostly affects the respiratory system but may easily affect bones, joints, nervous system, gastrointestinal system, and genitourinary system. To report tuberculosis, you must first report the primary infection, which is called a **Ghon's lesion**. Once the lesion has spread to another body area, is it considered a secondary lesion and should be coded in addition to the Ghon's lesion.

Zoonotic diseases are diseases that are transmitted from animals to humans. There are approximately 250 known organisms that cause zoonotic diseases. These diseases can be transmitted by fleas, flies, large and small, wild and domestic animals. A **bacterium** is a one-celled organism that can mutate and spread. There are several methods used to identify bacteria. They include gram stain, culture, and hanging drop, which is an unstained bacterium in a drop of liquid. A parasitic disease may develop internally or externally. But they all need a host in order to survive.

PRACTICE EXERCISE 11-1

Code the following.

1. Gastrointestinal anthrax

   Code(s) _____

2. Norwegian scabies

   Code(s) _____

3. Type II poliomyelitis, acute, nonparalytic

   Code(s) _____

4. Botulism

Code(s) _____

5. Primary tuberculosis of the lung, nodular, found in sputum

Code(s) _____

6. *Herpes simplex* dermatitis of the eyelid

Code(s) _____

7. Athlete's foot

Code(s) _____

8. Oral thrush

Code(s) _____

9. Pinworm infection

Code(s) _____

10. Oriental liver fluke disease

Code(s) _____

Neoplasms

Neoplasms are classified as benign or malignant (see Figure 11–2). They are also coded as primary or secondary. But not all neoplasms are coded as such. You may encounter carcinomas in situ, which simply means localized in position. Encoder Pro makes reporting of these codes very easy, especially when coding the **morphology** (histology) of the neoplasm. In order to code for neoplasms, enter into the Search box the term *neoplasm morphology*. As you can see, nothing happens, but click on "See Index Listing" and another detail box appears. Now click on the plus (+) sign to the left of the term "neoplasm." This dialog box gives you all the anatomical sites in alphabetical order. Now find the term "adipose tissue" located inside the dialog box. Click on the plus symbol, and you see that it reveals five additional codes. These are primary, secondary, benign, uncertain behavior, and unspecified. You can also find these codes by entering *neoplasm* into the Search box along with the anatomical site, such as *neoplasm bone*. But note that by doing it this way, you still need to search for a more specific code and it does not provide information on the neoplasm being primary or secondary. So, let's try coding for neoplasms.

PRACTICE EXERCISE 11-2

Code the following.

1. Malignant neoplasm of the transverse colon

Code(s) _____

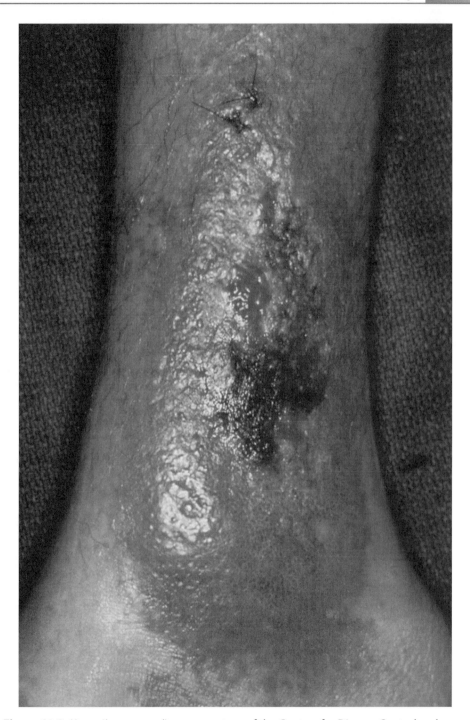

Figure 11-2 Kaposi's sarcoma (Image courtesy of the Centers for Disease Control and Prevention)

2. Primary cancer of the abdomen, with secondary cancer of the intrathoracic lymph nodes

   Code(s) _____

3. Multiple myeloma and immunoproliferative neoplasms in remission

   Code(s) _____

4. Chronic erythremia

   Code(s) _____

5. Carcinoma in situ of the trachea

   Code(s) _____

6. Benign neoplasm of the cervix uteri

   Code(s) _____

7. Chronic leukemia of unspecified cell type

   Code(s) _____

8. Kaposi's sarcoma of the soft tissue, malignant

   Code(s) _____

9. Malignant neoplasm of the base of the tongue, primary

   Code(s) _____

10. Malignant neoplasm of the upper-outer quadrant of the breast, female

    Code(s) _____

Endocrine System, Nutritional and Metabolic Diseases, and Immunity Disorders

The Endocrine System section deals with the body's glands and with hormones, which are secreted directly into the bloodstream. These codes include those associated with the thyroid, thymus, pituitary, and adrenal glands (see Figure 11-3). Nutritional and Metabolic Disorder codes deal with deficiencies of vitamins and minerals, along with the associated illnesses. These codes also include the body's inability to metabolize certain vitamins and minerals, as well as obesity codes.

PRACTICE EXERCISE 11-3

Code the following.

1. Vitamin A deficiency with keratomalacia

   Code(s) _____

2. Graves' disease with thyrotoxic storm

   Code(s) _____

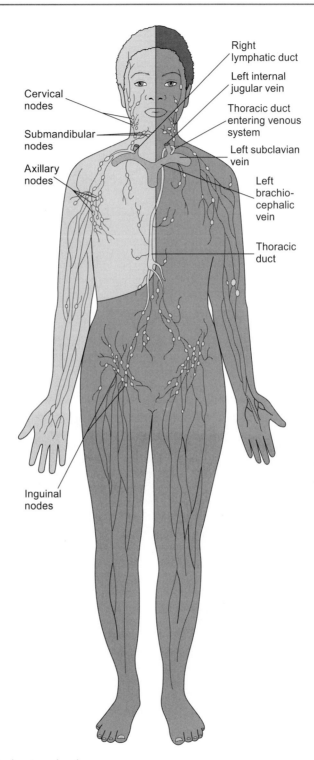

Figure 11-3 Endocrine glands

3. Thymic hypoplasia

   Code(s) _____

4. Diabetes Type II, uncontrolled, with peripheral circulatory disorders

   Code(s) _____

5. Hypercholesterolemia

   Code(s) _____

6. Wilson's disease

   Code(s) _____

7. Vitamin K deficiency

   Code(s) _____

8. Refenstein syndrome

   Code(s) _____

9. Simple goiter

   Code(s) _____

10. Vitamin A deficiency with night blindness

    Code(s) _____

Figure 11-4 Botulism Type A (Image courtesy of the Centers for Disease Control and Prevention)

Diseases of the Blood and Blood-Forming Organs

Diseases of the blood include codes that deal with anemias, coagulation disorders, and diseases associated with white blood cells (see Figure 11–4). Some codes within this section may need additional codes to identify the cause of the disease.

PRACTICE EXERCISE 11-4

Code the following.

1. Sickle-cell/Hb-C disease, without crises

   Code(s) _____

2. Pernicious anemia

   Code(s) _____

3. Splenic sequestration

   Code(s) _____

4. Allergic purpura

   Code(s) _____

5. Stokvis' disease

   Code(s) _____

6. Immune thrombocytopenia purpura

   Code(s) _____

7. Hemophilia C with secondary blood loss

   Code(s) _____

8. Factor V Leiden mutation

   Code(s) _____

9. Anemia in chronic kidney disease

   Code(s) _____

10. DIC syndrome

    Code(s) _____

Mental Disorders

When coding for mental disorders, we tend to think the worst, but that is not always the case. These codes are associated with senile dementia; drug- and alcohol-induced mental disorders, anxiety, and phobias. These codes also deal with drug abuse and sleep disorders, along with speech and language disorders. Web sites that may help you with coding questions are the American Psychological Association (http://www.apa.org) and the American Psychiatric Association (http://www.psych.org). Codes within this section may need to be reported with the cause of the underlying disease or physical condition of the patient.

PRACTICE EXERCISE 11-5

Code the following.

1. Night terrors

   Code(s) _____

2. Obsessive-compulsive personality disorder

   Code(s) _____

3. Catatonic type stupor, chronic

   Code(s) _____

4. Presenile dementia with delirium

   Code(s) _____

5. Moderate mental retardation

   Code(s) _____

6. Post-traumatic stress disorder

   Code(s) _____

7. Kleptomania

   Code(s) _____

8. Attention deficit disorder

   Code(s) _____

9. Stuttering

   Code(s) _____

10. Tension headache

    Code(s) _____

Diseases of the Nervous System and Sense Organs

When you think of the Nervous System, you automatically think of the brain and spinal cord, which is the central nervous system. But the peripheral nervous system is also part of the nervous system. Within this section, you will be reporting not only the type (purulent, aseptic/abacterial, chronic) but also the cause (bacterial, viral, mycobacterial, fungal) of specific diseases. Not only are the diseases associated with the type and cause, but hereditary and degenerative changes also play a part as we grow older. Codes within this section include diseases that are considered progressive. They include diseases that are a result of an underlying disease; in the case of underlying disease, you must report the underlying disease first.

PRACTICE EXERCISE 11-6

Code the following.

1. Retinal edema

   Code(s) _____

2. Cochlear otosclerosis

   Code(s) _____

3. Petit mal status

   Code(s) _____

4. Tinnitus

   Code(s) _____

5. Hereditary spastic paraplegia

   Code(s) _____

6. Chronic meningitis

   Code(s) _____

7. Quadriplegia

   Code(s) _____

8. Lumbosacral plexus lesions

   Code(s) _____

9. Myogenic ptosis

   Code(s) _____

10. Neural hearing loss

    Code(s) _____

Diseases of the Circulatory System

Diseases of the Circulatory System include the heart, coronary arteries, valves, and the electrical conduction of the heart (see Figure 11–5). These codes are based first on anatomical site, then disease. They include acute and chronic conditions. Some codes require a fifth digit, and the underlying disease may need to be reported.

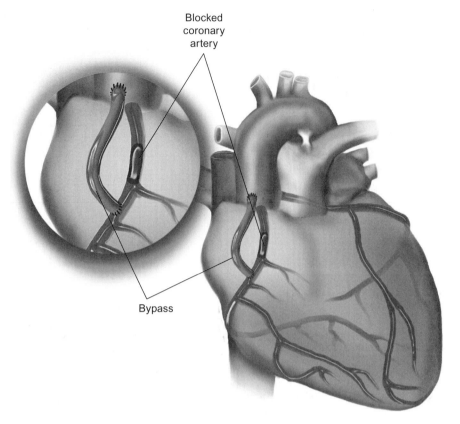

Blocked
coronary
artery

Bypass

Figure 11-5 Coronary artery bypass

PRACTICE EXERCISE 11-7

Code the following.

1. Cerebral embolism

Code(s) _____

2. Acute myocardial infarction

Code(s) _____

3. Myocardial degeneration

Code(s) _____

4. Atheroembolism of the lower extremity

Code(s) _____

5. Orthostatic hypotension

Code(s) _____

6. Internal hemorrhoids, without complication

   Code(s) _____

7. Deep vein thrombosis

   Code(s) _____

8. Rupture of an artery

   Code(s) _____

9. Dysphagia

   Code(s) _____

10. Vertigo

   Code(s) _____

Diseases of the Respiratory System

People tend to think of the Respiratory System as primarily the lungs, but the respiratory system includes much more than that. Diseases associated with the Respiratory System include those of the nasopharynx, lungs, and bronchial tube (see Figure 11–6). Some codes within this section must be reported with the underlying disease. Some codes include acute and chronic disorders.

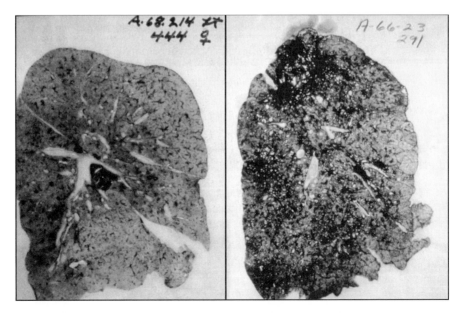

Figure 11-6 Coal worker's pneumonoconiosis (Image courtesy of the Centers for Disease Control and Prevention)

PRACTICE EXERCISE 11-8

Code the following.

1. Parapharyngeal abscess

   Code(s) _____

2. The common cold

   Code(s) _____

3. Interstitial emphysema

   Code(s) _____

4. Pleurisy

   Code(s) _____

5. Asbestosis

   Code(s) _____

6. Allergic rhinitis due to dog hair

   Code(s) _____

7. Pneumonia due to adenovirus

   Code(s) _____

8. Pigeon fanciers' disease

   Code(s) _____

9. Iatrogenic pneumothorax

   Code(s) _____

10. Mechanical complication of tracheostomy

    Code(s) _____

Diseases of the Digestive System

The Digestive System is broken down into two divisions. The first division is called the alimentary tube, which consists of the oral cavity, pharynx, esophagus, stomach, and the large and small intestines. The second division is called the accessory organs. These include the salivary glands, teeth, tongue, liver, gallbladder, and pancreas. Each one plays an important part in the aid of digesting food (see Figure 11–7). Codes within this section are broken down by anatomical site, then disease.

PRACTICE EXERCISE 11-9

Code the following.

1. Moderate atrophy of the mandible

   Code(s) _____

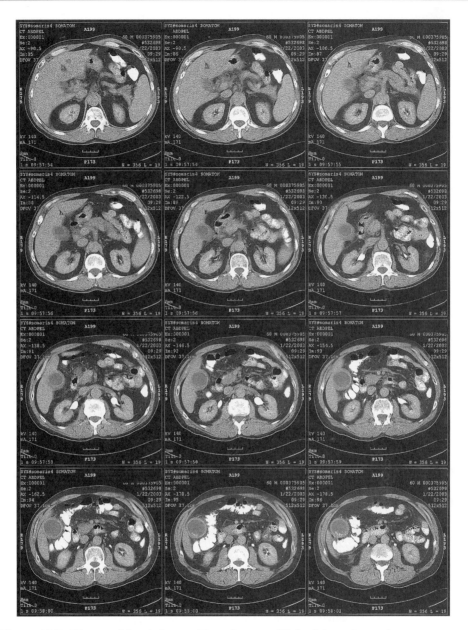

Figure 11-7 CT scan of the abdomen (Compliments of John P. Lampignano)

2. Alcoholic gastritis

   Code(s) _____

3. Acute appendicitis with peritoneal abscess

   Code(s) _____

4. Chronic cholecystitis

Code(s) _____

5. Acute peptic ulcer with perforation

Code(s) _____

6. Sialolithiasis

Code(s) _____

7. Dental caries, limited to the enamel

Code(s) _____

8. Bilateral inguinal hernia

Code(s) _____

9. Chronic ulcerative colitis, left side

Code(s) _____

10. Gallstones with obstruction, acute

Code(s) _____

Diseases of the Genitourinary System

The Genitourinary System includes the genitals and the urinary organs, which are the kidneys and urinary bladder. PKD (adult polycystic kidney disease) is an inherited renal disorder that affects from 1 in 400 to 1 in 1000 people. This disease accounts for 10% of cases with end-stage renal disease in United States. The kidneys form urine from blood plasma, which they do through filtration, reabsorption, and secretion. This section includes codes for the urinary system along with male and female genitals.

PRACTICE EXERCISE 11-10

Code the following.

1. Kidney stone

Code(s) _____

2. Acute prostatitis

Code(s) _____

3. Paralysis of the bladder

Code(s) _____

4. Primary amenorrhea

Code(s) _____

5. Endometriosis of the pelvic peritoneum

Code(s) _____

6. Small kidneys, bilaterally

Code(s) _____

7. Chronic renal failure

Code(s) _____

8. Hematuria, essential

Code(s) _____

9. Lump in the breast

Code(s) _____

Complications of Pregnancy, Childbirth, and the Puerperium

There are a lot of complications that can arise in the female due to pregnancy (anemia, diabetes mellitus) and childbirth (threatened labor, hemorrhage). They can even affect the **puerperium**, which is the period of 42 days following the birth of a child. During this 42-day period, the organs within the female return to their normal position. Codes within this section are classifiable to another section, so you must read each code carefully. Always remember to code the underlying cause first, and then report to the highest degree.

PRACTICE EXERCISE 11-11

Code the following.

1. Shock during labor and delivery, without mention of antepartum

Code(s) _____

2. Twin pregnancy, delivered

Code(s) _____

3. Spontaneous abortion, incomplete

Code(s) _____

4. Excessive weight gain in pregnancy

Code(s) _____

5. Normal delivery

Code(s) _____

6. Failure of lactation, antepartum complication

Code(s) _____

7. Varicose veins of the legs, complicating pregnancy and puerperium

Code(s) _____

8. Third stage postpartum hemorrhage, with delivery

Code(s) _____

9. Abdominal pregnancy, without intrauterine pregnancy

Code(s) _____

10. Spontaneous abortion, complete, complicated by renal failure

Code(s) _____

Diseases of the Skin and Subcutaneous Tissue

Although the skin has two major divisions, these codes do not differentiate between them. However, some codes are reported first by anatomical site, others are reported by the disease (psoriasis) or condition (sunburn) (see Figure 11–8). When you report these codes, especially for dermatitis due to chemicals, you need to report them with the use of additional E-codes (Chapter 13).

PRACTICE EXERCISE 11-12

Code the following.

1. Pilonidal cyst, without abscess

Code(s) _____

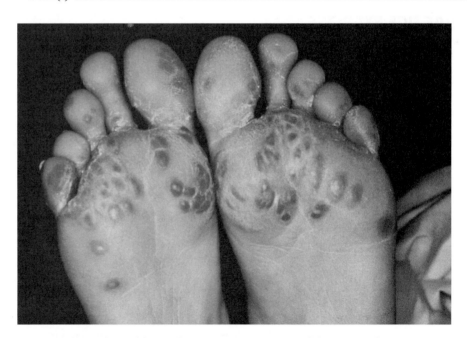

Figure 11-8 *Keratoderma blennorrhagica* (Image courtesy of the Centers for Disease Control and Prevention)

2. Ulcer of the calf

Code(s) _____

3. Hypertrophic scar

Code(s) _____

4. Sunburn, second degree

Code(s) _____

5. Cellulitis of the neck

Code(s) _____

6. Boil located on the wrist

Code(s) _____

7. Contact dermatitis due to detergents

Code(s) _____

8. Sebaceous cyst

Code(s) _____

9. Herpes iris

Code(s) _____

10. Cradle cap

Code(s) _____

Diseases of the Musculoskeletal and Connective Tissue

The Musculoskeletal System includes the bones, joints, and muscles of the human body (see Figure 11–9). These codes are first listed by disease (arthropathy), then by anatomical site (hand, forearm). When reporting arthropathies, you must report the underlying disease first, then the arthropathy.

PRACTICE EXERCISE 11-13

Code the following.

1. Kyphosis, postural

Code(s) _____

2. Muscle cramp of the leg

Code(s) _____

3. Systemic lupus erythematosus due to nephritis

Code(s) _____

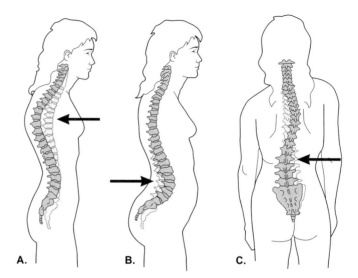

Figure 11-9 Abnormal curvatures of the spine

4. Recurrent dislocation of the shoulder

   Code(s) _____

5. Low back pain

   Code(s) _____

6. Trigger finger, acquired

   Code(s) _____

7. Cauliflower ear

   Code(s) _____

8. Degenerative spondylolisthesis

   Code(s) _____

9. Chronic osteomyelitis of the ankle and foot

   Code(s) _____

10. Complete rupture of rotator cuff

    Code(s) _____

Congenital Anomalies

Congenital anomalies literally mean deviating from normal at birth. In other words, these codes deal with birth defects. They are based on anatomical site, then anomaly.

PRACTICE EXERCISE 11-14

Code the following.

1. Subaortic stenosis

   Code(s) _____

2. Patau syndrome

   Code(s) _____

3. Madelung's deformity

   Code(s) _____

4. Renal dysplasia

   Code(s) _____

5. Multiple anomalies

   Code(s) _____

6. Spina bifida of the lumbar region

   Code(s) _____

7. Buphthalmos of a newborn

   Code(s) _____

8. Interruption of aortic arch

   Code(s) _____

9. Cleft palate, bilateral, complete

   Code(s) _____

10. Imperfect fusion of the skull

   Code(s) _____

Certain Conditions Originating in the Perinatal Period

Codes within this section deal with trauma encountered by the fetus or newborn. The trauma may be caused by the use of drugs or by the lack of oxygen at birth or even during the delivery. They also deal with premature and low birth newborns of low birth weight. Be sure to read the codes carefully. These codes may be used in conjunction with each other.

PRACTICE EXERCISE 11-15

Code the following.

1. Pulmonary hemorrhage

   Code(s) _____

2. Fetal alcohol syndrome

Code(s) _____

3. Neonatal tachycardia

Code(s) _____

4. Intraventricular hemorrhage, Grade IV

Code(s) _____

5. Breech delivery and extraction

Code(s) _____

6. Surgical operation on mother

Code(s) _____

7. Fracture of the clavicle

Code(s) _____

8. Respiratory failure of newborn

Code(s) _____

9. Meconium obstruction

Code(s) _____

10. Drug withdrawal syndrome in newborn

Code(s) _____

SYMPTOMS, SIGNS, AND ILL-DEFINED CONDITIONS

Codes that are listed under this classification are codes that mostly cannot be listed under any other section. Why? They are not a specific disease; they are symptoms associated with a disease or condition, but cannot be diagnosed as a disease. Here, you will find symptoms such as fever, dizziness, sore throat, and chest pain. These codes also include abnormal findings in diagnostic and laboratory results. The important thing to remember is that there may not be an identified cause for the abnormal condition or symptoms.

PRACTICE EXERCISE 11-16

Code the following.

1. Hallucinations

Code(s) _____

2. Splenomegaly

Code(s) _____

3. Precordial chest pain

Code(s) _____

4. Asphyxia

Code(s) _____

5. Mammographic microcalcification of the breast

Code(s) _____

6. Diarrhea

Code(s) _____

7. Headache

Code(s) _____

8. Coma

Code(s) _____

9. Febrile convulsions

Code(s) _____

10. Memory loss

Code(s) _____

Injury and Poisoning

Codes within the injury section are used to report a single or multiple injuries. The codes are very similar to CPT codes, with the inclusion of a more extensive injury such as loss of consciousness. The codes may also include more than one fracture (arm and leg, or three ribs). There are codes within this section that are not multiple injuries, but are considered complications due to a specific reason. All of these codes have one thing in common; they need to be reported with an E-code. An E-code gives further explanation as to the cause and effect of the injury. These codes are listed in Chapter 13 of this workbook. For practice exercises, do not report E-codes.

PRACTICE EXERCISE 11-17

Code the following.

1. Closed dislocation of the anterior elbow

Code(s) _____

2. Third-degree burn of the shoulder region

Code(s) _____

3. Traumatic amputation of the toe, with complications

Code(s) _____

4. Sunstroke

Code(s) _____

5. Rupture of an internal operation wound

Code(s) _____

6. Motion sickness

Code(s) _____

7. Poisoning by methadone

Code(s) _____

8. Contusion of the elbow

Code(s) _____

9. Infected blister on the foot

Code(s) _____

10. Concussion with loss of consciousness for 45 min

Code(s) _____

V-Codes

Physicians who report V-codes as the principle diagnosis usually do not get reimbursed, as these codes are not intended as a primary code. But home health services may report V-codes as primary. These codes are used to report patients who have come in contact with communicable diseases (for instance, hepatitis), when specific treatment is obtained (chemotherapy), or when a problem arises that influences a person's health status. Do *not* use code V15.82 for a history of tobacco use as a primary diagnosis, even if the patient is being treated for tobacco use. In this case, use code 305.1 if the patient is a current smoker.

PRACTICE EXERCISE 11-18

Code the following.

1. Family history of lung cancer

Code(s) _____

2. Treatment for gambling

Code(s) _____

3. Special screening for malnutrition

Code(s) _____

4. Convalescence and palliative care following chemotherapy

Code(s) _____

5. Problems with hearing

   Code(s) _____

6. Family history of hearing loss

   Code(s) _____

7. Vaccination against the flu

   Code(s) _____

8. Exposure to venereal disease

   Code(s) _____

9. Person receiving speech therapy

   Code(s) _____

10. Marriage counseling

   Code(s) _____

CHAPTER REVIEW

I. True/False

Indicate whether the sentence or statement is true or false.

____ **1.** V-codes are always used as a primary code.

____ **2.** The digestive system is divided into three divisions.

____ **3.** E-codes provide no explanation for injuries.

____ **4.** There may not be an identified cause for an abnormal condition.

____ **5.** When reporting arthropathies, you never report the underlying disease first.

____ **6.** The term "in situ" means localized in position.

____ **7.** There are several methods used to identify bacteria.

II. Multiple Choice

Identify the letter of the code that best describes the condition.

____ **8.** Accidental poisoning by paint cleaner

   a. E862.9   c. E861.6

   b. 982.8, E862.9   d. 982.8

____ **9.** Accidental poisoning by Premarin with therapeutic use

   a. 962.2   c. 962.2, E 950.4

   b. 962.2, E858.0   d. 962.0, E932.2

___ **10.** Suicide attempt by poisoning using hemlock

    a. 988.2, E865.4   c. 988.2, E950.9

    b. 988.2   d. 988.2, E962.1

___ **11.** Poisoning by eating fool's parsley

    a. 988.2   c. 988.2, E980.9

    b. 988.2, E865.4   d. 988.2, E950.9

___ **12.** Accidental poisoning by using a muscle relaxant

    a. 968.0   c. 975.2, E858.6

    b. 975.2   d. None of the above

III. Coding Exercises

Use an encoder or coding manuals to code the following.

13. Primary neoplasm of the lower leg, with metastasis into the spinal column.

    Code(s) _____

14. Cystic fibrosis with gastrointestional manifestations

    Code(s) _____

15. Endomyocardial fibrosis

    Code(s) _____

16. Contusion of the chest wall

    Code(s) _____

17. Insomnia with sleep apnea

    Code(s) _____

18. Interstitial myositis

    Code(s) _____

19. Kaschin-Beck disease of the upper arm

    Code(s) _____

20. Chronic pyelonephritis, with lesion of renal medullary necrosis

    Code(s) _____

IV. Coding Cases

Code the following cases.

21. Shanna was seen as a new patient by Dr. Forbes. She complained of feeling fatigued and having a lot of past infections, some resulting in the loss of blood. Dr. Forbes ordered a series of tests and returned with a diagnosis of myeloid leukemia.

    Code(s) _____

22. Aaron developed a severe rash and itching on his arms. He became concerned when his arms started swelling and began to blister. His physician, Dr. Rosenthal, immediately examined Aaron's arms and prescribed an antihistamine and a topical astringent for contact dermatitis.

    Code(s) _____

23. Kevin, a 29-year-old, was seen by Dr. Fergerson. At the time of his examination, Kevin complained of having joint pain with fever off and on for several months. Upon examination, Dr. Fergerson discovered small eruptions on Kevin's hands, feet, and face. Further examination revealed that Kevin had spent the last three months doing research in a rain forest. Dr. Fergerson then obtained a blood specimen and discovered Kevin had contracted an infectious disease.

    Diagnosis: Yaws (nodular)

    Code(s) _____

24. Tiffany arrived at the emergency department, a victim of a motor vehicle accident. She suffered severe wounds to her lower leg. Upon examination, the ER physician ordered multiple x-rays of her lower extremity. Tiffany suffered from multiple crushing fractures of the knee and lower leg. Tiffany was scheduled for repair in the operating room.

    Diagnosis:

    1. Crushing injury to the knee and lower leg

    2. Multiple fractures to the lower limb, open

    3. Open fracture of the patella

    Code(s) _____

25. John was seen by Dr. Raymond for his yearly exam. John complained of feeling tired and thirsty for several weeks. He explained he had a family history of diabetes but was never diagnosed himself. Dr. Raymond performed a fingerstick test for glucose monitoring. John's blood sugar level was 250. Dr. Raymond then ordered a glucose tolerance test.

    Diagnosis: Diabetes mellitus, Type II

    Code(s) _____

Chapter 12
HCPCS Level II Coding

KEY TERMS

durable medical equipment (DME)	Level II codes LOPS	PET scan

LEARNING OBJECTIVES

After completing this chapter, the learner should be able to:

- Identify HPCS codes
- Assign correct coding procedures
- Understand the use of HCPCS modifiers
- Assign the correct level of codes
- Understand the use of J-codes

HCPCS LEVEL II CODES

HCPCS **Level II codes** are considered a national code, a standardized system for reporting supplies (e.g., wheelchairs) and services (e.g., injections) that are not listed in the CPT-4 codes. These codes are alphanumeric and are grouped into sections such as transportation, orthotic, and rehabilitation.

These codes are easily recognized as Level II because they consist of a single letter followed by four digits: for example, A6410. To use this code, enter it into the Search box of Encoder Pro. You will find there is a special coverage message under the Code Detail dialog box. This information gives additional information as to whether the code is payable for the sterile eye patch. You will also see there is a quantity alert. Therefore, you must read the special coverage information in order to know how many sterile eye patches are billable. Some codes are not covered under Medicare (A4206) and are bundled into the service. Now enter code A4206 into the Search box of the encoder. As you can see under the Code Detail box, Medicare does not cover this. To make it easier to select a HCPCS Level II Code, locate the view description on the black tool bar of Encoder Pro. Change the box to "book selections" and click on HCPCS. This will show the listing of codes and the subsections. Using Encoder Pro for a listing of HCPCS will help you identify the code range quickly. You may also use the Search box to locate HCPCS by entering modifiers and choosing HCPCS as your code set. Try both ways to see which method you prefer.

Transportation Services, Medical and Surgical Supplies, and Miscellaneous Supplies (A-Codes)

The one thing that the transportation services, medical/surgical supplies, and miscellaneous supplies have in common is they all start with the alphabetic letter A. Each one of these services provides something different. Transportation services include emergency and non-emergency transportation. They also include transportation by ambulance and helicopter. The medical/surgical supplies category contains codes for infusion pumps, vascular catheters, incontinence and ostomy supplies, respiratory, ESRD, dressings, and supplies for radiology procedures.

PRACTICE EXERCISES 12-1

Code the following HCPCS.

1. Nonelastic binder for an extremity

   Code(s) _____

2. Ostomy pouch, drainable, with faceplate attached, plastic, one

   Code(s) _____

3. Advanced life support, level II

   Code(s) _____

4. Syringe with needles, for external insulin pump, needle type

   Code(s) _____

5. Blood collection tube, vacuum, for dialysis, per 50

   Code(s) _____

6. Supply of injectable contrast material for use in echocardiography, per study

   Code(s) _____

7. Compression burn garment, foot to knee length, custom fabricated

   Code(s) _____

8. Skin barrier; solid, 6 × 6 or equivalent, each

   Code(s) _____

9. Chinstrap used with positive airway pressure device

   Code(s) _____

10. Wound cleansers, any type, any size

    Code(s) _____

Enteral and Parenteral Therapy (B-Codes)

Codes within this section (which all start with the letter B) deal with feeding a patient by means other than the alimentary canal. They include the route (gastrostomy), the food or nutritional solutions (based on calories), and the pumps to supply the necessary nutrition for the patient.

PRACTICE EXERCISE 12-2

Code the following HCPCS.

1. Parenteral nutrition supply kit; premix, per day

   Code(s) _____

2. Enteral feeding supply kit; pump fed, per day

   Code(s) _____

3. Enteral nutritional infusion pump, with alarm

   Code(s) _____

4. Parenteral nutrition solution; amino acids, 3.5% home mix

   Code(s) _____

5. Levine type stomach tube

   Code(s) _____

6. Parenteral nutritional additives, vitamins, trace elements, heparin, electrolytes, home mix, per day

   Code(s) _____

7. Food thickener, administered orally, per ounce

   Code(s) _____

8. Parenteral nutritional administration kit, per day

   Code(s) _____

9. Parenteral nutrition solution, lipids, 20%, with administration set, 500 cc

   Code(s) _____

10. NOC for enteral supplies

    Code(s) _____

C-CODES

Codes within this section are strictly for use at an outpatient hospital and are not used to report any other service. These codes are updated by the Centers for Medicare and Medicaid every four months. This section deals with codes for radiopharmaceuticals, catheters, defibrillators, and ocular implants, to name a few.

PRACTICE EXERCISE 12-3

Code the following supplies.

1. Catheter, transluminal atherectomy, directional

    Code(s) _____

2. Pacemaker, dual chamber, non-rate responsiveness

    Code(s) _____

3. Implantable tissue marker

    Code(s) _____

4. Injection, perflexane lipid microspheres, per 10 ml vial

    Code(s) _____

5. MRI with contrast, breast; unilateral

    Code(s) _____

6. Implantable lead for a neurostimulator

    Code(s) _____

7. Implantable screw for opposing bone-to-bone

    Code(s) _____

8. Implantable breast prosthesis

    Code(s) _____

9. Catheter, balloon dilatation, nonvascular

    Code(s) _____

10. Embolization protection system

    Code(s) _____

Durable Medical Equipment (E-Codes)

The **durable medical equipment (DME)** category deals with any equipment used to care for the patient at home. This includes crutches, hospital beds, respiratory equipment, compressors, stimulators, parts, and supplies.

PRACTICE EXERCISE 12-4

Code the following equipment or supplies.

1. Home blood glucose monitor

    Code(s) _____

2. Crutches, forearm, metal, with tips and handgrips, fixed

   Code(s) _____

3. Jaw motion rehabilitation system

   Code(s) _____

4. Heavy duty wheelchair, detachable arms, elevating leg rests

   Code(s) _____

5. Cervical head harness

   Code(s) _____

6. Implantable cardiac event recorder with memory, activator, and programmer

   Code(s) _____

7. Helmet, with face guard and soft interface material, prefabricated

   Code(s) _____

8. Nebulizer, with compressor

   Code(s) _____

9. Whirlpool, non-portable

   Code(s) _____

10. Negative pressure wound therapy electrical pump, portable

    Code(s) _____

Temporary Codes (G-Codes)

Temporary G-codes are national codes that are assigned for services and procedures before they become a standard code. They include codes for **PET scan** (positron emission tomography) and for monitoring and evaluations for **LOPS** (loss of protective sensation). Included in this section are codes for monitoring radioisotopes and anticoagulation times; these are usually only for a covered inpatient who has been fitted with a mechanical heart valve.

PRACTICE EXERCISE 12-5

Code the following services or procedures.

1. PET imaging, whole body; diagnosis esophageal cancer

   Code(s) _____

2. Services of occupational therapist in home health setting, 60 min

   Code(s) _____

3. Administration of influenza virus vaccine

   Code(s) _____

4. Colorectal screening for cancer, colonoscopy, high-risk patient

   Code(s) _____

5. Trimming of dystrophic nails, five

   Code(s) _____

6. Diagnostic mammography, producing direct digital image, bilateral, all views

   Code(s) _____

7. ESRD-related services for home dialysis for 10 days, for patient aged 22 years

   Code(s) _____

8. Administration of pneumococcal vaccine

   Code(s) _____

9. Wound closure, utilizing tissue adhesive only

   Code(s) _____

10. Insertion or repositioning of electrode leads for dual chamber pacing cardioverter defibrillator and insertion of pulse generator

    Code(s) _____

ALCOHOL AND DRUG SERVICES (H-CODES)

Codes within this section deal primarily with services related to the use of alcohol and drugs. They contain codes for assessments, interventions, rehabilitation, and skills training. Social services and therapists mostly use these codes.

PRACTICE EXERCISE 12-6

Code the following services or procedures.

1. Therapeutic behavioral services, per diem

   Code(s) _____

2. Alcohol and drug assessment

   Code(s) _____

3. Drug services; acute detoxification (residential addiction program), inpatient

   Code(s) _____

4. Prenatal care, at-risk assessment

   Code(s) _____

5. Community psychiatric supportive treatment, face-to-face, 15 min

   Code(s) _____

6. Sexual offender treatment service, 60 min

   Code(s) _____

7. Alcohol services; group counseling by a clinician

   Code(s) _____

8. Crisis intervention service, 90 min

   Code(s) _____

9. Respite care services, not in the home, per diem

   Code(s) _____

10. Drug screening; laboratory analysis of specimens for presence of drugs

    Code(s) _____

Drugs J-Codes

Drugs that are listed under this section are given by injection, inhalation, and orally. The codes also include chemotherapy drugs and immunosuppressive drugs. The drugs are listed under the chemical names given, not the brand name. Each code contains the dosage amount, and some contain the route of administration. Be sure to read each code carefully to ensure proper coding.

PRACTICE EXERCISE 12-7

Code the following.

1. Oral prednisone, 5 mg

   Code(s) _____

2. Tobramycin, 300 mg inhalation solution, administered through DME

   Code(s) _____

3. Injection of morphine sulfate, 10 mg

   Code(s) _____

4. Injection of 7 cc of gamma globulin, intramuscular

   Code(s) _____

5. Injection of tetracycline, 250 mg

   Code(s) _____

6. Interferon, alfa-n3 (human leukocyte derived) 250,000 IU, for chemotherapy

   Code(s) _____

7. Injection of Vitamin K

   Code(s) _____

8. Hormone patch for use as contraceptive

   Code(s) _____

9. Oral administration of 50 mg etoposide

   Code(s) _____

10. Arsenic trioxide, 1 mg

   Code(s) _____

Durable Medical Equipment (K-Codes)

All codes listed here in the K section are considered temporary codes. They deal with re-placement parts and accessories for wheelchairs or specialized orthotics. Many of these codes have been deleted and placed in the permanent codes.

PRACTICE EXERCISE 12-8

Code the following supplies.

1. Portable oxygen concentrator, rental

   Code(s) _____

2. Replacement battery for external infusion pump, owned by patient, silver oxide, 3 volt

   Code(s) _____

3. Wheelchair accessory, seat cushion, does not meet specific code

   Code(s) _____

4. Multiple density insert, direct formed, molded to foot, external heat source of 230 degrees, total contact with patient's foot, including arch, base layer ¼-inch material of Shore A 35 durometer, prefabricated, for diabetic patient only

   Code(s) _____

5. Automatic external defibrillator, with integrated electrocardiogram analysis, garment type

   Code(s) _____

6. Detachable, adjustable height arm rest, upper portion

   Code(s) _____

7. Pneumatic tire and tire tube

   Code(s) _____

8. Ultra lightweight wheelchair

   Code(s) _____

9. Supplies for external drug infusion pump, syringe type cartridge, sterile

   Code(s) _____

10. Two arm pads

    Code(s) _____

Orthotic Procedures (L-Codes)

Codes listed in the L section are first listed by anatomic site, then device or procedure. These codes reflect many types of prosthesis and orthotic devices. Some codes are to be used immediately after surgery (L6382), immediate postsurgical or early fitting of initial rigid dressing, including fitting alignment and suspension of components, and one cast change, elbow disarticulation or above elbow. Other codes are considered base codes that may be modified by adding another code from the "Additions" section.

PRACTICE EXERCISE 12-9

Code the following devices or procedures.

1. Foot, arch support, removable, premolded, longitudinal, bilateral

   Code(s) _____

2. Thoracic rib belt

   Code(s) _____

3. Custom fabricated AFO, plastic

   Code(s) _____

4. Mechanical hand, infant, terminal device, Steeper

   Code(s) _____

5. Ocular implant

   Code(s) _____

6. Orthopedic footwear, custom shoes, depth inlay

   Code(s) _____

7. Addition to lower extremity, below knee, acrylic socket

   Code(s) _____

8. Halo procedure, cervical halo incorporated into plaster body jacket

   Code(s) _____

9. Foot drop splint, recumbent positioning device, prefabricated, includes fitting and adjustment

   Code(s) _____

10. Shoulder disarticulation, passive restoration (complete prosthesis), with an upper extremity addition of a suction socket

    Code(s) _____

Pathology and Laboratory Test (P-Codes)

Codes within the Pathology and Laboratory section are used for procedures that are not normally performed. The codes are listed first by procedure.

PRACTICE EXERCISE 12-10

Code the following procedures.

1. Urine culture, bacterial, quantitative, sensitivity study

   Code(s) _____

2. Fresh frozen plasma, between 8 and 24 hr of collection, three units

   Code(s) _____

3. Hair analysis

   Code(s) _____

4. Whole blood for transfusion, one unit

   Code(s) _____

5. Red blood cells, irradiated, one unit

   Code(s) _____

6. Catheterization for collection of specimen, single patient, at home

   Code(s) _____

7. Infusion, plasma protein fraction (human), 5%, 50 ml

   Code(s) _____

8. Screening Papanicolaou smear, cervical, two slides, requiring interpretation by physician

   Code(s) _____

9. Cephalin flocculation, blood

   Code(s) _____

10. Travel allowance, one-way, in connection with medically necessary laboratory specimen collection drawn from homebound patient; prorated trip charge

    Code(s) _____

Temporary Q-Codes

Codes within this section include injections, supplies, and new technologies. The codes are considered more in-depth and precise than similar codes in other sections. Codes for casting supplies are reported by anatomical site, then by the age of the patient, and lastly by the type of material used for the cast. Be sure to read these codes carefully to report the correct procedure.

PRACTICE EXERCISE 12-11

Code the following.

1. Injection, corticorelin ovine triflutate, one dose

    Code(s) _____

2. Cardiokymography

    Code(s) _____

3. Injection of dopamine HCl, 40 mg

    Code(s) _____

4. Telehealth-originating site facility fee

    Code(s) _____

5. Collagen skin test

    Code(s) _____

6. Irrigation solution for treatment of bladder calculi, 500 mg

    Code(s) _____

7. Cast supplies, short arm cast, plaster, patient aged 10 years

    Code(s) _____

8. New technology intraocular lens, category 4 of Federal Register

    Code(s) _____

9. ALS vehicle used, non-emergency transport, no ALS level service furnished

    Code(s) _____

10. Cast supplies, hip spica, bilateral, plaster, patient aged 30 years

    Code(s) _____

Temporary S-Codes

All the codes within this section are codes that have not been placed in any other section. The codes cover a variety of services and procedures, such as asthma education (S9441), exercise classes (S9451), and foster care (S5140). There are no codes listed within this section that are approved by Medicare.

PRACTICE EXERCISE 12-12

Code the following services or procedures.

1. Genetic testing for Tay-Sachs disease

   Code(s) _____

2. Annual rectal exam, digitally

   Code(s) _____

3. Disposable contact lens, bilateral

   Code(s) _____

4. Medical records copying fee, 50 pages

   Code(s) _____

5. Prenatal vitamins, 30-day supply

   Code(s) _____

6. Storage of previously frozen embryos

   Code(s) _____

7. Portable peak flow meter

   Code(s) _____

8. Diabetic management program, group session

   Code(s) _____

9. Sales tax

   Code(s) _____

10. Nicotine patches, legend

    Code(s) _____

National T-Codes for State Medicaid Agencies

All codes within this section are strictly for the use of state Medicaid programs and are not recognized by Medicare. These codes deal with the rehabilitation and patient assistance given by and managed under the care of the Medicaid programs. These codes are only payable at the discretion of the individual state agency. Before using any code listed within this section, be very sure the code you are reporting is an acceptable code within your state. It is wise to use a code that contains the same description as the CPT-4 codes.

PRACTICE EXERCISE 12-13

Code the following.

1. Day habilitation, waiver; per diem

   Code(s) _____

2. Hospice long-term care, room and board only; per day

   Code(s) _____

3. Substance abuse modification

   Code(s) _____

4. Home health aide; one visit

   Code(s) _____

5. Supply, not otherwise specified

   Code(s) _____

6. Utility services to support medical equipment and assistive technology waiver

   Code(s) _____

7. Case management, 1 hr

   Code(s) _____

8. Washable diapers; 10

   Code(s) _____

9. Non-emergency transportation; patient escort

   Code(s) _____

10. Administration of intramuscular medication by a health care agency; per diem

    Code(s) _____

Vision, Hearing, and Speech (V-Codes)

When coding for vision care supply, it is important to remember that the CPT code for a permanent prosthesis or a supply of glasses, contacts, or low vision lenses should be reported with the addition of the specific lens listed within this section. Codes that deal with aphakic temporary glasses should be coded strictly from the CPT-4 codes. Codes that deal with hearing, speech, and language are strictly for nonphysician services only. Services for these codes deal with repair, dispensing, and programming of hearing aids or speech devices. Codes that deal with hearing and speech are not covered under Medicare.

PRACTICE EXERCISE 12-14

Code the following procedures.

1. Ear mold/insert, not disposable

   Code(s) _____

2. Purchase of frames for glasses

   Code(s) _____

3. Processing, preserving, and transporting corneal tissue

Code(s) _____

4. Hand-held low vision aids and other nonspectacle-mounted aids

Code(s) _____

5. Dysphagia screening

Code(s) _____

6. Fitting, orientation, and checking of hearing aid

Code(s) _____

7. Prosthetic eye, plastic, custom made

Code(s) _____

8. Contact lens, gas permeable, bifocal, bilateral

Code(s) _____

9. Specialty bifocal by report

Code(s) _____

10. Ear impression, unilateral

Code(s) _____

HCPCS LEVEL II NATIONAL MODIFIERS

Level II national modifiers are similar to other modifiers you have learned. The purpose is the same, which is to explain in more detail the procedures performed. These modifiers detail anatomic sites, such as the left foot, great toe (TA), or the upper right eyelid (E3). The complete listings of HCPCS Level II national modifiers are listed in the back of the HCPCS manual. These codes may also be used in outpatient settings.

PRACTICE EXERCISE 12-15

Code the following.

1. Right foot, fourth digit

Code(s) _____

2. Left side

Code(s) _____

3. Waiver of liability statement on file

Code(s) _____

4. Right coronary artery

Code(s) _____

5. Lower left eyelid

Code(s) _____

6. Left hand, fourth digit

Code(s) _____

7. Right foot, great toe

Code(s) _____

8. Upper right eyelid

Code(s) _____

9. Right hand, third digit

Code(s) _____

10. Ambulance service furnished directly by a provider of service

Code(s) _____

CHAPTER REVIEW

I. True/False

Indicate whether the sentence or statement is true or false.

_____ **1.** HCPCS Level II codes are a standardized system.

_____ **2.** Some HCPCS codes are not billable under Medicare.

_____ **3.** Transportation codes do not include transportation by helicopter.

_____ **4.** National T-codes deal with patient rehabilitation.

_____ **5.** National modifiers may be used in an outpatient setting.

II. Multiple Choice

Identify the letter of the code that best describes the service or supply.

_____ **6.** Supply of radiopharmaceutical diagnostic imaging agent, technetium Tc 99m arcitumomab/vial

a. C1201   c. C1122

b. C1080   d. C1722

_____ **7.** Wheelchair commode seat

a. E0968   c. E0958

b. E0950   d. E0830

_____ **8.** Injection of oxytocin, five units

a. J2271   c. J2590

b. J0610   d. J1570

___ **9.** AFO, spring wire, dorsiflexion assist calf band, custom fabrication

   a. L1685   c. L2020

   b. L1900   d. L1620

___ **10.** Ostomy pouch, urinary, for use on barrier with flange, two pieces, each

   a. A5505   c. A4774

   b. A4637   d. A5073

___ **11.** Enteral feeding supply kit; gravity fed, two days

   a. B9000   c. C1716

   b. B4036   d. B4036 × 2

III. Coding Exercises

Use an encoder or coding manuals to code the following.

12. IV pole

   Code(s) _____

13. Wound cleansers, any type, any size

   Code(s) _____

14. Home blood glucose monitor

   Code(s) _____

15. PET imaging, whole body; restaging; esophageal cancer

   Code(s) _____

16. Community psychiatric supportive treatment program, per diem

   Code(s) _____

17. Breast prosthesis, mastectomy form

   Code(s) _____

18. Whole blood for transfusion, per unit, four units received

   Code(s) _____

19. Set-up portable x-ray equipment

   Code(s) _____

20. Surgical trays

   Code(s) _____

21. Lead pacemaker, transvenous VDD single pass

   Code(s) _____

22. Electronic elbow, Hosmer, switch controlled

   Code(s) _____

IV. Coding Cases

Code the following cases.

23. Charley, who has been in a wheelchair for several years, needed a new seat cushion. He telephoned All American DME services and they supplied Charley with a 4-inch cushion.

    Code(s) _____

24. Duane was diagnosed with esophageal cancer several weeks ago. Today he is scheduled for a PET imaging of the whole body as an initial staging.

    Code(s) _____

25. Dr. Kiley, an orthopedic specialist, examined Brett today for an ankle-foot orthotic. After the exam, Dr. Kiley decided to make a Perlstein type orthotic with custom fabrication for Brett.

    Code(s) _____

26. Rita received a right-side mastectomy for breast cancer. Today, she is being fitted with a custom breast prosthesis, which is molded to her.

    Code(s) _____

27. Amy, aged 14 years, has been treated for pernicious anemia for the last several months, without improvement. Today, her physician prescribed cyanocobalamin cobalt (Co57) as a radiopharmaceutical and also ordered a PET scan. (Code only the radiopharmaceuticals.)

    Code(s) _____

Chapter 13
External Causes of Injury and Poisoning

KEY TERMS

accident	nontraffic accident	poisoning
air transport	passenger	railway vehicle
injury	pedal cycle	watercraft
motor vehicle accident (MVA)	pedestrian	

LEARNING OBJECTIVES

After completing this chapter, the learner should be able to:

- Understand the purpose of E-codes
- Properly apply E-codes
- Understand the Table of Drugs and Chemicals
- Understand definitions of terms associated with E-codes

PURPOSE OF E-CODES

When you code with E-codes, you must first understand their purpose. They detail the circumstances in which an **accident** (an unforeseen mishap), **injury** (trauma to some part of the body), or **poisoning** (introduction of a toxic substance into the body) took place. These codes inform the insurance companies, employers, or physicians how an injury occurred and where it took place. These codes are not intended as a primary code, and most insurance companies do not reimburse for an E-code. They should be used to add more detail of the event or circumstance. Codes within this section are based on the type of accident or injury, such as vehicle accident, environmental, homicide, or suicide. Then the injured person's circumstances further specify the code. These include a pedestrian, employee, or **passenger** (occupant of a motor vehicle), to name a few. Other categories include accidental poisoning and acts of war; everything that would cause an injury is listed in this section.

Vehicle Accidents

This section includes codes that are classified as vehicle accidents. They consist of a three-digit code that represents a large group of related accidents or injuries associated with vehicles. The different types of vehicles—railway, motor vehicle, watercraft, air transport; nontraffic and other road vehicles—further divide these codes. Before we start to code, let's learn the definitions of different vehicle and vehicle accidents. A **railway vehicle** is a transportation vehicle that is operated on rails (train, streetcar). A **motor vehicle accident (MVA)** is considered to be any transport accident involved in a motor vehicle (cars, trucks). A **watercraft** is considered to be any device for the purpose of transporting passengers or goods on the water. An **air transport** is a device for transporting passengers or goods in the air (airplane, balloon, and military aircraft). A **nontraffic accident** is a motor vehicle accident that takes place other than on a public highway (e.g., off-road trails). To ensure proper reporting, these codes must be assigned a fourth digit that identifies the specific person injured. This would include a **pedestrian**, who is any person on foot, pedal cycle, or riding in or on a motor vehicle, railway train, and so forth. A **pedal cycle** is a transportation vehicle that is operated on rails (train, streetcar).

The fourth digit is identified as .0–.9 in the ICD-9 manual and is included within the code description in Encoder Pro. Coders using the ICD-9 manual should read the guideline in order to identify the specific exclusions. These exclusions are included within Encoder Pro. E-codes also deal with the place of occurrence. These codes range from E849 through E849.9. Although every place of occurrence is a little hard to develop codes for, they have been grouped together. Take code E849.6 (public building); this code is intended for all buildings that are used by the general public. Examples of this would be restaurants, schools, theaters, airport, banks, churches, and the like.

PRACTICE EXERCISE 13-1

Code the following.

1. Pedestrian injured in a motor vehicle accident involving a collision with a train

   Code(s) _____

2. The rider of an animal-drawn vehicle being thrown from the vehicle at a racecourse

   Code(s) _____

3. Drowning of a crew member due to accidental fall from a ship

   Code(s) _____

4. Accident to a crewmember due to an explosion in the boiler room on a steamship at sea.

   Code(s) _____

5. Accident to a passenger of a train, caused by a fallen tree on the railway

   Code(s) _____

Accidental Falls, Fire, and Flames

Most codes within this section include the mandatory fourth digit. In reporting accidental injuries, you may report more than one code to give exact descriptions of whom the injury happened to, how the injury occurred, and where the injury occurred. As in code E883 (fall into hole or other opening in surface) would apply to any cavity, pit, hole, or shaft, and does not require a fourth digit. But code E884 (other fall from one level to another) reports the exact item the patient fell from, such as a cliff, chair, or bed, necessitating the fourth digit. When coding for fire and flames, you may report where the fire was located (E890) along with the cause of the fire (E891.3).

PRACTICE EXERCISE 13-2

Code the following.

1. Accidental burn caused by a bonfire at home

   Code(s) _____

2. Accidental fall from a window of an apartment building

   Code(s) _____

3. Accidental fall caused by pushing and shoving by another person at a stadium

   Code(s) _____

4. Explosion caused by conflagration at a factory

   Code(s) _____

5. Fire caused by smoking a cigarette in bed

   Code(s) _____

Natural and Environmental Factors

Codes within this section are used to report injuries caused by nature and the environment. These include injuries due to heat, cold, hunger, and thirst, among others. Codes that do not include a fourth digit are three digit codes only.

PRACTICE EXERCISE 13-3

Code the following.

1. Injury caused by a tornado

   Code(s) _____

2. Injury caused by a jellyfish on the beach

   Code(s) _____

3. Injury caused by a sudden change in air pressure while flying in an airplane

Code(s) _____

4. Sunstroke

Code(s) _____

5. Injury caused by a dog bite in a backyard

Code(s) _____

Submersion, Suffocation, Foreign Bodies, and Other Accidents

Codes that deal with submersion, suffocation, and foreign bodies are usually those injuries associated with children. Codes listed under "Other Accidents" are injuries that happen in the workplace or at home. These accidental injuries involve machinery, household appliances, hot liquids, and even radiation.

PRACTICE EXERCISE 13-4

Code the following.

1. Accidental injury caused by a circular saw, at work

Code(s) _____

2. Accidental burn caused by teapot, at home while pouring tea

Code(s) _____

3. Accidental suffocation by a plastic bag

Code(s) _____

4. Accident caused by a sewing machine

Code(s) _____

5. Injury caused by falling rock while at a mountain resort

Code(s) _____

ACCIDENTAL POISONING AND ADVERSE EFFECTS

Codes within these sections report accidental poisoning from drugs, chemicals, and even food. They can be used to report the wrong drug taken, given, or overdosed. Poisonings are listed in two places within the CPT-4 manual. The first location is within the E-codes, and the second location is in the Table of Drugs and Chemicals, which is Section II of the CPT-4 manual. When using Encoder Pro, you must enter *poisoning* within the Search box and know exactly what type of drug or chemical is the cause. The more extensive list within the CPT-4 manual is within the Table of Drugs and Chemicals. To learn to correctly report these codes, let's take a look at the E-codes. This section lists the drugs by the classification. The Table of Drugs and Chemicals lists the drugs alphabetically, which is easier to use. It also lists the external cause, which includes poisoning, accident, therapeutic use, suicide, assault, and undetermined. Accidental poisoning is defined as the accidental overdose of a wrong substance, given or taken. When coding for poisonings, you must code for the cause of the poisoning (980–989). Therapeutic use of a drug is the correct administration of the drug that caused an adverse effect. A suicide attempt is considered a self-inflicted injury. Injuries that are categorized as an assault are those inflicted by another person with the intent to injure or even kill. "Undetermined" should be used only if the cause of the injury or poisoning cannot be determined to be self-inflicted or accidental.

Let's look at an example. Find the code for nitrogen gas poisoning, E869.0. As you can see listed in the Table of Drugs and Chemicals, the code for the actual chemical is 987.2, but the accidental poisoning is code E869.0. There is no code for nitrogen gas listed under the heading of Therapeutic Use because there is no therapeutic use for this chemical. Therefore, the cause of the injury must be considered an accident; suicide attempt, or assault or it has not been determined. So let's practice coding.

PRACTICE EXERCISE 13-5

Code the following.

1. Poisoning caused by ingesting shrimp

    Code(s) _____

2. Accidental poisoning by ampicillin

    Code(s) _____

3. Accidental poisoning caused by cosmetics

    Code(s) _____

4. Accidental poisoning caused by taking digoxin

    Code(s) _____

5. Accidental poisoning caused by the tetanus vaccine

    Code(s) _____

Misadventure to Patients During Surgery and Medical Care

When you think about a surgical procedure, you tend to think only of the procedure itself. But, in reality, a lot of surgical instruments and equipment are used. Many things can go wrong with these, such as equipment failure, lack of sterilization, and even an accidental cut or hemorrhage during surgery. This section includes all of the misadventures that can possibly happen to any patient during surgery and aftercare.

PRACTICE EXERCISE 13-6

Code the following.

1. Mechanical failure of a transfusion

   Code(s) _____

2. Mismatched blood in transfusion

   Code(s) _____

3. Accidental perforation during endoscopic examination

   Code(s) _____

4. Mechanical instrument failure during heart catheterization

   Code(s) _____

5. Performance of an inappropriate operation

   Code(s) _____

Surgical and Medical Procedure as the Cause of Abnormal Reaction or Later Complication without Misadventure at the Time of Procedure

Patients who undergo surgery often experience side effects, which can cause abnormal reactions. This section includes those misadventures and complications due to surgery. It does not include complications caused by the administration of anesthesia, that was properly administered (E937.0–E938.9).

PRACTICE EXERCISE 13-7

Code the following.

1. Later complications of a heart transplant

   Code(s) _____

2. Abnormal reaction to a urinary catheterization

   Code(s) _____

3. Complication after the amputation of an arm

   Code(s) _____

HOMICIDE AND INJURY INFLICTED BY OTHER PERSONS, LEGAL INTERVENTION

Codes within the section of homicide and injury are strictly those injuries that are inflicted by another person whose main intent is to injure or kill. These codes include every type of weapon and category of perpetrator who is inflicting the injury. Codes that use words such as "assault" are considered an injury and not homicide. Legal intervention codes refer to injuries due to a legal action. These would include an arrest or maintaining order on the part of any law enforcement agency, including military, that inflicts injury upon another person.

PRACTICE EXERCISE 13-8

Code the following.

1. Assault by a stab wound to the chest at a nightclub

   Code(s) _____

2. Legal execution by electrocution at prison

   Code(s) _____

3. Assault during an unarmed fight on a golf course

   Code(s) _____

4. Injury due to legal intervention, by a revolver

   Code(s) _____

5. Death caused by unarmed fight

   Code(s) _____

Injury Undetermined Whether Accidental or Inflicted

Codes within this section are solely for the purpose of coding undetermined injuries. This includes injuries that are unintentional or not determined, attempted suicide, or an assault. If the cause of death is undetermined, it is reported by using code E989.

PRACTICE EXERCISE 13-9

Code the following.

1. Injury caused by a handgun

   Code(s) _____

2. Poisoning by taking tranquilizers at home

   Code(s) _____

3. Injuries at work caused by exhaust gas from a car in the garage

   Code(s) _____

4. Injury caused by jumping in front of a moving car

   Code(s) _____

5. Injury caused by a paintball gun at the playground

Code(s) _____

Injury Resulting from Operations of War and Terrorism

Codes that deal with injuries resulting from war are used to code those injuries inflicted on civilians. They may also be used to report injuries to military personnel, but they must be injuries during the time of war operations. Death resulting from those injuries should be reported using code E999.0. When reporting acts of terrorism, these injuries must result from unlawful use of violence against another person or property. This includes the coercion of a government or civilian population. To report a death caused by terrorism, code E999.1 should be reported.

PRACTICE EXERCISE 13-10

Code the following.

1. Injury due to biological warfare during time of war

Code(s) _____

2. Terrorism involving an aircraft as a weapon

Code(s) _____

3. Terrorism caused by the use of anthrax

Code(s) _____

4. Injury resulting in death, caused by artillery shell

Code(s) _____

5. Injury caused by war, after cessation of hostilities

Code(s) _____

CHAPTER REVIEW

I. True/False

Indicate whether the sentence or statement is true or false.

____ **1.** E-Codes are not intended to be used as a primary code.

____ **2.** When reporting poisonings, you must report the cause of the poisoning.

____ **3.** Injuries that are inflicted by another person would be listed under the heading of "misadventure."

____ **4.** Poisonings are listed in two separate sections of the CPT manual.

____ **5.** A barge is considered a watercraft.

___ **6.** Patients who undergo surgery may experience side effects that can cause abnormal reactions.

___ **7.** Words such as "assault" are never considered an injury.

___ **8.** Accidental poisoning is described as an accidental overdose of the wrong substance, given or taken.

II. Multiple Choice

Identify the letter of the code that best desribes the condition in question.

___ **9.** Accidental puncture during a surgical operation

a. E863.9   c. E862.2

b. E870.0   d. E883

___ **10.** Accidental fall into a well at home

a. E883.1   c. E890, E849

b. E883.1, E849.6   d. E883.1, E849.0

___ **11.** Heat exhaustion due to weather

a. E900   c. E919.6

b. E904.2   d. E913.0

___ **12.** Legal execution

a. E970   c. E978

b. E973   d. E972

___ **13.** Attempted suicide with a handgun

a. E 970   c. E965

b. E960   d. E955.0

___ **14.** Accidental drowning in a lake while swimming

a. E849.8   c. E849.4

b. E849.6, E910   d. E910, E849.8

III. Coding Exercises

Use an encoder or coding manuals to code the following.

15. Explosion aboard a commercial aircraft while taking off, injuring crew members

Code(s) _____

16. Injury caused by an x-ray machine

Code(s) _____

17. Fall from a tricycle at home, resulting in an injury

Code(s) _____

18. Accidental poisoning caused by mixing insecticides

Code(s) _____

19. Accident caused by fireworks

Code(s) _____

20. Accidental overdose of heroin taken at a nightclub

Code(s) _____

IV. Coding Cases

Code the following.

21. When on vacation in New York City, April decided to take a carriage ride around the park. While April was enjoying her ride, the horse got spooked and bolted. April fell off the carriage and injured her arm and leg.

Code(s) _____

22. Julianna was polishing her silverware, preparing for a special dinner she was giving. The more she polished, the more she became ill. She decided to go to the ER and as she left her home, she noticed her hands had became swollen and inflamed. Upon arrival at the ER, she had difficulty breathing. Dr. Hammond examined Julianna and gave her a good prognosis. She had accidentally poisoned herself with the polishing compound she was using to clean the silverware. He prescribed medication and told Julianna to return if the symptoms did not subside within a few hours.

Diagnosis: Accidental poisoning by polishing agents.

Code(s) _____

23. Jack and Jane decided to go skiing. Jane had never skied before, and decided to start at the kiddie slopes. Nevertheless, she fell off her ski and injured her ankle.

Code(s) _____

24. Kerry was in a motor vehicle accident three days ago and seemed fine. Today she feels dizzy and lightheaded. She telephones her physician to schedule an appointment. While speaking with the physician, he tells her it could be a late effect of the car accident she had three days ago.

Code(s) _____

25. Steve, John, and Abe decided to have some fun by going to a hockey game. When their team won, the crowd began to swarm the players. John fell as the crowd rushed over him onto the playing field.

Code(s) _____

26. While on a camping trip high in the mountains, Peter became very ill. He decided to go to a clinic at the bottom of the mountain in a small village. During the examination, the physician discovered Peter had never been camping there before.

Diagnosis: Mountain sickness due to a prolonged visit at high altitude

Code(s) _____

Chapter 14
Reimbursement

LEARNING OBJECTIVES

After completing this chapter, the learner should be able to:

- Identify components of an HCFA claim form
- Identify components of a UB92 claim form
- Understand the difference between Medicare Part A and Part B
- Understand the reimbursement process

UNDERSTANDING THE REIMBURSEMENT PROCESS

When a patient enters the physician's office, the usual routine is to inform the physician that the patient has arrived. But behind the scenes within the physician's office, many things have to happen before the patient enters to be examined. The insurance coverage for the patient has to be verified, along with the type of coverage for the patient. The coverage includes the amount of deductibles (amount of money patient must pay before insurance reimbursement), co-insurance (amount of money the insurance will not cover, usually 20%) and other pertinent information. Office personnel have to establish the type of health plan the patient has in force, such as an HMO or PPO, which are the largest types of health plans beside Medicare.

Types of Health Plans

Medicare is a federally funded health plan for persons 65 years of age and older or the medically disabled. It is commonly known as Social Security. This is because the money that funds Medicare is taken from the employee in payroll taxes by the employer and submitted to the Social Security Administration (SSA). In turn, SSA is responsible for handling the funds. Individuals who are covered under Medicare are called beneficiaries. The Medicare program itself consists of **Medicare Part A**, which pays for the hospital facility, home health care, skilled nursing facility, respite and hospice care and **Medicare Part B**, which pays for physician services, outpatient, hospital, laboratory services, and diagnostic and therapeutic services. Although Medicare is a federally funded program for healthcare, it does not include coverage for all services and procedures. Coverage must be deemed medically necessary.

Physicians might or might not participate in Medicare. Medicare **participating physicians (Par)** agree to accept an allowed charge as payment in full for their services. **Non-participating physicians (Non-Par)** are reimbursed at a lower rate of payment. The reimbursement from Medicare is posted on the Medicare web site (http://cms.hhs.gov/physicians/default.asp). This list contains all CPT codes that are payable for participating and non-participating physicians. This is called the Medicare **Fee Schedule**. The fee schedule is also printed in the Federal Register at http://www.access.gpo.gov.

Health Maintenance Organization

A Health Maintenance Organization (**HMO**) is a prepaid health care delivery system. Patients who are enrolled in an HMO must receive services from participating physicians, hospitals, and other providers contracted with the HMO network. Patients who seek services outside the HMO network are not covered under the network plan. Services may also require a pre-authorization from the HMO before coverage applies. Patients who are enrolled in an HMO also must pay a required fee (**co-pay**), which is an out-of-pocket expense collected when services are provided. This co-pay is usually higher when the patient seeks medical treatment from an emergency room rather than the network physician. The co-pay is usually waived if the patient is admitted into the hospital from the emergency room. In these cases, the hospital must contact the HMO within three days for authorization to treat the patient.

Preferred Provider Organization

A preferred provider organization (**PPO**) is another health care delivery system. It also contracts with physicians, hospitals, and other providers. This type of organization is different because it negotiates provider services at a discounted rate. Patients within the PPO network are required to make co-pays and may have a deductible. Deductibles are a patient's out-of-pocket expenses that must be paid before benefits begin. Co-pay is out-of-pocket expense paid by the patient each time services are rendered. Members of the PPO are allowed to seek services that are outside the organization, but must pay a higher co-pay and deductible. The reimbursement is also lower for services to an out-of-network provider.

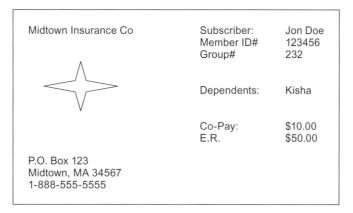

Figure 14-1 Sample insurance card

Insurance Identification Card

When a beneficiary of a health insurance organization receives an identification card, it contains information necessary for the provider to submit a claim to the insurance company (see Figure 14-1). This information includes the insured's name, identification number, and the date on which the coverage began. It also contains the type of coverage and amount of co-pay owed by the patient at the time services are rendered. Additional information might be the physician's name and telephone number if the coverage is an HMO plan. Some identification cards include a group number to identify a specific employer or coverage. When additional services are provided under the coverage, such as vision care, dental, or prescription coverage, these are also listed on the insurance card, along with the co-pay for each service. Located on the back of the insurance card is the address and telephone number of the insurance company. This is to let the provider know where to submit the claim and how to contact the carrier for verification of coverage. It is always good practice to copy both sides of the identification card and place the copies in the patient's medical record.

COMPLETING THE CMS-1500 CLAIM FORM

The 1500 claim form, formally known as the CMS 1500 and the HCFA claim form, is a paper claim submitted to insurance companies by the providers (see Figure 14–2). It is a standard form used for the purpose of submitting charges incurred by the patient. The claim forms are used to report a patient's diagnosis and physician services. The 1500 claim form is used to report services within an outpatient setting, while the UB-04 form identifies a hospital inpatient. Although this claim information is increasingly being transmitted electronically, it is always good to know the basic procedure for completing a claim form. So, let's get started.

Each box on the CMS-1500 claim form is numbered and includes the specific information that is needed to complete the form. Complete the form using the insurance card in Figure 14–1 and information given in Table 14–1.

Current Procedural Terminology (CPT) © 2006 American Medical Association. All Rights Reserved.

Figure 14-2 The CMS-1500 claim form (Courtesy of Centers for Medicare and Medicaid Services, www.cms.hhs.gov)

Current Procedural Terminology (CPT) © 2006 American Medical Association. All Rights Reserved.

Anesthesia Services

When a provider is an anesthesiologist, there is some additional or supplemental information that can be entered into the 1500 claim form. This should be entered into box 24 of the 1500 claim form. The supplemental information includes: the anesthesia duration in hours and minutes with the start and end times; narrative description of unspecified codes; identifiers for NDC (national drug codes), which is N4; vendor product number, which is VP; and Global Trade Item Number (GTIN), which is OZ. Some services do not have an identifier; in that case, enter two blank spaces before entering additional information. Refer to Figure 14-3 for specific examples of the claim form.

Explanation of Benefits (EOB)

An **explanation of benefits** is known as an EOB. Each time a claim is forwarded to an insurance company for payment, the insurance company sends back an explanation for each service provided for the patient. These EOBs will vary as to which information is given to the provider, but most will contain information needed to post the payment for the claim. Information that is necessary to post payments are the patient's name or patient's account number, the date(s) of service, procedure performed, any deductibles, co-pays, amount billed, amount approved, and payments made. Some include the patient balance. Insurance companies also include explanations (usually numeric) for denied, rejected, or downcoded claims. Other necessary information provided is the number of the check sent to the provider. This information should be included on each patient's account when posting payments. It is always necessary to include the check number when a claim is being appealed. An appeal is a formal request to the insurance company for reconsideration of payment for a specific claim. Claims that are denied will have a reason code given by the insurance company as for the denial. This is usually due to a lack of eligibility, the procedure not being a covered benefit, or the procedure not having been pre-authorized by the insurance company. Rejected claims may need missing information to adjudicate the claim. In these cases, the claim must be corrected and rebilled to the insurance company in a timely manner. All insurance companies have a specific time from the patient's date of service in which to submit the claim for payment. Each company will vary in its definition of timely filing, so it is important to submit claims immediately. Downcoding is when the insurance company pays the fee for a lesser CPT code but does not show that they have reduced the code itself to the lower-paid service. Always remember to check the CPT codes when posting payment to avoid overlooking a code that has been downcoded.

Remittance Advice

A **remittance advice (RA)** is an explanation of how electronically transmitted claims were adjudicated by the insurance company. The provider will receive the RA and the patient will receive the explanation of benefits. In any remittance advice is a claim control number, which is assigned by the provider when a claim is transmitted electronically. This claim control number contains the same information as stated above for an explanation of benefits.

TABLE 14-1 COMPLETING THE CMS-1500 FORM

Box 1	Indicate the type of health insurance by placing an X in the appropriate box.
Box 1a	Enter the insured's ID number. (123456)
Box 2	Enter the patient's name. (Doe, Jon)
Box 3	Enter patient's date of birth (MM/DD/CCYY) and sex (M).
Box 4	Enter the insured's full last name, first name, and middle initial. (Doe, John)
Box 5	Enter the patient's mailing address and telephone number. Do not use commas, periods, hyphens, or spaces as separators in the telephone number. Use a hyphen in the 9-digit zip code. (P.O. Box 132, Midtown MA 34567-0011 18885555555)
Box 6	Enter an X in the appropriate box to show the patient's relationship to the insured. The box signifying "Other" may include employee, ward, or dependent as identified by the insured's plan.
Box 7	Enter the insured's address, which may be different than the patient's address listed in box 5, and telephone number. (13366 N 65th Street, 18885555555)
Box 8	Enter X in the appropriate boxes for the patient's marital status and for whether the patient is employed or a student.
Box 9	When additional health care coverage exists, enter the insured's name (last, first, middle initial). If no additional coverage is present, leave this box blank.
Box 9a	Enter the policy or group number of the other insured.
Box 9b	Enter the other insured's date of birth (DOB and place an X to indicate the insured's sex.
Box 9c	Enter the other insured's employer's name or school name.
Box 9d	Enter the other insured's insurance plan or program name.
Box 10 a–c	Enter an X in the correct box to indicate whether one or more of the services are the result of a condition or injury that occurred. If injury is the result of an automobile accident, the state postal code must be shown.
Box 10d	When the payor requires the Condition Code, this box must be completed; otherwise, leave blank
Box 11	Enter the insured's policy or group number. (232)
Box 11a	Enter the insured's DOB (02-15-1984) and place an X to indicate the insured's sex.
Box 11b	Enter the insured's employer's name or school's name. (The ABC Refrigeration Group)
Box 11c	Enter the insured's plan or program name.
Box 11d	Place an X in the "Yes" box if 9 through 9d (Other insured) were completed.

Current Procedural Terminology (CPT) © 2006 American Medical Association. All Rights Reserved.

Box 12	Enter "Signature on File" or "SOF" and enter date the patient authorized release of information (usually on the patient's first encounter). If there is no signature on file, leave blank or enter "No Signature on File."
Box 13	Enter "Signature on File, SOF or No Signature on File" for authorizing payment.
Box 14	Enter the 6-digit or 8-digit date of the first date of the present illness, injury or pregnancy. For pregnancy, enter the date of the last menstrual period.
Box 15	Enter the first date the patient had the same or similar illness. Previous pregnancies are not considered a similar illness. Leave blank if unknown.
Box 16	If patient is employed and unable to work, a date for the "from-to" must be completed to show the dates that the patient is unable to work.
Box 17	Enter the name and credentials of the referring physician.
Box 17a	The other identification number of the referring provider should be entered in 17a. The qualifier indicating what the number represents should be reported in the qualifier field to the immediate right of 17a.

	Qualifier Codes	
	OB	State License number
	1B	Blue Shield Provider Number
	1C	Medicare Provider Number
	1D	Medicaid Provider Number
	1G	Provider UPIN Number
	1H	Champus Identification Number
	E1	Employer's Identification Number
	G2	Provider Commercial Number
	LU	Location Number
	N5	Provider Plan Network Identification Number
	SY	Social Security Number
	X5	State Industrial Accident Provider Number
	ZZ	Provider Taxonomy

Box 17b	Enter the HIPAA National Provider Identifier Number.
Box 18	Enter the hospital dates. (MM-DD-YY)
Box 19	Leave Blank.
Box 20	Enter an X in the YES box if billing for purchased services and charges (otherwise enter NO).
Box 21	Enter the patient's diagnosis.
Box 22	List the original reference number for resubmitted claims.

TABLE 14-1 (CONTINUED)

Box 23	Enter the authorization number, referral number, mammography precertification number or CLIA number.
Box 24	Enter the date of service "From" and "To." (MM-DD-YY) (03-27-07 to 03-27-07) If only one date of service is provided, you may leave "To" empty.
Box 24B	Enter the place of services (Outpatient office code is 11) that identifies where the services were rendered. Place of services codes are available at: www.cms.hhs.gov.
Box 24C	For whether services were an emergency, enter Y for yes and N for no. (Emergency as defined by federal, state, payer contracts)
Box 24D	Enter the CPT or HCPCS code and modifier, if applicable, for the effective date of service.
Box 24E	Enter the diagnosis code reference number that relates the date of service and the procedure performed to the primary diagnosis. When multiple services are performed, the primary reference number for each service should be listed first as 1 or a 2 or a 3 or a 4. Do not use commas between the numbers. (Diagnosis is 401.10 and 250.00)
Box 24F	Enter the charge for each listed service, without commas. If the number amount is a whole number, enter 00 in the cents area. (Procedure code 99213, charge is $135.00)
Box24G	Enter the number of days or units the services were provided. If reporting a fraction of a unit, use the decimal point. (Days 1)
Box 24H	For whether the claim is Early & Periodic Screening and Treatment related, enter Y for "Yes" or N for "No" in the unshaded area of the field.
Box 24I	Enter the qualifier identifying if the number is a non-NPI. The other ID# of the rendering provider should be reported in 24J. The qualifier number is the same as in 17a. There will always be providers without an NPI who will need to report the non-NPI identifiers on their claim forms.
Box 24J	The individual rendering the service should be reported in this field. (NPI is 0321)
Box 25	Enter the Federal Tax ID Number (Employer Identification Number or Social Security Number) of the provider. Enter an X in the appropriate box to indicate which number is being reported. (EIN is 326233)
Box 26	Enter the patient's account number if the provider has assigned one.
Box 27	Enter an X in the "YES" box to show the provider accepts assignment.

Current Procedural Terminology (CPT) © 2006 American Medical Association. All Rights Reserved.

Box 28	Enter the total charges for the services. (Charge $135.00)
Box 29	Enter the total amount paid by the patient or other providers. (Patient paid $10.00)
Box 30	Enter the balance due. (Balance due is $125.00)
Box 31	Enter the legal signature of the provider or representative. You may enter "SOF" or "Signature on File" and the date.
Box 32a–b	Enter the name and address of the location where services were provided into box 32. Enter the NPI number of the service facility location in 32a. Enter the two-digit qualifier as defined in box 17a.
Box 33	Enter the provider's billing name, address, and phone number.
Box 33a–b	Enter the NPI number of the billing provider into box 33a. Enter the two-digit qualifier identifying the non-NPI number, followed by the ID number.

TABLE 14-2 LIST OF DIAGNOSIS RELATED GROUPS

DRG	DRG TITLE
006	Carpal Tunnel Release
056	Rhinoplasty
060	Tonsillectomy &/or Adenoidectomy only, age 0 to 17 yr
128	Deep Vein Thrombophlebitis
128	Hypertension
143	Chest Pain
195	Cholecystectomy
232	Arthroscopy
238	Osteomyelitis
290	Thyroid Procedures
302	Kidney Transplant
316	Renal Failure
360	Vagina, Cervix & Vulva Procedures
440	Wound Debridement For Injuries
524	Transit Ischemia
531	Spinal Procedures

Current Procedural Terminology (CPT) © 2006 American Medical Association. All Rights Reserved.

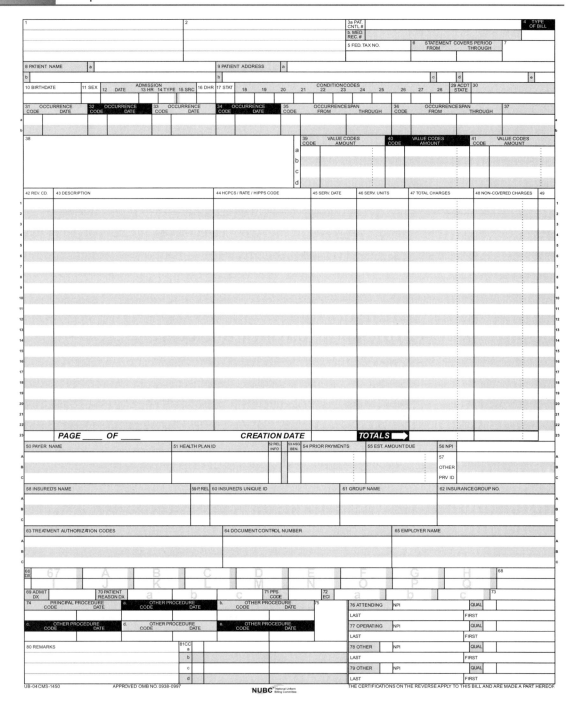

Figure 14-3 The UB-04 claim form (Courtesy of the National Uniform Billing Committee, www.nubc.org)

TABLE 14-3 COMPLETING THE UB-04 CLAIM FORM

Box 1	Enter the provider name, address, telephone, fax, and country code.
Box 2	Enter the name, address, and ID of the facility where the payment is to be sent.
Box 3a	Enter the patient control number (assigned by the facility).
Box 3b	Enter the patient medical record number.
Box 4	Enter the type of bill (refers to initial or rebill).
Box 5	Enter the federal tax number.
Box 6	Enter the date the statement covers (from date, to date).
Box 7	Leave blank.
Box 8a	Enter the patient identification.
Box 8b	Enter the patient name.
Box 9a	Enter the patient street.
Box 9b	Enter the patient city.
Box 9c	Enter the patient state.
Box 9d	Enter the patient zip code.
Box 9e	Enter the patient country code.
Box 10	Enter the patient date of birth.
Box 11	Enter patient sex (F—female, M—male).
Box 12	Enter the admission date in military time.
Box 13	Enter the admission hour in military time.
Box 14	Enter the type of admission or visit. (1—emergency, 2—urgent, 3—elective)
Box 15	Enter the source of admission. (1—physician referral, 2—clinic referral, 3—HMO, 4—transfer from a hospital, 5—transfer from SNF, 6—transfer from another facility, 7—emergency room)
Box 16	Enter the discharge hour in military time.
Box 17	Enter the patient's discharge status. (01—routine to home, 03—discharge to SNF, 05—home with home health care, 07—left against medical advice, 20—expired)
Box 18–28	Enter the condition codes.
Box 29	Enter the accident state.
Box 30	Leave blank.

TABLE 14-3 (CONTINUED)

Box 31–34	Enter the occurrence code and date. (01—auto accident, 04—employer related accident, 11—onset of symptoms)
Box 35–36	Enter the occurrence span code from date to date.
Box 37	Leave blank.
Box 38	Enter the name and address of the person responsible for payment.
Box 39a–c	Enter the value code and amount.
Box 40a–c	Enter the value code and amount.
Box 41a–c	Enter the value code and amount.
Box 42	Enter the revenue code.
Box 43	Enter the description of service provided.
Box 44	Enter the HCPCS.
Box 45	Enter the service date.
Box 46	Enter the number of units of service.
Box 47	Enter the total charges.
Box 48	Enter the non-covered charges.
Box 49	Leave blank.
Box 50	Enter the primary, secondary, and then tertiary insurance.
Box 51	Enter the Health plan ID.
Box 52	Enter the release of information for primary, secondary, and tertiary insurance.
Box 53	Enter the assignments of benefits for primary, secondary, and tertiary insurance.
Box 54	Enter prior payments from primary, secondary, and tertiary insurance.
Box 55	Enter the estimated amount due from the primary, secondary, and tertiary insurance.
Box 56	Enter the NPI.
Box 57	Enter the primary, secondary, and tertiary providers' ID numbers.
Box 58	Enter the primary, secondary, and tertiary insureds' names.
Box 59	Enter the patient's relationship, primary, secondary, and tertiary.
Box 60	Enter the insured unique ID, primary, secondary, and tertiary.
Box 61	Enter the insurance group name for the primary, secondary, and tertiary.

Box 62	Enter the insurance group number for the primary, secondary, and tertiary.
Box 64	Enter the document control number.
Box 65	Enter the employer name, primary, secondary, and tertiary.
Box 66	Enter the diagnosis version qualifier.
Box 67	Enter the principal diagnosis code.
Box 67a–q	Enter any other diagnoses.
Box 68	Leave blank.
Box 70	Enter the patient's reason for the visit code.
Box 71	Enter the PPS code.
Box 72	Enter the external cause of injury code.
Box 73	Leave blank.
Box 74	Enter the Primary procedure code and date.
Box 75a–e	Enter any other procedures codes and dates.
Box 76	Enter the attending physician's ID. (Last name then first name)
Box 77	Enter the operating physician's ID. (Last name then first name)
Box 78–79	Enter ID and name of any other physician who treated the patient.
Box 80	Leave blank.
Box 81a–d	Enter the qualifying then value code

Diagnosis Related Group

A **diagnosis related group (DRG)** is a group of patients with a similar diagnosis or conditions. This is a classification system used by hospitals and based on a relative value guide. Each related group is assigned a DRG code, as seen in Table 14–2, which is equal to a certain value by which reimbursement is calculated. These groups are based on calculations made from the patient's age, sex, diagnosis, comorbidities, and complications.

COMPLETING THE UB-04 CLAIM FORM

The UB-04 claim, formerly known as the UB-92, is primarily used for hospital inpatients (see Figure 14–3). Although not all hospitals use the same reporting of diagnoses and procedures, most hospitals use the revenue codes for the DRG payment plan. More and more hospitals are now strictly using the HCPCS codes for reimbursements. Table 14–3 lists the step-by-step instructions for completing the UB-04 Claim Form.

Current Procedural Terminology (CPT) © 2006 American Medical Association. All Rights Reserved.

This UB-04 form is slightly different from the old UB-92 claim form. It provides more detailed information related to the patient's hospital stay. These claim forms are transmitted electronically to those payors who can receive electronic transmission. Payments on transmitted claims are received in approximately two weeks, compared to submitting claims manually. Insurance companies have, by law, one month to respond to a claim once it is received.

CHAPTER REVIEW

I. True or False

Read each statement and decide whether it is true or false.

____ 1. Deductibles are a patient's out-of-pocket expenses.

____ 2. The UB-04 claim form is for outpatient billing.

____ 3. You should always use hyphens and commas when completing a UB-04 claim form.

____ 4. An EOB is the same as an explanation of benefits.

____ 5. Rejected claims may have missing information needed to adjudicate the claim.

____ 6. Claims are never downcoded.

____ 7. There is sometimes a claim control number in a remittance advice.

____ 8. Insurance companies have 45 days to respond to a claim.

____ 9. Medicare Part A pays for outpatient services.

____ 10. Medicare is federally funded.

II. Matching

Match the correct claim form to the correct box information

    a. UB-04   b. 1500 claim form

____ 11. Box 5, federal tax number

____ 12. Box 25, federal tax number

____ 13. Box 11, insured's policy or group number

____ 14. Box 24, date of service

____ 15. Box 9b, insured's date of birth

____ 16. Box 1, provider name

____ 17. Box 30, balance due

____ 18. Box 46, number of units

____ 19. Box 51, health plan ID number

____ 20. Box 2, patient's name

Appendix:
Practice Exercises

These exercises may or may not include the use of codes from chapters or body systems covered in this workbook. This appendix may be used as additional practice exercises or as quizzes to test your ability to properly code procedures. All exercises may be coded using coding manuals or an encoder program for extra practice. Answers are given in the instructor's manual.

Name _____

Date _____

PRACTICE EXERCISE 1: EVALUATION AND MANAGEMENT

Code the following cases using an encoder or coding manuals.

1. A new patient presented to the office of Dr. James. After completing a detailed history and examination, Dr. James determined this new patient has a severe upper respiratory infection.

   Code _____

2. During a brawl at the local tavern, Dean received a hit on the head with a chair. He went to an area emergency department for a severe headache. While in the ER, the physician on call performed a problem focused history and examination, placed three sutures within the occipital lobe, and released Dean.

   Code _____

3. Tammy has been a patient of Dr. Carlos's for the past three years. Recently, she has developed a mild skin irritation on her left arm. Dr. Carlos was called to the nursing home to examine the rash on Tammy's arm.

   Code _____

4. Mr. and Mrs. Lawson recently had their first child, who is now six months old. Mrs. Lawson took the infant to see Dr. Henry for their annual check-up. After examination, Dr. Henry concluded the infant was a normal, healthy six-month-old.

   Code _____

5. Dr. Tom spent one hour on the phone with other health professionals coordinating care for an established patient. This was a team conference.

   Code _____

6. A patient was brought into the Emergency Department for treatment related to a myocardial infarction.

   Code _____

7. A patient presented to the emergency department after falling off a two-story building he was working on. The patient complained of severe back, head, and neck pain. The attending physician performed a comprehensive history and examination and ordered multiple x-rays of each of the three areas. After reviewing the interpretation, the physician determined the patient had a mild concussion and a fracture of the cervical spine at the C-2 level.

   Code _____

8. Jenny has had a problem with her gallbladder for the past six months. She has recently seen her physician, who referred her to Dr. Capps, a general surgeon. After Dr. Capps consulted with Jenny's physician for 30 minutes, they both determined to schedule surgery to remove the gallbladder.

   Code _____

9. Deanna presented to her physician to remove six sutures on her arm. At the office, the nurse removed the sutures.

Code _____

10. Mr. Hobbs went to see Dr. Denton for a renewal on his blood pressure medication.

Code _____

Name _____

Date _____

PRACTICE EXERCISE 2: EVALUATION AND MANAGEMENT

I. Matching

Match the modifier with the correct procedure.

    a. 50   e. 21
    b. 57   f. 51
    c. 26   g. 80
    d. 54   h. 66

___ **1.** Prolonged evaluation and management

___ **2.** Surgical team

___ **3.** Professional component

___ **4.** Bilateral procedures

___ **5.** Assistant surgeon

___ **6.** Surgical care only

___ **7.** Decision for surgery

___ **8.** Multiple procedures

II. Coding

Code the following cases using an encoder or coding manuals.

 9. Simple repair, wound, extremities 8.0 cm

   Code(s) _____

10. Incision and drainage, leg, hematoma

   Code(s) _____

11. Arthrodesis, lateral extracavitary technique, including minimal diskectomy to prepare interspace, thoracic

   Code(s) _____

12. Repair of nail bed

   Code(s) _____

13. Excision, tumor, soft tissue of back

   Code(s) _____

14. Open treatment of patellar dislocation, without patellectomy

   Code(s) _____

15. Mastotomy with exploration of abscess, deep

   Code(s) _____

16. Excision, excessive skin and subcutaneous tissue, both legs

    Code(s) _____

17. Incision and drainage, complex, postoperative wound infection

    Code(s) _____

18. Full thickness graft, free, including direct closure of donor site, trunk; 40 sq cm

    Code(s) _____

19. Arthroplasty, temporomandibular joint, with autograft

    Code(s) _____

Name _____

Date _____

PRACTICE EXERCISE 3: CPT ANESTHESIA AND MUSCULOSKELETAL

Code the following cases using an encoder or coding manuals.

1. Application, cast, figure eight, long arm, shoulder to hand

   Code(s) _____

2. Open treatment of calcaneal fracture with internal fixation and removal of foreign body, complicated

   Code(s) _____

3. Arthroscopy; knee, diagnostic, without synovial biopsy

   Code(s) _____

4. Osteotomy, femur, supracondylar; without fixation, bilateral

   Code(s) _____

5. Release of a hamstring, proximal

   Code(s) _____

6. Arthrodesis, anterior interbody technique, including minimal diskectomy to prepare interspace; thoracic (T-5,6,7) including Lumbar (L-1,3,5), with anesthesia

   Code(s) _____

7. Reconstruction of mandibular rami, horizontal, without graft

   Code(s) _____

8. Electrical stimulation to aid bone healing; noninvasive

   Code(s) _____

9. Intubation, emergency procedure

   Code(s) _____

10. Strapping of the ankle and foot

    Code(s) _____

11. Manipulation of the knee, with traction, under general anesthesia

    Code(s) _____

12. Release of two intrinsic muscles of the hand

    Code(s) _____

13. Fracture, elbow; open treatment with internal fixation, fracture of proximal end of ulna, with dislocation of radial head

    Code(s) _____

14. Kyphectomy, circumferential exposure of spine and resection of three vertebral segments with posterior arthrodesis, with casting

    Code(s) _____

15. Reconstruction of orbital walls, rims forehead nasoethmoid complex following intra- and extracranial excision of benign tumor of cranial bone, with multiple autografts, total area 35 sq cm, with orbital prosthesis made by an outside laboratory

Code(s) _____

Name _____

Date _____

PRACTICE EXERCISE 4: CPT ANESTHESIA

Code the following cases using an encoder or coding manuals.

1. Anesthesia for a femoral artery ligation, including a bypass graft of the upper leg

   Code(s) _____

2. Anesthesia on a patient with a severe systemic disease for a bone marrow aspiration and biopsy on the anterior iliac crest

   Code(s) _____

3. Anesthesia on a one-year-old, who is not expected to live, for an intracranial subdural tap

   Code(s) _____

4. Anesthesia for a diagnostic arteriography

   Code(s) _____

5. Anesthesia given to an 89-year-old man, burned over 20% of his total body

   Code(s) _____

6. Anesthesia for a heart-lung transplant

   Code(s) _____

7. Anesthesia on a patient with a mild systemic disease for a needle biopsy of the thyroid

   Code(s) _____

8. Anesthesia for a sternal debridement on a patient who suffered a coronary during the initial procedure, who was otherwise healthy

   Code(s) _____

9. Anesthesia for electroconvulsive therapy

   Code(s) _____

10. Anesthesia on a one-year-old healthy infant for a repair of a cleft palate. The procedure took 2 hr in Miami, Florida. Procedure has a basic value of 2.

    Code(s) _____

11. Anesthesia given to a patient with a severe systemic disease for a percutaneous liver biopsy. The procedure has a basic value of 2 and took 15 min to perform, in Vermont.

    Code(s) _____

Name _____

Date _____

PRACTICE EXERCISE 5: CPT INTEGUMENTARY SYSTEM

Code the following cases using an encoder or coding manuals.

1. Simple repair, superficial wound; extremities, 7.8 cm

   Code(s) _____

2. Removal of skin tag, abdominal area, 17 lesions

   Code(s) _____

3. Mastopexy

   Code(s) _____

4. Full thickness graft, free, including closure of donor site, cheeks, 23 sq cm

   Code(s) _____

5. Puncture aspiration of abscess, cyst, without guidance

   Code(s) _____

6. Anesthesia for arthroscopic procedure of foot and ankle

   Code(s) _____

7. Excision of benign tumor; arm, 2.5 cm, with complex reconstruction repair

   Code(s) _____

8. Anesthesia for bone marrow aspiration and biopsy, posterior iliac crest

   Code(s) _____

9. Fine needle aspiration with imaging guidance

   Code(s) _____

10. Excision, ischial ulcer, with primary suture

    Code(s) _____

11. Reconstruction of nail bed with graft, right hand, fourth digit

    Code(s) _____

12. Excision, malignant lesion, including margins, three lesions, 1.0 cm, .05 cm, and 1.2 cm, neck

    Code(s) _____

13. Anesthesia for open repair of malunion of humerus

    Code(s) _____

14. Insertion, implantable contraceptive capsules

    Code(s) _____

15. Radical mastectomy; including pectoral muscles, axillary lymph nodes

    Code(s) _____

16. Removal of tissue expander, without insertion of prothesis

Code(s) _____

17. Initial incision of escharotomy

Code(s) _____

18. Incision and drainage of a complex postoperative wound infection

Code(s) _____

Name _____

Date _____

PRACTICE EXERCISE 6: CPT MUSCULOSKELETAL SYSTEM

Code the following cases using an encoder or coding manuals.

1. Replantation of the right foot for complete amputation, under general anesthesia
   Code(s) _____
2. Closed treatment of three rib fractures, uncomplicated
   Code(s) _____
3. Excision of torus mandibularis
   Code(s) _____
4. Excision of an abdominal wall tumor 3.0 cm, under anesthesia
   Code(s) _____
5. Tendonesis of long tendon of the right biceps
   Code(s) _____
6. Removal of a foreign body located in the pelvis, subcutaneous
   Code(s) _____
7. Exploration of penetrating wound of the neck, separate procedure
   Code(s) _____
8. Exploration of a penetrating wound of the chest, separate procedure
   Code(s) _____
9. Exploration of a penetrating wound of the abdomen, separate procedure
   Code(s) _____
10. Exploration of a penetrating wound on an extremity, separate procedure
    Code(s) _____
11. Excision of epiphyseal bar, with autogenous soft tissue graft obtained through the same fascial incision
    Code(s) _____
12. Superficial biopsy of a muscle
    Code(s) _____
13. Biopsy of a deep muscle
    Code(s) _____
14. Biopsy of the sternum using a trocar, superficial
    Code(s) _____
15. Biopsy of a bone; open, superficial, of the ilium
    Code(s) _____

16. Biopsy, open, of the vertebral body; thoracic

   Code(s) _____

17. Biopsy of the cervical vertebral body, open

   Code(s) _____

18. Therapeutic injection of the sinus tract, as a separate procedure

   Code(s) _____

19. Diagnostic sonogram of the sinus tract

   Code(s) _____

20. Removal of a foreign body in the tendon sheath; simple

   Code(s) _____

21. Complicated removal of a foreign body in a muscle

   Code(s) _____

22. Therapeutic injection for carpal tunnel

   Code(s) _____

Name _____

Date _____

PRACTICE EXERCISE 7: CPT MUSCULOSKELETAL SYSTEM

Code the following cases using an encoder or coding manuals.

1. Aspiration of a three-ganglion cyst
   Code(s) _____

2. Application of a femoral halo
   Code(s) _____

3. Removal of an external fixation system, under anesthesia
   Code(s) _____

4. Cartilage graft; nasal septum
   Code(s) _____

5. Bone graft
   Code(s) _____

6. Low density stimulation to aid bone healing; noninvasive
   Code(s) _____

7. Arthrotomy, temporomandibular joint
   Code(s) _____

8. Radical resection of malignant tumor, soft tissue on the face
   Code(s) _____

9. Excision of a facial bone for a bone abscess
   Code(s) _____

10. Excision of torus mandibularis
    Code(s) _____

11. Application of an oral surgical splint
    Code(s) _____

12. Reduction of the forehead; contouring only
    Code(s) _____

13. Reconstruction by contouring of a benign tumor of the cranial bone
    Code(s) _____

14. Arthroplasty of the temporomandibular joint with an allograft
    Code(s) _____

15. Secondary revision of orbitocraniofacial reconstruction
    Code(s) _____

16. Osteotomy, mandible, segmental with genioglossus advancement

Code(s) _____

17. Closed treatment of a nasal bone fracture, without manipulation

Code(s) _____

18. Closed treatment of a skull fracture, without operation

Code(s) _____

19. Closed treatment of a nasal bone fracture, with stabilization

Code(s) _____

20. Open treatment of nasoethmoid fracture, without external fixation

Code(s) _____

21. Open treatment of a depressed frontal sinus fracture

Code(s) _____

22. Open treatment of an orbital fracture, without implant (except blowout)

Code(s) _____

Name _____

Date _____

PRACTICE EXERCISE 8: CPT MUSCULOSKELETAL SYSTEM

Code the following cases using an encoder or coding manuals.

1. Percutaneous treatment of a fracture of malar area, including zygomatic arch and malar tripod, with manipulation
   Code(s) _____

2. Closed treatment of a mandibular fracture with interdental fixation
   Code(s) _____

3. Closed treatment of a temporomandibular dislocation with a wire fixation
   Code(s) _____

4. Radical resection of a tumor located in the soft tissue of the thorax
   Code(s) _____

5. Partial excision of a rib
   Code(s) _____

6. Excision of the first cervical rib, with sympathectomy
   Code(s) _____

7. Sternal debridement
   Code(s) _____

8. Hyoid myotomy and suspension
   Code(s) _____

9. Division of scalenus anticus, with resection of a cervical rib
   Code(s) _____

10. Reconstructive repair of pectus excavatum; open
    Code(s) _____

11. Uncomplicated closed treatment of one rib fracture
    Code(s) _____

12. Closed treatment of a fracture to the sternum
    Code(s) _____

13. Posterior arthrodesis of L4–S1, utilizing morselized autogenous iliac bone graft, harvested through separate fascial incision and pedicle screw fixation
    Code(s) _____

Name _____

Date _____

PRACTICE EXERCISE 9: CPT RESPIRATORY

Code the following cases using an encoder or coding manuals.

1. Thoracotomy, limited, for biopsy lung

   Code(s) _____

2. Excision of nasal polyp, simple

   Code(s) _____

3. Total lung removal

   Code(s) _____

4. Surgical endoscopy, with sphenoidotomy of the nasal tissue

   Code(s) _____

5. Laryngoscopy, direct, operative, with biopsy

   Code(s) _____

6. Removal of a foreign body, intranasal, requiring anesthesia, general

   Code(s) _____

7. Emergency tracheostomy; transtracheal

   Code(s) _____

8. Rhinectomy; partial

   Code(s) _____

9. Submucous resection, with cartilage scoring

   Code(s) _____

10. Therapeutic pneumothorax

    Code(s) _____

11. Pneumonostomy; with open drainage of abscess

    Code(s) _____

12. Total lung lavage, unilateral

    Code(s) _____

13. Complex nasal hemorrhage control, anterior with packing

    Code(s) _____

14. Sinus endoscopy, surgical, with biopsy and dacryocystorhinostomy

    Code(s) _____

15. Intubation, endotracheal, as an emergency procedure

    Code(s) _____

16. Removal of lung, total pneumonectomy

Code(s) _____

_____

Name _____

Date _____

PRACTICE EXERCISE 10: CPT RESPIRATORY AND CARDIOVASCULAR

Code the following cases using an encoder or coding manuals.

1. Splenectomy; total

   Code(s) _____

2. Bone marrow; aspiration only

   Code(s) _____

3. Removal of mediastinal tumor

   Code(s) _____

4. Coronary artery bypass, vein only, five coronary venous grafts

   Code(s) _____

5. Pericardiocentesis; initial

   Code(s) _____

6. Insertion of permanent pacemaker with transvenous electrodes; atrial and ventricular

   Code(s) _____

7. Pulmonary endarterectomy, with embolectomy, with cardiopulmonary bypass

   Code(s) _____

8. Insertion of intra-aortic balloon assist device through the ascending aorta

   Code(s) _____

9. Repair of blood vessel with vein graft; lower extremity

   Code(s) _____

10. Bypass graft; vein, using synthetic graft; axillary-femoral

    Code(s) _____

Name _____

Date _____

PRACTICE EXERCISE 11: CPT DIGESTIVE SYSTEM

Code the following cases using an encoder or coding manuals.

1. Glossectomy; composite procedure with resection of the floor of the mouth and mandibular resection, without radical neck dissection

   Code(s) _____

2. Change of a gastrostomy tube

   Code(s) _____

3. Total hepatectomy; left lobectomy with a liver allotransplantation; orthotopic from a living donor

   Code(s) _____

4. Repair of a lumbar hernia

   Code(s) _____

5. Excision of a lesion of mesentery, with a single resection of the small intestine

   Code(s) _____

6. Gastric bypass for morbid obesity, with short limb

   Code(s) _____

7. Chemical destruction of a lesion of the vestibule of the mouth

   Code(s) _____

8. Placement of a nasogastric tube by a physician, with fluoroscopic guidance

   Code(s) _____

9. Total colectomy; abdominal, with ileostomy

   Code(s) _____

10. Ligation of multiple internal hemorrhoids

    Code(s) _____

11. Excision of a sacrococcygeal tumor

    Code(s) _____

12. Exploration and biopsy of the colon

    Code(s) _____

13. Diagnostic endoscopy, with delivery of thermal energy of the lower esophageal sphincter for treatment of gastroesophageal reflux disease

    Code(s) _____

Name _____

Date _____

PRACTICE EXERCISE 12: CPT URINARY SYSTEM

Code the following cases using an encoder or coding manuals.

1. Manometric studies through nephrostomy, with radiologic supervision

   Code(s) _____

2. Cystourethroscopy, with biopsy

   Code(s) _____

3. Aspiration of bladder by needle

   Code(s) _____

4. Renal allotransplantation, implantation of graft with recipient nephrectomy

   Code(s) _____

5. Dilation of female urethra, including suppository and instillation; initial

   Code(s) _____

6. Cystotomy; for simple excision of bladder diverticulum, multiple procedures

   Code(s) _____

7. Laparoscopy, surgical; ureterolithotomy

   Code(s) _____

8. Suture of kidney wound

   Code(s) _____

9. Drainage of perirenal abscess

   Code(s) _____

10. Aspiration and injection of renal cyst by needle

    Code(s) _____

Name _____

Date _____

PRACTICE EXERCISE 13: CPT OBSTETRICS

Code the following cases using an encoder or coding manuals.

1. Colposcopy of the vulva, with biopsy
   Code(s) _____

2. Colposcopy of the vulva, with six biopsies
   Code(s) _____

3. Fitting and insertion of a pessary
   Code(s) _____

4. Removal of cerclage sutures, under anesthesia
   Code(s) _____

5. Colposcopy of the cervix, with a biopsy
   Code(s) _____

6. Total abdominal hysterectomy, with an anterior/posterior colporrhaphy and an enterocele repair
   Code(s) _____

7. The marsupialization of a Bartholin's gland cyst
   Code(s) _____

8. Partial removal of the vaginal wall, vaginectomy
   Code(s) _____

9. Vaginal removal of a 230 gm uterus
   Code(s) _____

10. Treatment of a septic abortion that was completed surgically
    Code(s) _____

11. External cephalic version without tocolysis. Code only the version.
    Code(s) _____

12. Treatment of an incomplete abortion that was treated surgically during the second trimester
    Code(s) _____

13. Unlisted procedure, maternity care and delivery
    Code(s) _____

14. Cauterization and introduction of contrast for a hysterosalpingography
    Code(s) _____

15. Cesarean delivery with postpartum care, and a ligation of fallopian tubes done at the same operative session

    Code(s) _____

16. Diagnostic hysteroscopy

    Code(s) _____

17. D&C performed on a patient with dysfunctional uterine bleeding

    Code(s) _____

18. Drainage of left ovarian cyst, abdominal approach

    Code(s) _____

19. The patient presents with a perineal abscess of the vulva. The physician performs an incision and drainage.

    Code(s) _____

20. The patient is undergoing clinical brachytherapy and has an insertion of Heyman capsules.

    Code(s) _____

21. The physician performs a surgical laparoscopy with fimbrioplasty.

    Code(s) _____

22. Colpocentesis

    Code(s) _____

23. Surgical hysteroscopy with lysis of multiple intrauterine adhesions

    Code(s) _____

24. A patient who has delivered twice by means of cesarean section receives complete obstetrical care and vaginal delivery services that include the postpartum care.

    Code(s) _____

25. Amniocentesis. Code only the procedure, not the radiological service.

    Code(s) _____

26. Vaginal delivery with episiotomy and use of forceps

    Code(s) _____

27. Dilation and curettage of cervical stump

    Code(s) _____

28. Intrauterine cordocentesis. Do not code the radiological portion of the procedure.

    Code(s) _____

29. Induced abortion by dilation and evacuation

    Code(s) _____

30. Antepartum care only after vaginal delivery, eight visits

    Code(s) _____

Name _____

Date _____

PRACTICE EXERCISE 14: CPT GENITAL SYSTEM

Code the following cases using an encoder or coding manuals.

1. Inguinal exploration for undescended testis
   Code(s) _____

2. Antepartum care for five visits
   Code(s) _____

3. Fetal shunt placement, including ultrasound guidance
   Code(s) _____

4. Electroejaculation
   Code(s) _____

5. Fitting and insertion of an intravaginal support device
   Code(s) _____

6. Laser surgery for destruction of a lesion of the penis; simple
   Code(s) _____

7. Diagnostic amniocentesis
   Code(s) _____

8. Vaginal hysterectomy, with removal of tubes and ovary
   Code(s) _____

9. Bilateral vesiculotomy; complicated
   Code(s) _____

10. Colposcopy and biopsy of the vulva
    Code(s) _____

11. Multifetal pregnancy reduction
    Code(s) _____

12. Pelvic examination, under anesthesia
    Code(s) _____

13. Intersex surgery, female to male
    Code(s) _____

14. Repair of an incomplete circumcision
    Code(s) _____

15. Surgical laproscopy; orchiectomy
    Code(s) _____

Name _____

Date _____

PRACTICE EXERCISE 15: CPT RADIOLOGY AND NERVOUS SYSTEM

Code the following cases using an encoder or coding manuals.

1. Myocardial perfusion imaging (planar) stress exercises and redistribution, with interpretation and report

   Code(s) _____

2. Intracranial angiography, radiological supervision and interpretation

   Code(s) _____

3. Total body radiation treatment, oral

   Code(s) _____

4. Magnetic resonance imaging, brain, during intracranial procedure to remove tumor without contrast, followed by contrast material and further sequence

   Code(s) _____

5. Gastroesophageal reflux study

   Code(s) _____

6. Surgery of complex intracranial aneurysm, intracranial approach using computed tomography guidance for stereotactic localization

   Code(s) _____

7. Therapeutic lumbar puncture for drainage of cerebrospinal fluid, needle

   Code(s) _____

8. Radiation treatment, five treatments with hypothermia, externally generated, superficial

   Code(s) _____

9. Ultrasound, abdominal, B-scan

   Code(s) _____

10. Intravascular ultrasound on a non-coronary vessel, with radiological supervision and interpretation; two vessels

    Code(s) _____

Name _____

Date _____

PRACTICE EXERCISE 16: CPT LABORATORY AND PATHOLOGY

Code the following cases using an encoder or coding manuals.

1. ABO Blood typing
   Code(s) _____

2. Transfusion of white blood cells
   Code(s) _____

3. Bone marrow tissue culture for neoplastic disease
   Code(s) _____

4. Intramuscular chemotherapy administration, without anesthesia
   Code(s) _____

5. Routine EEG, 30 min, awake and asleep
   Code(s) _____

6. Bleed time
   Code(s) _____

7. Urea nitrogen, urine
   Code(s) _____

8. Urinalysis, automated with microscopy
   Code(s) _____

9. Therapeutic lithium level
   Code(s) _____

10. Acute hepatitis panel
    Code(s) _____

11. Injection of antibiotic
    Code(s) _____

12. Alcohol drug test, urine
    Code(s) _____

13. Pregnancy test, urine, visual comparison
    Code(s) _____

14. Rheumatoid factor, qualitative
    Code(s) _____

15. Peripheral vein stimulation panel with physician supplied agent, injected subQ
    Code(s) _____

16. Immunoassay, analyze, quantitative, by radiopharmaceutical technique

Code(s) _____

17. Bone density study, radiopharmaceutical, multiple sites, single photon absorptiometry

Code(s) _____

Name _____

Date _____

PRACTICE EXERCISE 17: CPT MEDICINE SECTION

Code the following cases using an encoder or coding manuals.

1. Gastric intubation and aspiration, for treatment

   Code(s) _____

2. Fitting of spectacles, bifocal

   Code(s) _____

3. CPR

   Code(s) _____

4. Physician services for outpatient cardiac rehabilitation, with continuous ECG monitoring, one session

   Code(s) _____

5. Wada activation test for hemispheric function, including electroencephalographic monitoring

   Code(s) _____

6. Home visit for intramuscular injections

   Code(s) _____

7. Electrical stimulation, 30 min, ultrasound application

   Code(s) _____

8. Rapid desensitization procedure, 1 hr

   Code(s) _____

9. Nasal function studies

   Code(s) _____

10. Hypnotherapy

    Code(s) _____

11. MMR injection, subcutaneous, 3-month-old

    Code(s) _____

12. Typhoid vaccine, live, oral

    Code(s) _____

13. Intramuscular injection of antibiotic

    Code(s) _____

14. Left heart catheterization by left ventricular puncture

    Code(s) _____

15. Actinotherapy

Code(s) _____

16. Tensilon test for myasthenia gravis

Code(s) _____

Name _____

Date _____

PRACTICE EXERCISE 18: ICD-9 CM DIAGNOSTIC

Code the following cases using an encoder or coding manuals.

1. Spider finger
   Code(s) _____

2. Snoring
   Code(s) _____

3. Rheumatoid osteoarthritis of the hand
   Code(s) _____

4. Contusion of the lumbar region
   Code(s) _____

5. Contusion of the thoracic region
   Code(s) _____

6. Open biopsy of adrenal gland
   Code(s) _____

7. Unilateral repair of inguinal hernia
   Code(s) _____

8. Biopsy of a patella bone
   Code(s) _____

9. CAT scan of abdomen
   Code(s) _____

10. Lobotomy and tractotomy
    Code(s) _____

11. Repair of scleral fistula
    Code(s) _____

12. Pleurectomy of the lung
    Code(s) _____

13. Fast pulse
    Code(s) _____

14. Paralysis, progressive
    Code(s) _____

15. Nausea
    Code(s) _____

16. Malformation of the inner ear

    Code(s) _____

17. Phobic disorder

    Code(s) _____

18. Congenital cyanosis

    Code(s) _____

19. Writer's cramp

    Code(s) _____

20. Emotional blindness

    Code(s) _____

21. Hairy tongue

    Code(s) _____

22. Pernicious anemia

    Code(s) _____

23. Diastasis of cranial bones

    Code(s) _____

24. Excessive eating

    Code(s) _____

25. Mud fever

    Code(s) _____

26. Senile dementia, with depression

    Code(s) _____

27. Coxsackie endocarditis

    Code(s) _____

28. Midtarsal fusion

    Code(s) _____

29. Metal polisher's disease (unspecified)

    Code(s) _____

30. Intrinsic asthma, with acute exacerbation

    Code(s) _____

31. Chronic pyelnephritis, without lesions

    Code(s) _____

32. Repair of esophageal strictures

    Code(s) _____

33. Fetal pulse oximetry

    Code(s) _____

34. Administration of tetanus antitoxin in a hospital

    Code(s) _____

35. Suture of laceration of a kidney

Code(s) _____

36. Shingles, affecting many nerves

Code(s) _____

37. Wichmann's asthma

Code(s) _____

38. Open wound (laceration) of the toe

Code(s) _____

39. Neurogenic bowel

Code(s) _____

40. Congestive left heart failure

Code(s) _____

41. Cerebral embolism, with infarction

Code(s) _____

42. Repair of the brain

Code(s) _____

43. Excision of a deep cervical lymph node

Code(s) _____

44. Pyeloscopy

Code(s) _____

45. Kyphoplasty

Code(s) _____

46. Arthrodesis of the shoulder

Code(s) _____

47. Application of a plaster splint

Code(s) _____

48. CPR in a hospital

Code(s) _____

49. Pancreatic steatorrhea

Code(s) _____

50. Tinnitis (objective)

Code(s) _____

Name _____

Date _____

PRACTICE EXERCISE 19: ICD-9 CM PROCEDURE CODE

Code the following cases using an encoder or coding manuals.

1. Removal of a foreign body from the peritoneal cavity

   Code(s) _____

2. Injection of an antibiotic

   Code(s) _____

3. Transabdominal gastroscopy (diagnostic)

   Code(s) _____

4. Suture of the thyroid gland

   Code(s) _____

5. Intranasal antrotomy

   Code(s) _____

6. Tonsillectomy and adenoidectomy

   Code(s) _____

7. Removal of a heart assist system

   Code(s) _____

8. Repair of a direct inguinal hernia

   Code(s) _____

9. Revision of a stoma of small intestine

   Code(s) _____

10. Appendectomy

    Code(s) _____

11. Vaginoscopy

    Code(s) _____

12. Replantation of scalp

    Code(s) _____

13. X-ray of the entire skeleton

    Code(s) _____

14. Application of a pressure dressing

    Code(s) _____

15. Training in the use of a lead dog for the blind

    Code(s) _____

16. Injection of a steroid

Code(s) _____

17. Cerebral thermography

Code(s) _____

18. Reattachment of a muscle

Code(s) _____

19. Closed reduction or fracture of the femur, without internal fixation

Code(s) _____

20. Open biopsy of a kidney

Code(s) _____

21. Flexible sigmoidoscopy

Code(s) _____

22. Repair of vertebral fracture

Code(s) _____

23. Probing of lacrimal punctum

Code(s) _____

24. Unilateral breast implant

Code(s) _____

25. Separation of conjoined twins

Code(s) _____

Glossary

A

A-mode: A one-dimensional view of the body structure

accident: An unforeseen occurrence

Add Code icon: An icon in Encoder Pro that enables the user to create sticky notes, add a code to the notepad, or to bookmark a frequently used code

add-on code: Additional work performed in addition to the primary procedure

adrenal gland: A gland that regulates electrolyte balance and the metabolism of proteins, fat, and glucose

air transport: A device for transporting passengers or goods in the air

allergic/immunologic: Pertaining to allergies and the immune system

allograft: The transplant of tissue from an individual

analgesia: The loss of or absence of normal sensation of pain

anesthesia: Partial or complete loss of sensation

aneurysm: The abnormal dilation of a blood vessel due to a weakening of its wall

annotations: A dialog box that enables the coder to view more information regarding specific professional services

arthroplasty: Repair of a joint

autograft: The transplant of tissue from the patient's own body

B

bacterial: The actual development of a disease caused by a bacterium

bacterium: A one-celled organism that mutates and spreads

basic unit (B):   A value given according to the complexity of a service

Bethesda System: A system used to report cellular changes

bookmarks: A reference for codes frequently used by a user

B-scan: A two-dimensional view of a structure with two-dimensional displays

C

cadaver: A dead body used for dissection

carotid body: Refers to the body of the adrenal gland

cardiography: The recording of the electrical functions within the heart muscle

cardiovascular: Pertaining to the heart and blood vessels

category: In CPT-4, contains codes for the procedure being performed on an anatomic site

category II codes: Codes intended for a collection of data

category III codes: Temporary codes that are assigned based on new technology and procedures

cervix uterus: The neck of the uterus

chief complaint: A concise statement made by the patient describing the symptom, problem, or other reason for the visit or encounter

chromatography: A separation of at least two or more chemical compounds

closed treatment: Not surgically opened to view

color coding legend: An Encoder Pro feature that enables the coder to quickly identify all codes associated with a specific color code

comminuted fracture: The fracture of a bone which has splintered

compound fracture: A fracture in which parts of the fragments of bone protrude through the skin

comprehensive examination: A complete examination of a single organ system or a general multisystem examination

comprehensive history: A level of patient history consisting of a chief complaint, extended history of present illness, complete review of systems, and complete past family and social history

conscious sedation: A state of depressed consciousness

constitutional: General appearance of the patient

consultation: Verbal or written orders requesting advice on a specific problem or illness

continuous caudal analgesia: An analgesia that is injected continuously into the sacral hiatus during childbirth

contrast: Substance, not administered orally or rectally, used to view the body's internal organs or their structures.

co-pay: An out-of-pocket expense collected at the time services are provided

corpus uterus: The main body of the uterus, located above the cervix

CPT-4:   Current Procedural Terminology, 4th Edition

critical care: Patients requiring a higher level of treatment within a hospital

cytogenetic: Promoting the production of more cells

cytopathology: The study of cell disease

D

debridement: A cleaning of skin tissue

deductible: A patient's out-of-pocket expense that must be paid before benefits begin

dentoalveolar: Pertains to the alveolus of the tooth and the tooth itself

dermis: The middle layer of skin, which is the thickest layer

detailed examination: An extended examination of both the affected area and related organ system

detailed history: A level of patient history which includes a chief complaint, an extended review of systems, and a past family and social history

diagnostic radiology: Using a radiologic device to obtain a diagnosis

diagnostic ultrasound: A technique used to view the internal structures of the body by the application of sound waves

diagnosis related group (DRG):   Group of patients with similar diagnosis or condition

dialysis: Cleansing of the blood

Doppler: A two-dimensional image

dosimetry: A calculation in the measurement of doses in radiation

duodenum: The lower opening of the stomach, with the esophagus being the top opening of the stomach

durable medical equipment (DME):   Assisted medical devices designed for patients to use at home

E

echocardiography: An ultrasound of the heart

electromyogram: The graphic record of the muscle activity during rest and voluntary movements as a result of electrical stimulation

elements of an examination: Levels used to indicate the extent of an examination

E/M: See Evaluation and Management (E/M) section

embolism: Obstruction of a blood vessel that is caused by a blood clot, bacteria, plaques, fat, or air

encoder programs: Specialized computer program that allows for fast code selection

endocrine: Pertains to glands that secrete into the blood system

EOB: See Explanation of Benefits (EOB)

epidermis: The outermost layer of the skin

epididymis: A long coiled tube on the posterior surface of each testis

epidural: Spinal block

eponym: Procedure or thing named after a person

esophagus: A hollow muscular tube that carries food from the mouth to the stomach

ESRD: End stage renal disease

established patient: Someone who has been seen by the physician within three years

expanded problem focused examination: A limited exam of the affected body area or organ system with an additional examination to a related organ system.

expanded problem focused history: Chief complaint and brief history of the patient's presenting problem or illness

explanation of benefits (EOB):   An explanation for each service provided to the patient

external fixation: Stabilization extends out through the skin; made with pins, rods, etc.

extracorporeal: Outside the body

Evaluation and Management (E/M) section: Section within the CPT manual that describes the levels of services performed by a physician

F

face-to-face time: The amount of time a physician spends with the patient or family face-to-face

fee schedule: A list that contains all CPT codes that are payable for participating and non-participating physicians

fiber-optic endoscope: A device that allows for the transmission of light along plastic or glass fibers

fluoroscope: A device in which the image has been interposed between the x-ray and a fluorescent computer screen

G

gastrointestinal: Pertains to the organ system that deals with the stomach and intestines

general anesthesia: A state of total unconsciousness

genitourinary: Pertains to the organ system that deals with the genitals and urinary organs

Ghon's lesion: The primary infection of tuberculosis

global: A technical and professional component

greenstick fracture: A fracture of bone that is partially bent and partially broken

guidance: Any device used to assist a physician during a procedure

guidelines: Direct instructions on the proper use of all the codes within a section

H

hematologic/lymphatic: Organ system that deals with the blood and lymph nodes

history of present illness (HPI):   A chronological description of the development of the patient's present illness from the first sign of onset

HMO: Healthcare Maintenance Organization

hydration: The addition of water and other substances introduced into the tissues in an attempt to rehydrate a patient

I

ICD-9:   International Classification of Diseases, 9th Edition

indented codes: Codes that contain part of the primary procedure

index: A guide used to locate specific procedure codes

infectious: Transmittable with or without skin contact

infiltration anesthesia: An anesthesia that is injected into the nerve endings to reduce sensation in a localized area

infusion: Fluids introduced into the body

injury: Trauma to a part of the body

inpatient: One who has been formally admitted into a healthcare facility

integumentary: Organ system that deals with the skin

internal fixation: The placing of rods, pins, etc., into the bone to stabilize an open fracture

introitus: The opening to the uterus from the vagina

K

key components: Elements of obtaining levels of an examination

L

late effects code: Condition reported as a sequelae to the cause of an injury

lesions: Various types of skin disorder

Level II codes: National codes for reporting supplies

local anesthesia: Loss of sensation over a particular area

LOPS: Loss of protective sensation

M

manipulation: A method used to restore a fractured bone to its original alignment by applying manual force to skin through the use of straps

Medicare: Federally funded health plan for persons 65 years of age and older or the medically disabled

Medicare Part A: A federally funded program that pays for a hospital facility, home health care, skilled nursing facility, respite and hospice care

Medicare Part B: A federally funded program that pays for physician services, outpatient hospital, laboratory services, and diagnostic and therapeutic services

microbiology: The study of microorganisms

M-mode: A one dimensional view that records movement

modality: An application of a therapeutic agent (ultrasound) or regimen (exercise)

modifier: A further explanation of services or procedures provided

modifying unit (M): A unit that characterizes the patient's physical condition

morphology: The study of the form of neoplasms

motor vehicle accident (MVA): any transport accident involved in a motor vehicle (cars, trucks)

musculoskeletal: Pertaining to the muscles and bones

MVA: Motor vehicle accident

myocardium: Pertaining to the heart muscle

N

necrosis: Dead skin tissue

neurologic: Pertaining to the nerves or nervous system

neurostimulator: A pulse generator that transmits electricity to the nerves of the muscles

new patient: A patient who has not been seen by the physician for at least three years

non-face to face time: Services provided by a physician without requiring the presence of the patient, such as a review of medical records

non-participating physician (Non-par): A physician who is not contracted with an insurance company

nontraffic accident: A motor vehicle accident that takes place other than on a public highway

notepad: Icon used only to store temporary codes

nuclear medicine: The use of radioactive substance for diagnosis and treatment

nystagmus: A disease of the eyes that causes the eye to move back and forth involuntarily

O

open treatment: Surgically opened to view

ophthalmologic: Pertaining to the eyes

otolaryngology: The study of the ears, nose and throat

outpatient: A person who has not been formally admitted into a hospital

overcoding: Services performed are charged at a level that is higher than actually performed

oviduct: Fallopian tube

P

panel: Multiple laboratory tests grouped together as one test

paranasal sinuses: Resonating chambers for the voice

parasite: An organism that lives at the expense of its host

parathyroid gland: Glands that regulate calcium and phosphorus metabolism

participating physician (Par):   A physician who is contracted with an insurance company

passenger: Occupant of a motor vehicle

past family social history: A review of the patient's family and social history

patient-controlled analgesia: An analgesia that permits the patient to self-administer at his or her own rate by using an infusion pump

patient status: Third factor in a code assignment

pedal cycle: A transportation vehicle that is operated on rails (train, streetcar)

pedestrian: Any person on foot, pedal cycle, or riding in or on a motor vehicle, railway train, etc.

pericardium: The fibrous sac containing the heart

PET scan: Positron emission tomography scan

pharynx: The passageway for air traveling from the nose to the larynx

physical status unit: A unit that indicates the patient's physical condition

place of service: The place or setting in which the service was provided

poisoning: An introduction of a toxic substance into the body

PPO: Preferred Provider Organization

preemptive analgesia: Analgesia administered before surgery to reduce pain and the amount of recovery time

problem focused examination: A limited examination of a body area or organ system

problem focused history: A level of the patient's history that includes a chief complaint, brief history, or present illness

professional component: The radiologist performs or supervises the procedure and completes the interpretation, followed by a written report

prolonged service: Services performed in addition to the allotted time

prophylactic: A preventative measure taken against disease

prostate: A single gland located below the urinary bladder

psychiatric: Pertaining to the diagnosis and prevention of mental illness

public building: Any building used by the general public

puerperium: The period of 42 days following the birth of a child

Q

qualifying circumstances: A relative value code given for special circumstances in the administration of anesthesia

qualitative: A test that determines whether a drug is or is not present

quantitative: A test that determines whether a drug is present and provides results based on numeric values

R

radiologist: A physician who specializes in radiology

radiology: Division within the medical field that uses various types of imaging techniques

railway vehicle: A transportation vehicle that is operated on rails (train, streetcar)

real-time: A two-dimensional view of movement of a structure

regional anesthesia: Loss of sensation in a particular area

reimbursements: The amount an insurance company will pay the primary physician for services provided

remittance advice (RA): An explanation of how the claims that were transmitted electronically were adjudicated by the insurance company

relative value guide: A comparison of anesthesia services

respiratory: An organ system that allows for the exchange of oxygen and carbon dioxide

review of systems (ROS): An inventory of the body systems obtained through a series of questions seeking to identify signs and symptoms that the patient may be experiencing.

S

search box: Enables the user to search for specific code or code range in a particular code set, when a code or code range is known

section: In CPT-4, main body of material being listed

shunt: An artificial passage created to divert the flow of fluids

skeletal traction: Force applied directly to the bone through the application of pins

skin traction: Manual force applied to the skin with the use of straps

stand-alone code: A code that contains the full description of a procedure

sticky notes: Reminder notes the user creates for selected codes

subcategory: In CPT-4, contains codes for identifying the approach to a procedure

subheading: In CPT-4, contains codes for the location of an anatomic site on which the procedure is being performed

subcutaneous: The deepest layer of skin, which lies under the dermis

subsection: In CPT-4, a division of a section into smaller sections

subsequent hospital care: Each additional day a patient is hospitalized

surgical package: A group of procedures that have been bundled or grouped together under one code

synonyms: Words that have the same meaning

T

tandem: A stainless steel tube used to restrict radioactivity

technical component: Used when the radiologist has only performed a procedure and has not read the end results

therapeutic: A healing obtained through treatment

therapeutic drugs: Commonly known as maintenance drugs

therapeutic nuclear medicine: A division of medicine that deals with the administration of radiopharmaceuticals

therapeutic radiology: Application of radiation to obtain healing

thrombus: A blood clot that obstructs any blood vessel

thromboendarterectomy: The surgical removal of a blood clot from an artery

thymus gland: A lymphatic organ located in the mediastinal cavity

time: The amount a physician spends, based on minutes or hours

time unit (T):   A division of time based on 15 minutes

toolbar: Buttons and icons displaying command features

tracheostomy: A surgical creation of an opening into the trachea

trocar: A sharp instrument contained in a cannula for the use of extracting fluids

turbinates: Coil-shaped bone within the nasal cavity

type of service: A clinical or non-clinical service provided to a patient

U

unbundling: A surgical package that is coded separately

undercoding: A term used when the highest level of coding has not been achieved

urinalysis: A test performed on urine

urodynamics: The study of the storage of urine in the bladder

uvula: A small muscle that hangs at the back of the throat above the root of the tongue

V

vagina: Serves as the birth canal

vas deferens: The ductus deferens, extends from the epididymis into the abdominal cavity through the inguinal canal, behind the urinary bladder

vertebral interspace: The non-bony compartment between two vertebral bodies, contains the intervertebral disk

viral: Pertains to a specific virus

vulva: The external portion of the female genitals

W

watercraft: Any device for the purpose of transporting passengers or goods on the water

X

xenograft: A transplant of tissue obtained from an animal

Z

zoonotic: Diseases that are transmitted from animals to humans

Index